WE, US, AND THEM

Cultural Frames, Framing Culture

Robert Newman, Editor
Justin Neuman, Associate Editor

WE, US, AND THEM

Affect and American Nonfiction from Vietnam to Trump

Douglas Dowland

University of Virginia Press • *Charlottesville and London*

University of Virginia Press
© 2024 by the Rector and Visitors of the University of Virginia
All rights reserved
Printed in the United States of America on acid-free paper

First published 2024

9 8 7 6 5 4 3 2 1

Library of Congress Cataloging-in-Publication Data

Names: Dowland, Douglas, author.
Title: We, us, and them : affect and American nonfiction from Vietnam to Trump /
    Douglas Dowland.
Description: Charlottesville : University of Virginia Press, 2024. | Series: Cultural
    frames, framing culture | Includes bibliographical references and index.
Identifiers: LCCN 2023052296 (print) | LCCN 2023052297 (ebook) |
    ISBN 9780813950839 (hardcover) | ISBN 9780813950846 (paperback) |
    ISBN 9780813950853 (ebook)
Subjects: LCSH: American prose literature—20th century—History and criticism. |
    Nationalism in literature. | National characteristics, American, in literature. |
    Synecdoche. | BISAC: LITERARY CRITICISM / Subjects & Themes / Politics |
    LITERARY CRITICISM / American / General
Classification: LCC PS374.N288 D69 2024 (print) | LCC PS374.N288 (ebook) |
    DDC 810.9/005—dc23/eng/20231220
LC record available at https://lccn.loc.gov/2023052296
LC ebook record available at https://lccn.loc.gov/2023052297

Cover art: Heart-shaped barbed wire, rawpixel.com; paper pieces,
Gradient Background/shutterstock.com
Cover design: David Fassett

For my students

CONTENTS

ACKNOWLEDGMENTS

No scholar does it alone. There are so many people to thank, especially Angie Hogan at the University of Virginia Press, who shepherded this book from manuscript to what is in your hands—or on your screen—today. My thanks to Jane M. Curran for copyediting the manuscript. And I am of course indebted to the peer reviewers commissioned by the press, series editors Robert Newman and Justin D. Neuman, and press director Eric Brandt for their continuous support. My thanks as well to J. Andrew Edwards at the press for seeing this book through to fruition, Rebecca McCorkle for writing the index, and David Fassett for designing a wonderful cover.

I would also like to acknowledge the assistance of Ohio Northern University for the sabbatical that allowed me to begin this book and for their granting me the Sara A. Ridenour Endowed Chair of Humanities so that I could finish it. In particular, I would like to thank the faculty and staff of the Heterick Memorial Library at Ohio Northern University for their assistance and their expeditious interlibrary loan service.

Many of these chapters benefited from being presented at the American Literature Association, the Modern Language Association, and the Northeast Modern Language Association. I am thankful to the audiences of these conferences for their insightful questions and positive feedback. The chapter on John Steinbeck first appeared as "Hawkish Reading: John Steinbeck and the Vietnam War" in *Criticism*, published by Wayne State University Press, and the chapter on J. D. Vance first appeared as "The Politics of Resentment in J. D. Vance's *Hillbilly Elegy*" in *Texas Studies in Literature and Language*. My thanks to *TSLL*'s editors for awarding the latter its Tony Hilfer Prize for Outstanding Article.

Joshua Gooch read this entire book and commented voluminously. The least I can do is return the favor in kind.

This is the second book my senior foster dog, Joanie, has listened to me read aloud, helping me catch a sentence that was going too long or a section that was starting to drift, and knowing the right time to step away from the desk and take a reflective, refreshing walk. That the Thompson chapter proved to be her favorite may suggest a trans-species connection between Chihuahuas and the textual style of gonzo journalists.

WE, US, AND THEM

INTRODUCTION

The Problem of Strong Nationalism

ON JULY 11, 2017, the *New York Times* published an article entitled "How We Are Ruining America." Its author, the columnist David Brooks, lamented how "members of the college-educated class have become amazingly good at making sure their children retain their privileged status." The "upper-middle class," he writes, "have embraced behavior codes" that place children at the forefront: mothers "breast-feed their babies at much higher rates . . . and for much longer periods," and families spend more time and money on their children than lower-middle class families. The upper-middle class, Brooks insists, have "become fanatical" at insuring that their children stay upwardly mobile. They are "devastatingly good at making sure the children of other classes have limited chances to join their ranks." It is the way in which the upper-middle class protects their own against a shrinking sphere of opportunity that Brooks insists is one of the ways in which "we" are "ruining" the entire nation.[1]

Brooks's "we" matters here. It is a lazy, "unrigorous 'we' of the traditional critic who projects his/her subjective impressions and analyses on all members of the audience" (Diamond 390). As such, it is a "we" that is not so much interested in constructing a comprehensive polity as it is in hailing anyone who might be affectively disposed—shares a similarly vague grievance, is irked in a general way by some contemporary event—to turn around when the writer textually calls out, "Hey, you there!" (Althusser 118). It is a "we" just specific enough to locate mutual discontent and to affectively sustain further discontenting. Reading narratives like these, one feels, time and time again, that the writer's use of "we," "us," and "them" is really a "factitious but powerful sense of community which buttresses but also conceals the narcissistic claims of the critic" (Diamond 390). The writers who produce such narratives may see a national problem. They may visit its location or interview its people. They may undertake or examine research. But ultimately all of these efforts are secondary to what the writer personally feels the nation is. While the scope of such writing may be national, this scope is always reduced to the first person. And not only is it reduced to the first person, it is further reduced to the intense reactions, the strong affects, of that writer's reading of the nation.

Brooks's article—like the nonfiction I study throughout this book— derives explanatory power only because it is individually bold and replete with personal conviction. As a result, its narrative energy stems from a deliberately orchestrated drama of "us" and "them." Brooks accomplishes this hyperbolically: it is not just that upper-middle-class parents are good at insuring their children have opportunities; they are "amazingly" and "devastatingly" good at doing so. It is not just that the upper-middle class is privileged; it is that they "sit atop gigantic mountains of privilege" and only offer "teeny step ladders for everybody else." The evidence of this, for Brooks, is found in a tumultuous sea of "cultural signifiers." "To feel at home in opportunity-rich areas," he writes, requires being cradled from an early age to understand "the right barre techniques, sport the right baby carrier, have the right podcast, food truck, tea, wine and Pilates tastes, not to mention the right attitudes about David Foster Wallace, child-rearing, gender norms and intersectionality"—all of these function as "status rules" that "erect shields against everybody else." In such prose, we are to infer that the sheer magnitude of such a list—so many practices presented as problems—shows how "ruined" America is: not just its food and drink, but what it buys and how it travels, how it dances, how it listens, what it reads, how it thinks—all of these to Brooks are signs of national decline.

Yet, as Christa J. Olson and other rhetoricians remind us, magnitude— either positive or negative—is a "simultaneously sturdy and fragile thing" (185). Brooks's magnitude comes from his hasty inventorying and the "fearless generalizing" of what he inventories as signs of national decline (Kinsley). It depends on an ever-sliding terminology (what begins as the "college-educated" morphs into the "upper-middle" class, which are not exactly synonymous). And it relies on, as Michael Kinsley notes, Brooks's "show-off use of commercial brand names as a shorthand for demographic nuances."[2] Indeed, the particular inventory of "How We Are Ruining America" seems to index cultural practices not adopted by Brooks's generation—really, it indexes the bourgeois trends of late-2010s Manhattan rather than the enduring, far-reaching practices that constitute national culture. Parse any one item of Brooks's inventory, and the house of cards falls. For what holds it together is the thin glue of strong affect.

As the penultimate evidence of how "we" are "ruining" the nation, Brooks offers an anecdote of visiting a Manhattan sandwich shop with a friend. As they review the menu, he watches his friend's "face freeze up" as she is "confronted with sandwiches named 'Padrino' and 'Pomodoro' and ingredients like soppressata, capicollo and a striata baguette." Brooks suggests that they go somewhere else for lunch—his friend "anxiously nodded yes." This anecdote is the climax of Brooks's article, to him proof of a ruined nation in which "American upper-middle-class culture is now laced with cultural signifiers that are completely illegible unless you happen to have grown up in this class." Based on his reading of his friend's affects—what he sees not as mild curiosity but as intense confrontation, a nodding yes that shows not disinterest in the menu but an anxious panic, a face that "freezes" as if in a fight-or-flight reflex—Brooks confirms his thesis that what is ruining America is not structural nor economic, but informal and cultural. The sandwich shop and its ingredients are a synecdoche of wholesale national ruination, of a nation laced with impure "cultural signifiers" that humiliate and exclude those not in the know. The issue, to Brooks, is not money nor politics, but access to "rarefied information." And this access is not a matter of mere snobbery, he insists. Instead, the menu reveals something insidious and exclusionary. It is not a sign of American multicultural diversity but one of American elitism. It does not invite people to try the cuisine. The menu instead says, Brooks tells us, "You are not welcome here."

His article concludes with an indictment—that "we in the educated class have created barriers to mobility. . . . The rest of America can't name them, can't understand them. They just know they're there." If the writer of narratives like these uses the word "we" selectively, they also use the word "they" in an equally unrigorous but powerful way. Brooks's use of the word "they" has shifted, by the article's conclusion, from the lower-middle class to "the rest of America." It is a "they" that may begin small but becomes evermore large and vague, shifting from "a reputable pronoun to a vague substitute for identifiable people" (Konda 193). Indeed, such writers use the word "they" to entrap or expel as many others as possible: no wonder why "the disembodied 'they' has long been a popular identifying trait of conspiracism" (193). The exactness of the writer's categories is not as important as their use to perpetuate a feeling of being attacked. The orchestrated drama of "we" and "them" that propels writing like this concludes with the "us" and the "them" farther away than they were before, even less discernable than they were at the beginning, and trapped in a conflict that seems without resolution.

To "ruin" means many things. Ruination mars, decays, spoils, pollutes. It not only signals the collapse of a nation but destroys the hopes of its citizens. What interests me about Brooks's article—and the narratives I study throughout this book—is how their display of affective conviction insulates them from an honest exploration of their concern. Once the "informal" becomes the target, nothing concrete—no policy, no legislation, no practice—need be offered. Through their affective sleight of hand, the writer retains his power to criticize while never needing to detail a solution. Underneath Brooks's vague call is an arrogance that cannot see how its own prose is a form of hoarding. It need not do—and none of the narratives I study in this book ever do—the serious labor of imagining a new "we" that remedies the problem they put forward.

Is spending time with your family and children a sign of fanaticism? Are Italian cured meats a sign of snobbery? Is the menu of a Manhattan sandwich shop representative of an entirely "ruined" United States?[3] What is of interest to me in this book is how narratives like these inevitably answer such questions with a yes, the way in which affect motivates their peculiar linking of parts to a whole to provide and sustain their answer. What propels such answers is an intense yet ugly narrative energy based on the certainty of one's worldview and the conviction that the nation is not who your neighbors are but what you feel in your gut. The explanatory power of such narratives comes from their ability to paint a landscape of intense feelings that emanate from within them. The nation such narratives evoke is not one that seeks out what is larger than the individual self. Instead, these narratives relish in making personal opinion the arbiter of the entire nation. They do so through a perverse form of close reading, reading not so much for unity but disunity, not so much creating a shared national pathos but one that is antipathetic toward others.[4] In a way, it is fortunate that Brooks is a narcissist but not a monomaniac. For "ruining," what Brooks claims "we" are doing, is but a hair different affectively from the "ruined" nation that needs a demagogue to be made great again. On the one hand, Brooks's hysteria is laughable. On the other hand, move this hysteria out of a lazy reading of a sandwich shop and onto a presidential campaign platform, and it is no longer laughable but toxic. Either way, the emotional intensity of its writing leads to a variety of antidemocratic conclusions.

The question "What is America?" requires an honest, multifaceted engagement to answer. It requires tolerance, ingenuity, and an appreciation of ambiguity—the realization that the nation is more than the sum of its parts. The writers I explore in this book eschew these requirements. To them, the nation is simple, literal, and self-evident. Their narratives, in their peculiar construction of "us" and "them," come to an "either" or an "or": a pessimism, if not a depression, the feeling that nothing can be done, or a destructiveness, a spitefulness, that the only way to save America is to make it less democratic. Their prose demonstrates the danger of what Louis Althusser calls "obviousness as obviousness": their conclusions are so evident to themselves that they presume their audience will, like themselves, find it "inevitable and natural" to think "'That's obvious! That's right! That's true!'" upon reading such conclusions (116). But it is only through the avoidance of the complexities of reality that one can find their conclusions to be obvious, right, and true. Prose of this type commits the worst form of ideologizing, one that deprives others of the freedom to be different, to be part of a community, perhaps even the right to exist. What is most worrisome about these narratives is how they encourage, in their arsenal of affects, citizens to either passively retreat from, or actively denounce, their fellow Americans.

Strong Nationalisms

In its simplest sense, nationalism is the style through which the nation is imagined. The word "style" is paramount here, for nationalism is not just the conception of one as part of a nation—and others as part of it, too—but the manner in which the nation is conceived as minimal or essential, horizontal or vertical, banal or profound. What these styles reveal is how nationalism is an "angle of participation in processes larger than ourselves" (Massumi 214). And what these styles reveal is how "America," insofar as it exists, does so in the participatory, affective space of synecdoche, in the space between part and whole. For as Benedict Anderson notably writes, it is through nationalism that "communities are to be distinguished, not by their falsity/genuineness, but by the style in which they are imagined," and that the nation "is *imagined* because the members of even the smallest nation will never know most of their fellow-members, meet them, or even hear of them, yet in the minds of each lives the image of their communion" (6, emphasis in original). For Anderson, nationalism emerges in moments in which people "think of themselves as living lives *parallel* to those of other substantial groups of people—if never meeting, yet certainly proceeding along the same trajectory" (188, emphasis in original). As such, the nation is a source of "emotional legitimacy" that is derived from the envisioning of ourselves as being together, a vision that is both my own and extends far beyond myself (see Anderson 4).

As Anderson notes, nationalism comes about when states orchestrate measures for the reading of its subjects: the map, the census; and when certain modalities of reading become prevalent: the newspaper, the museum. Equally important for my purposes, nationalism comes about when the discursive production of the nation comes to serve as a site of emotional legitimacy. For instance, Sara Ahmed notes how a phrase such as "the nation mourns" induces "the nation as a shared object of feeling through the orientation that is taken towards it" (*Cultural Politics* 13). To say that "the nation mourns" is to arrange diverse lives into parallel ones—it tells me that I should mourn because others are, and that in our doing so simultaneously, our shared emotions create the legitimacy of both myself and others beyond my line of sight. The act of mourning, the affect of mourning, becomes one of the many emotional legitimacies through which I express myself as part of a broader whole. Thus to evoke the nation is to show how the "power of nationalism to motivate and agitate is grounded in lived experience" and to realize how its "emotional universes that encompass shared lives" are constructed (Cox 141).

Because nationalism is a site of affective work, it perpetually varies in intensity. That the affective investment in the nation can traverse "both utopian national identification and cynical practical citizenship" should serve as a reminder that nationalism is not the staid, singular practice critics too often take it to be (Berlant, *Queen* 14). For nationalism encompasses an entire range, from "a flag which is being consciously raised with fervent passion" to the flag which is "hanging unnoticed on a public building" (Billig 8). The solidarity of feeling that comes from nationalism can be expansive or exclusive, beautiful or ugly. As Steven Grosby writes, "Some may view their nation as standing for individual liberty, while others may be willing to sacrifice that liberty for security. Some may welcome immigrants while others may be hostile to immigration" (5). Indeed, nationalism is likely both simultaneously and in ways that seem contradictory—take the nationalist who favors immigration for some but not for others. Indeed, it is nationalism's ability to be consistent and inconsistent simultaneously that should compel our study of it. As Lauren Berlant writes, the "popular form of political optimism" known as the "American Dream" emerges from innately contradictory senses of the public and the private sphere: indeed, the very imagining is predicated upon "imagining itself national only insofar as it feels unmarked by the effects of [its] national contradictions" (*Queen* 4). Thus instead of categorizing nationalisms as consistent or inconsistent, right or wrong, it proves more valuable to follow Anderson's insistence to read nationalism for the style in which the nation is conceived.

Nationalism, Michael Billig writes, always possesses a "Jekyll and Hyde duality" (7). Elsewhere, I have studied the nation's Jekyll-like tendencies. In this book, I am studying its Hyde. The portraits of the nation I study in this book are not a horizon that is expanding and inviting but that of a setting sun: starker, darker, ultimately receding. The writers of this style of nationalism do not attempt to moderate their frenetic edge, do not pause to doubt themselves. The America they see is complacent, corrupt, on the verge of being unredeemable. Yet their solutions to national problems are vague and unimplementable or moral and draconian. The nation they produce lacks imagination. And in the intense emotion that drives such productions, they disconnect themselves from others for whom the nation is not so central or extreme. They are so certain that America is what they say that their interpretations do not allow for neighbors. All in all, in their promulgation of an "us" and a "them," this strain of nonfiction narrows the circle of the American "we" (see Hollinger).

John Steinbeck, wading through the mud of South Vietnam, finds national purpose in the war being fought there, yet even as he is surrounded by American soldiers, he cannot restrain himself from zealously attacking the war's protestors at home. Hunter S. Thompson, as he travels America as part of the 1972 McGovern presidential campaign, writes of how the entire nation is like what he sees in its political elite: ugly, violent, and gullible, far more interested in the calculus of winning than the guaranteeing of freedom. James Baldwin, parsing the Atlanta child murders of 1979–81, comes to the conclusion that the nation is not politically salvageable or morally redeemable. Under the guise of explaining the rise of a nativist right in response to the election of Barack Obama, J. D. Vance, a Yale-trained lawyer, West Coast lobbyist, and, at present, United States senator, rediscovers a forgotten America, a nation whose prominence stems not from its diversity but from its ability to resent someone for something. And David Sedaris, upon the election of Donald Trump to the presidency, finds his temper short and his body aching. In his attempts to make jest of the doom to come, his glibness toward the new commander in chief costs him first his acquaintances, then his father, and, finally, a close friend.

Narratives like these are examples of what I call strong nationalism. The political scientist Maria Todorova provides a variety of adjectives—"extreme, expansionist, messianic, integral, radical, exclusive"—that describe it (686). Strong nationalism is not interested in the middle of the road nor the moderate: strong nationalists find the nation in its extremes and seek to expand them. To think of strong nationalism's tactics in this way is to realize that it is not reducible to any one party or movement. Indeed, this book shows how mainstream liberals, subcultural populists, documenters of the nation's fraught relationship with civil rights, neoconservative spokespeople, and wry progressive essayists all participate in its peculiar affective intensity. Strong nationalism is not exclusive to one race, class, or gender. Its operations can be witnessed whenever a particularly "phobic majoritarian public sphere" is constructed that "continuously elides or punishes the existence of subjects who do not conform to the phantasm of normative citizenship" it insists upon (Muñoz 4). Strong nationalism is not necessarily conservative, but it is always politically conserving in its textual attempts to narrow and purify its "we" and demarcate and exclude its "them." It is evident in Amiri Baraka's chant "It's nation time!" at the Congress of African Peoples conference of 1972, whose theme was "unity without uniformity" (Robinson 98–99). It is evident in the "incredulous maternal disappointment" of Brook Van Dyke, the lesbian separatist who chastised the contemporary gay rights movement for, as she saw it, losing traction because lesbians want to simply "fit in" through same-sex marriage and military service (Levy). And it is evident any time that one group reduces another to parts so that they cannot participate in the national whole (see Enloe 87).[5]

Cumulatively, strong nationalists cannot see that the "we" of the nation is "built out of many smaller, overlapping, or contending forms of togetherness" (Costello 14). Strong nationalists find intolerable the idea that nationalism can have "local inflections, subjunctive moods, and lateral assemblages" (Saint-Amour 455). For strong nationalists, explanatory power does not come from the ambiguity inherent in the nation as a diverse, imagined community. Instead, it comes from the literal, unambiguous, and exclusive interpretations of the nation they create. To maintain explanatory power, strong nationalists synecdochically construct a nation that fundamentally misattunes the relationship between "us" and "them": their narratives turn America into a matter of "us" or "them," with the "them" being utterly unrepresentative of "us." They reject the idea of the nation as a "multifaceted democracy" that is able to inculcate "diverse satisfactions and different degrees of autonomy" (Connolly 55). The nation that emerges from the rhetoric of strong nationalism is seldom plural, diverse, or densely textured. It has strong gates but lacks a rich inner life. Its rhetoric is "stagey and brittle, more bravado than strength" (Esty ix). It is not interested in creating a sphere of "mutual responsibility, significant interaction, and a cooperative spirit" (May 170). In their narratives, if there is talk of mutual responsibility, it is vague and lacking a policy to structure it; if there is significant interaction, it only leads to hostility. Strong nationalists ask us to imagine very little. Indeed, much strong nationalist writing does little more than present readers with the familiar "and ask them to recognize it" (Issenberg). Strong nationalisms do not gain explanatory power from explaining anew. Instead, they gain it by dramatically confirming what the strong nationalist already knows. Strong nationalism produces a nation not of an imagined community but a nation that is not interested in imagining at all.

The strong nationalist use of synecdoche is paradoxical, for it uses the potential of a part to represent a whole to reject the idea that the nation can mean many things to many people. Whereas the relationship between the part and the whole in weaker forms of nationalism may be conjectural or merely suggestive, for the strong nationalist, it is terse, serious, and insistent. As a result, its figurative language lacks hues: it relies on a chiaroscuro of all or nothing. Readings that might suggest something broader than a binary of falsity/genuineness are taken to be soft and "narrated as a proneness to injury" that cannot withstand the strong nationalist's rigor (Ahmed, *Cultural Politics* 2–3). Strong nationalists empty the diverse contents of the nation by deriding multifaceted others as "false" and use their own personal "genuineness" as the measure that others can never match. What proves intriguing about the narratives I study in this book is how they anchor genuineness through the demonstration of the falsity of others—a reactive posture that presumes its own virtues through the depiction of others' vices. Thus strong nationalism "excels at coding the various forms of identarian uncertainty subtending liberal democracy—like differences among accounts of 'the people' or between 'people' and self—not as signs of democratic possibility but as threats" (Johnson 2). And because of this, strong nationalist solutions are ultimately antidemocratic. Strong nationalisms demonstrate how, as Rachel Greenwald Smith writes, "the content of democracy—the belief that citizens participate in the governing of their country—[has] been sacrificed in order for individuals to feel like autonomous, liberal subjects" (306).

Whereas the nonfiction of weak nationalism relishes the nation's ambiguities, the nonfiction of strong nationalism reduces these ambiguities to binaries. It does so with a voice that is filled with conviction, using a rhetoric that is hijacked to suit their purpose. The voice of the people, when commandeered by strong nationalists, neither reports nor hears "the people." Nor is it especially interested in hearing "the people," for strong nationalism's rigor is not meant to stitch but to sever. As Sara Ahmed writes, strong nationalists employ a maxim of "spare the rod, spoil the nation" (*Willful Subjects* 130). The extremity of their reading functions as a rod that accuses, reproofs, corrects, and disciplines, as if such readings "kept the body of the nation whole" (131). Strong nationalists derive strength from the definitiveness of their reading, the ways in which they corporeally correct the national body, assigning the "us" or "them" to be embraced or scolded. Indeed, for strong nationalists, intolerance offers a fount of narrative energy, as sustained enmity propels the description of "them" and narrows the band of "us." As Toni Morrison notes of classic American fiction, in this book I note how the nonfiction of strong nationalism uses a myriad of techniques dedicated to exposing others as Other: "estranging language, metaphoric condensation, fetishizing strategies, the economy of stereotype, allegorical foreclosure" (58). As if these tactics reveal a mutual sameness, such readings show how fervently strong nationalists commit to the "fantasy of the nation as a whole social body" (Ahmed, *Willful Subjects* 131). There may even be an element of pride in strong nationalists' intolerance, as if its ugly intensity shows "the need to believe in belief, to make a commitment to commitment . . . to consistently take the position, on whatever topic, which enabled and even called forth the maximum passion" (Grossberg, *We Gotta Get Out* 271). To strong nationalists, the nation is not only "the cathexis of a singular element" to stand in for the whole; it is also the energy of cathexis—the cognitive and affective energy such substitution of part for whole brings—that propels the intense attachments and detachments of their prose

(Laclau 97). Strong nationalists are uninterested in the new or the original: they are interested in repeating the same chord again and again, content in the familiarity of their shrill noise. Strong nationalism is not dense nationalism: it does not gain explanatory power through complex theses with supporting paragraphs. Strong nationalism is a thin nationalism: its explanatory power comes from the loud chord of a single affect it can strike repeatedly as proof of its bombast.

Affect and Affect Theories: Or, Affect Is a Theory

As Melissa Gregg and Gregory J. Seigworth note in *The Affect Theory Reader*, there are, at present, at least eight configurations of affect theory in the humanities and social sciences, each with their own alliances and each with their own resistances to the others (6–8). And, as Gregg and Seigworth note, the future portends that "there will always be more; undoubtedly there *are* more—as other means of inquiry are invented to account for the relational capacities that belong to the doings of bodies or are conjured by the world-belongingness that gives rise to a body's doing" (9, emphasis in original). That there is such a panoply of configurations indicates that no single definition of the word "affect" suffices: each configuration will define the word and its relationship to other keywords such as "emotion" and "mood" differently. All in all, this lack of a single definition signals affect's centrality to a variety of disciplines. Affect theory's configurations offer the reminder that affect is a matter of "what," but it is more importantly a matter of "why" and "how."

My use of the word "affect" in this book is derived primarily from the work of Silvan Tomkins, which may be best thought of as a resistance to the Freudian orthodoxy that insists that drive is the source of often-unconscious human emotionality (see Flatley, *Affective Mapping* 12–13). Inspired by both Charles Darwin and midcentury cybernetic theory, Tomkins reframed affect as having both a biological origin and an endlessly social outcome. As Donovan O. Schaefer writes, Tomkins's understanding of affect is one that "is better understood not as fixed, but as compounding" (*Evolution* 38). It is the accumulating plasticity of affect that has drawn a wide gamut of critics to Tomkins, including Eve Kosofsky Sedgwick and Adam Frank, who brought Tomkins into the humanities with their 1995 essay "Shame in the Cybernetic Fold." To critics such as Sedgwick and Frank, "Tomkins offers a matrix for mapping the contingent connections between bodies and histories—the veins of affect animating our values" in ways that do not reduce those affects to a consistent, deterministic explanation (Schaefer, *Evolution* 39). Tomkins does so primarily by paying attention to the ongoing flux of affect: how affects are registered as meaningful or meaningless by a person or between people, how affects magnify some objects and demagnify others (thus performing amplification and reduction at the level of affect similar to synecdoche at the level of rhetoric), how affects show part of our internal selves but also play into broader cultural scripts we may endorse or eschew. As such, affect is a stew of responses in which (rational) thinking and (emotional) feeling are always, inseparably, fused.

For Tomkins, an affect is as much an answer as it is the site of further questioning. "The individual whose affect is engaged is inevitably thereby confronted with such questions as 'What is happening?' 'What is going to happen?' 'How sure am I of what seems to be happening and what will happen?' 'What should I do?' These are theoretical questions in that they involve interpretation of empirical evidence, the extrapolation into the future, the evaluation of both interpretation and extrapolation and application of knowledge to strategy" (Tomkins, *Affect* 2:369). Affects both appraise and anticipate: in other words, they are not mere reactions but cogitations upon what has been reacted to. Affects not only respond to what has happened but speculate and in doing so frame what may happen next. Affects respond with intensity but also lay the ground for further or diminished intensity to come. Affects question the nature of their response and ponder about their appropriateness. Affects call to action and prepare for further calls to action.

The questions that Tomkins claims affects raise are, to me, the very same questions literary and cultural critics see at work—and perform in their own work—in the act of reading. These are questions of plot and emplotment, of story and discourse, of motivation, character, and characterization. Most importantly, what I derive from Tomkins's description of affect is that an affect is primarily a reading. *An affect is the incitement to read.* It is what ignites the urge to discourse on whatever has stimulated it. Importantly for both Tomkins and myself, the incitement to read comes with a theory of reading to sustain this incitement. Thus, when I write that Steinbeck's writing on Vietnam displays hawkishness, for example, I mean not only that Steinbeck finds his hawkishness incited by certain objects, but that his incitement to read urges him to further discourse on his hawkishness, and that in both, a general theory of hawkishness is evident in his synecdochical choices, in what he sees as parts that represent a whole. Through such synecdochical choices, the incitement to read demonstrates an attachment to an object, one in which the object is something more than the object, as a part connected to the whole. To me, this is all the more intriguing given that synecdochical choices are ones that connect the personal to the national, something that seems simultaneously part of the self and much more than oneself. In their being affected, the writers in my archive respond to certain objects in a purely personal way. Yet these writers also attempt to apply their affecting beyond themselves in their insistence that their personal response is indicative of the nation. In other words, throughout *We, Us, and Them* I trace how these authors work their responses into entire theories of the nation.

Their doing so offers not only a reminder of the speculative, discursive potential inherent in the nation as a concept, but a reminder as well of affect's ever-present penchant to read and theorize beyond its immediate surroundings. And their doing so not only reveals the "somewhat fluid relationship" between affect and object that is key to Tomkins's understanding of affect, it also reveals the always fluid relationship between self and community that manifests as the style through which the nation comes into being and is sustained (see Flatley, *Affective Mapping* 17). Jonathan Flatley paraphrases this fluid relationship as "a kind of subject-object confusion," and I find it useful to think of it not as confusion but as the sort of fusion about which Sara Ahmed writes so productively, the ways in which affect consists of the "sticking of signs to bodies" (Flatley, *Affective Mapping* 17; Ahmed, *Cultural Politics* 13). What we see in the affects that saturate one's reading of the nation are the ways in which objects—activities, places, even other people—are interpreted as public symbols of the writer's own private America. We see how their attachment to an object is invested with affect, how it is stuck *to* an object and how the object becomes stuck *with* the affect—which is perhaps a too elegant way of saying that in studying affect, what we come to see is how signs become stuck to bodies, and how this sticking is in itself always worth parsing for its particular relationship to the sign and the body.

Tomkins's parsing of affects has often been misunderstood as an attempt to categorize affect into discrete categories or to reduce affect to mere facial expression—the latter being more the work of Tomkins's successors than himself. Even Gregg and Seigworth seem to disparage

Tomkins for being "generally more prone to a categorical naming of affects" rather than a highly theorized description of their architecture (7). Such misunderstanding selectively forgets that Tomkins often introduces affects in pairs that could never be reduced to one single name ("surprise-startle," for instance) and that he insists any object could not only yield an affect but also create linkages across affects. All the same, we should not think of the assigning of a name to an affect as a fault to which we are prone: as Hil Malatino evocatively writes, naming is "both a resolution and an incipience" (12). Similarly, in this book, my use of a single affect in each chapter is not intended to reduce an author to a sole affect but to make apparent an intensity that is worth exploring not only in a key text but as a component of a broader understanding of the interlocking and contradicting affects that constitute the nation. I very much agree with Malatino that "no affective commons is possible in the absence of such naming, such recognition. Collective naming is the way that feelings become public, which is to say that it is the way that feelings come to have transformative force" (12). Without naming we cannot begin to see the affective commons in front of us—and without naming, we cannot begin to formulate the critical commons so needed to interpret and transform the sphere of the nation.

It is Tomkins's insight that the purpose of reading an object is primarily to diminish the risk of negative affect (see Frank and Wilson 92–93). In this book, the thoroughness of the attempt to ward off negative affect is seen in the frenetic, haphazard, reactionary way in which the authors I study attempt to thwart any possibility of being personally challenged by what they observe of the nation. What they see is such a challenge to their theory of the nation that it must be radically torqued or totally expunged from their vision—it is such a threat to their sense of the world that the only defense is going on the offense. The narratives that flow from this position demonstrate what Tomkins sees as the paradox of affect, that affects become "strong" "by virtue of the continuing failures of its strategies to afford protection" from their being challenged (*Affect* 2:323). The authors whose narratives I study in this book find their theories of the nation are roused and confirmed in ways that they are not resolved but intensified. What the adamancy of the affects shown through their synecdochical reading reveals is the hardening of their point of view instead of the development of further sophistication. The certainty with which their reading concludes seems to stand on an even shakier foundation than it did at its beginning. And overall, while the interpretations they make may be bold or certain, the anxiety from which they originate is never truly expunged. It is the paradoxical fragility of strong affect that, even as its expositors find themselves all the more confirmed in their theory of the nation, that we feel less confident because of their very confirmation. The strength of what they see is strong only for them and fellow travelers—for us, what they see induces only further skepticism. Affects of the type I explore in this book reveal how "affect is the missing term in an adequate understanding of ideology" (Grossberg, *We Gotta Get Out* 82), for we see how the affects that should spur interpretation only work to confirm one's view of the world; how affect, like any strategy of reading, solidifies ideology.

Strong Affects

The intervention of my previous book was to show how, as Tomkins writes, it is paradoxically the very weakness of the affects—and how weak affects loosely organize a theory of the world—that makes weak nationalism effective, as weak affects "are neither intense enough nor recurrent enough to prompt the generation of more than a crude general description of the phenomena themselves" (*Affect* 2:312). Weak affects calibrate ourselves to the world and allow us to be receptive to it. For Tomkins, a weak affect was the most "effective" because "if it breaks down only occasionally, it can be revised and yet remain relatively weak" (324). It is weak affects' very lack of intensity that allows one to avoid the false interpretation that the world is one way and one way alone. Weak affects are malleable and subject to revision: they are able to account for the world as it was, as it is, and as it might be in the future.

By contrast, strong affects are fixed, inflexible theories of the world. If weak affects provide nothing more than a general description, strong affects wrench weird specifics and absolute boundaries from the vagaries of life. If weak affects can be revised, strong affects are not only final; they return to their finality time and time again through duplication, repetition, and rumination. And if weak affects break down occasionally to no great bother, when strong affects face the possibility of revision, all hell breaks loose. What fills in the transferential space between part and whole for strong nationalists are the hysterical projections of a ruined nation that is evident in their readings of it. As an example of strong affect, Tomkins writes of the person whose desire to avoid being hit by a car first leads him to avoid busy streets, then to avoid leaving the house in the daytime, such that "if his house were to be hit by a car, he would have to seek refuge in a deeper shelter" (*Affect* 2:324). The person so worried about being hit by a car sees everything to be such a threat that the only thing he can do is ensconce himself in a stronger barrier. And much like how the person who has retreated to a deeper shelter may write vehemently of traffic collisions, a similar tenor is found in strong nationalists' depiction of America. Even when based on direct observation, the thinness of their depiction seems as if it could have been made within the shelter of one's home. Practitioners of strong affect live in what Adam J. Frank and Elizabeth A. Wilson call a "monochromatic world" (95). Theirs is a world composed of one color, of one affect. Strong nationalists may be interested in the nation, but only in one way: the intricacies of demography, the inflections of locality, the flux of immigration seldom interest them, and if so, only in a secondary way that supports rather than problematizes their universalist, strong reading. The reader of such prose may feel an odd uncanniness: the nation a strong nationalist depicts seems familiar but also disconnected from reality. This is because a monochromatic world is not the real world: it is missing coloration, saturation, and hue. The strong nationalists' world is certain in its interpretation but never lively or vibrant. The confidence of its representation comes from its inflexibility.

The problem of strong affect is the problem of strong nationalism. Strong nationalist affect ignores the participatory nature of the nation, realizing individual vision at the expense of diverse communities. The explanatory power of weak nationalism is its defamiliarizing capacity. In the moods of such writing it is possible that a "new 'we' has come into being, one that enables, in its turn, a different 'I' to be experienced and articulated" (Flatley, "How a Revolutionary Counter-Mood" 510). "Things matter in a new way, a way that is manifestly and consciously plural" (510). But what strong nationalism offers is a way in which things matter in the same old way, that they are confirmed as the most familiar and most stale version of "I," not only no different than before, but now even more hostile toward becoming anything more than what it ever was. As Silvan Tomkins writes, strong affect is "vulnerable to signs, parts, and similarities" as modes of constructing its theory of the world (*Affect* 3:532). Reduced to monochrome, everyone looks the same; reduced to chiaroscuro, everyone looks like a stereotype in strong nationalist prose. Its use of the word "we" is bereft of the word's democratic under-pinnings and is more interested in sustaining a dogma through which the author's use of "the national 'we' magically enables the 'I' of the na-tional to do things it can never hope to be able to do as an individual 'I'" (Hage 13). The strong nationalist similarly abuses the word "us," for in that word "representational function becomes political as well as sym-bolic," a way of entrusting someone "to represent our own best selves" and "act *on our behalf*" so that they may "achieve things that are beyond us" (Slotkin 498, emphasis in original). Speaking for "us" presumes a con-nection between "us" and "them," a claustral space where we come into being because we have been authentically engaged. But the strong na-tionalist perverts the horizontal idealism of this for vertical, demagogic purposes. Strong nationalists do not engage with the real "us."[6] Instead, they use synecdoche to speak in ways to demarcate a "them." They do not create spheres of representativeness—they instead create spheres of unrepresentativeness.

Strong affects promote a "flexible absolutism," the framing of "new and internally diverse cultural positions as 'eternal absolutes'" to be safe-guarded at all costs (Harding 275). Strong affects do not reflect: they react, by any means necessary, to affirm their world. So while strong national-ists may hold the nation near and dear to their hearts, in the way they do so, they override and reject a broader, communal sense of it. This is a concern, for as Rick Altman writes, "When patriotism is reduced to the identifiable style of a specific constellated community, then the stage of unisonality has clearly been superceded" (202). There is no room for new citizens in a nation constructed through strong affect. Its reliance on inflexible rules and eternal absolutes, even as it amplifies parts to wholes, reduces the nation to the gut feeling of a single person that no neighbor can broach and no expert can qualify. As Fintan O'Toole writes, "The gut is a tyrant. Intuition is both inherently unpredictable and, as a basis for public policy, inherently anti-democratic. It does not have to account for itself—any more than divine inspiration can be questioned by believ-ers. It is not open to contradiction because it is entirely personal" (14). It is through such gut feeling, through such strong affect, that we see the strong nationalists' attempts at the "miniaturization of community" through their constricting "the radius of identification" of what and who counts as American (Collins 15). In their monopolistic conception of the world, strong affect pushes others out of the way, leaving the strong nationalist the lone individual who knows they are correct because they are the only person remaining.

Reading Strong Nationalisms

Much of what I study in this book is how writers of this type of "America" take artifacts, from menus to monuments, from trials to elections, and synecdochically endow them with what they perceive as an innate Americanness, how "the scraps, patches, and rags of daily life [are] repeatedly turned into the signs of a national culture" in ways that are both "pedagogical" and "performative" (Bhabha 297). In the thrall of strong affect, some items come into microscopic view while the broader field that allows for a macroscopic view disappears. The portrait of the nation that strong nationalists depict—the nation they read—seems cropped: what would give it perspective is missing. Writers of this particular type of America thus expose the problem of synecdochical writing.[7] As Michel de Certeau observes, "synecdoche makes more dense: it amplifies the detail and miniaturizes the whole" (101). The efficiency of synecdoche makes the world understandable. But that efficiency comes with a risk that the weak nationalist eschews and the strong nationalist embraces: it is in their amplification and miniaturization that the strong nationalist's part becomes misattuned from the whole. Whereas weak nationalism is conjectural and universalizing, strong nationalism raises the individual to the exemplar and thus risks obsessing over strange particulars. To paraphrase Robert L. Ivie, strong nationalists do not put metaphor to good use. Instead, their strong affects narrow the space between the metaphorical and the literal, "denying the inevitable ambiguity and constitutive force of our linguistic choices" (Ivie 72). Strong affects generate distortion, exaggeration, and hysteria because of their attempt to generalize what is, in reality, an incommensurate world. And as Sara Ahmed notes, strong affect "may respond to the particular, but it tends to do so by aligning the particular with the general: 'I hate you because you are this or that,' where the 'this' or 'that' evokes a group that the individual comes to stand for or stand in for" (*Cultural Politics* 49). One way to refute a critique of your way of life is to miniaturize the critique; one way to insist on your vision of the world is to amplify it to the point that it alone can be representative. The affective forcefulness of strong nationalist prose obscures how, in their substitution of a part for a whole, strong nationalists reduce the whole, turning people into abstractions. Yet in the pang their narratives affectively elicit, every abstraction feels personal.[8] Indeed, strong nationalists are prone to lengthy taxonomic elaborations over insignificant minutiae as to delineate others such that "every single person should be vetted to the most extreme standard" (Stern 124). In strong nationalism, synecdoche "fulfill[s] the task of particularization" that strong nationalists believe will demonstrate its superiority over the ambiguities of the universal (Tamir 54).

Strong nationalism's use of synecdoche produces an affective gravitas that threatens to consume more complex readings of the nation. As Maurice Blanchot notes, nationalism "tends always to integrate everything, all values, that is how it ends up being integral, the sole value" (qtd. in Hill 21). Strong nationalists use the integrative potential of synecdoche to pave over representations they see as false: they engage in "the production of the common to a repetition of the same or a process of unification" (Hardt and Negri 182). As Michael Hardt and Antonio Negri note, strong nationalists take complex concepts such as love of fellow citizens and convert them into "the pressure to love most those like you and hence less those who are different" (182). They believe that the only way to make a nation is by "setting (or pushing) aside differences and alterity in order to form a united national people, a national identity" (183). Thus in their representation of the "true" America, strong nationalists reduce the nation to a sole source and a desire for a sole authority (who might be a democrat but is more likely a demagogue) to perpetuate its reading as "the sole value" from which the nation can be constructed. Strong nationalists' use of synecdoche does not attempt to imagine a horizon as much as it does the verticality of "truest" representation of which all others are inferior copies.

In effect, strong nationalists' use of synecdoche is not to produce a true representation but to abuse its tactics to produce the sole representation. This is how strong nationalists monopolize the conversation. They use synecdoche to dramatically traffic in "the birth and death of whole worlds, whole political orders, whole systems of human values" (Hofstadter 29), all the while drawing their drama from what might seem to be an odd use of the particular as evidence for it. They turn complex situations into either/or dichotomies and turn a complex rhetoric into caricature, cliché, and stereotype. They will not concede a single point for they suspect that ambiguity and flexibility is "the strait gate through which newness would enter" (Saint-Amour 443–444). In both their use of language and the nation that emerges from it, strong nationalist prose is ugly—I mean this in the way that Elisabeth R. Anker describes the "ugly freedoms" strong nationalists admire in which "principles and actions of freedom are granted preeminence even when they support widespread subjugation" (6). It is the way in which the narratives I study disregard the damage they do in the name of national virtue that makes the America they endorse ugly—and there is often a recurring strange pride in their doing so, as if the way in which they "legitimate mass harm . . . to uphold freedom as an always celebrated virtue" (6) enacts the truest nationalism. Strong nationalists use rhetoric to produce an arhetorical world "where no metaphors would be needed, where thing, thought, memory, imagination, and language would all coalesce in the oneness" of the nations' "eternity" (Vendler 233). This is a far cry from the sort of "imagined community" that Benedict Anderson articulates, for it is not a community where individual contributions cohere into a whole, but a sea of sameness, where its citizens are indistinct, mere copies of the oneness of the nation. In strong nationalism the very rhetoric that is supposed to bring us together is deployed not only to put us at cross-purposes, but to eradicate the variety of thought and feeling that makes an "us" the cornerstone of democracy.

This cross-purpose is evident in depictions of the nation that center on strong affects of hawkishness, bile, futility, resentment, and depression. The first chapter of this book explores the strong affect of hawkishness through John Steinbeck's Vietnam journalism. Drawing upon theories from Cold War rhetoric and contemporary political theory, I use Steinbeck's journalism to articulate the role of "hawkish reading" that reads the world through what affect theorists would call a "strong theory" of aggression. It does so by weaponizing the rhetoric of synecdoche, taking its premise that a part can represent a whole, as the justification to intervene and escalate conflict. I argue that hawks are readers who vigilantly scan their world for the proof of their totalizing and tautological theory that the best response to potential aggression is to preempt it with their own. To do so, hawks employ synecdoche in ways that do not diminish but instead escalate conflict. In this way, hawkishness reminds us of how, as Benedict Anderson writes, the rhetoric of nationalism makes it possible for "so many millions of people, not so much to kill, as willingly to die for such limited imaginings" (7).

The second chapter explores what I call Hunter S. Thompson's "bilious reading" of the nation. Bilious reading engages in a synecdochical, populist construction of a narrow elite of "them" to whom the nationalist can only react with excessive anger and bad temper, a rhetoric that relies on "profanity, *ad hominem* invective, and hyperbolic imagery of graphic—and often sexualized—violence" (Jane 533). At an affective level, what bile produces is not wholly divisive but offers moments of "savage agreement" (534) in which fellow populists agree that mainstream life is corrupt and unregenerate. Closely reading his reportage of the "Battle of Aspen," *Fear and Loathing on the Campaign Trail '72*, and his 1976 essay on the rise of Jimmy Carter for their bile, I show how Thompson practices a populism under the guise of a subcultural ethos. As a strong nationalism, Thompson's bile shows how synecdoche is used to create what he calls "the terrible logic of it all": how elite parts fit together in ways that create a monstrous whole that, in sum, shows the "Death of the American Dream" (Thompson in Torrey and Simonson 182). Drawing on political theory, I explore how bile's "terrible logic" is indeed "a particular moralistic imagination of politics, a way of perceiving the political world that sets a morally pure and fully unified—but ultimately fictional—people against elites who are deemed corrupt or in some other way morally inferior or institutions that support the 'wrong' people" (Müller 19–20). In its doing so, bilious reading shows how populism cannot transcend vitriol to become a multifaceted political movement.

The third chapter examines James Baldwin's last book-length nonfiction essay to understand how he became, by the mid-1980s, a futile reader. Examining the two narratives he produced about the Atlanta murders of 1979–81, first as a *Playboy* article entitled "The Evidence of Things Not Seen" and second as a 1985 book-length exploration with the same title, I study how Baldwin's affective trajectory shifted from a weak civic nationalism in the 1960s to his embrace of Black nationalism in the 1970s, and ultimately his conviction that it was better to exit the nation than continuing to urge its reform. The *Playboy* narrative offers a perfect example of what scholars have called Baldwin's "strategic exceptionalism": his insistence that the problems of race were reflective of national problems that the nation itself could remedy (see Wall 36). In particular, the *Playboy* narrative is highly reliant upon a strong nationalist connection between the child and the nation's future, which I unpack through the works of Sara Ahmed and Lee Edelman. By contrast, the book-length version, completed after the trial, exposes how Baldwin gave up on the nation as a source of the future. Through Albert O. Hirschman's theorizations of futility and exit, I explore how Baldwin takes the nation's collective uninterest in seeking true justice for the Atlanta child murder victims as the reaffirming of its racist and classist past. Thus to Baldwin, the nation becomes that for which no prose can solve. Through his use of synecdoche, Baldwin's futile reading seals off any ambiguity that may defamiliarize or engender a new reading of the nation: what it depicts is final and terminal. In doing so, he reveals how futility is a mode of reading driven by a strong affect that denies the possibility for progress and immobilizes the expectation that the future will be better than the present. As an incitement to discourse, futile reading is not melancholic or reparative but definitive and conclusive: it aims to show an entire history without progress, a nation without possibility, a world without redemption.

The fourth chapter examines the politics of resentment in J. D. Vance's *Hillbilly Elegy*. The memoir's foundational premise is that Vance's life experiences are representative of not just one swath of the nation—the "hillbillies" who migrated to the industrial north in the 1950s—but also their succeeding generations, the struggles of the Rust Belt and blue-collar Americans more generally, their abandonment of progressive politics, and, ultimately, an entire nation in decline. Vance's use of synecdoche allows him to take on multiple voices, sliding from exemplary hillbilly to concerned middle-class citizen, from atypical to typical American. His narrative is dependent upon his strategic pivoting from one synecdoche to the other, exhorting the collapse of urban communities on the one hand while indicting suburban consumerism on the other, all the while claiming to represent an undefined—yet truly "American"—morality that is beyond exhortation or indictment. The effect of such synecdochical leaps is that it quickly—and deliberately—becomes impossible to figure out the whole for which Vance, as a part, exactly speaks. In particular, I explore how Vance, throughout *Elegy*, uses synecdoche to drag others down and in doing so perpetuates a strong nationalism based on denying others the power to represent the whole. Synecdoche, as it is deployed by the resentful, works to maintain an us/them dichotomy between those who are unfairly entitled and those who supposedly lack entitlement. At the same time, in the way it affixes parts to wholes, resentment seeks to cover up the contradictions that come with such dichotomies, not only to erase its own entitlement, but so that it may continue attacking others.

I conclude by examining the strong affects that constitute Trumpism and contributed to its rise. I study how these affects increasingly infringe upon a reader by exploring David Sedaris's writing on the 2016 presidential election. His essay "A Number of Reasons I've Been Depressed Lately" indexes how Trumpist strong affect encroaches upon Sedaris, rewriting his understanding of his friends, family, and, ultimately, himself. The depression he eventually comes to feel shows how Trumpism comes to negatively overhaul American popular culture and daily life. Trumpism hijacks not only the conversation but also the fundamental premises of what it means to be an American, slashing out at milder forms of national identification. Sedaris's trademark wit, especially his irony, comes to fail him in a nation in which all participatory affects are strong, in which all is literal. What Sedaris's essay ultimately shows, I argue, is how liberals fail to go beyond the mere rejection of Trumpism, how those like Sedaris falter in their offering an alternative to Trumpist strong affect. Sedaris's wit does not throw a towel over strong nationalism's ever-widening fire, and the depression Sedaris comes to feel only shows how irony runs aground in the face of democratic disaster.

Overall, the problem of strong nationalism shows how "the domain of citizenship, which had expanded in the post–World War II years to bring in, for the first time, broader and broader ranges of Americans, began to shrink" (Rodgers 198). Its prose enables a nation that shrinks "into smaller, more partial contracts: visions of smaller communities of virtue and engagement—if not communities composed simply of one rights-holding self" (198). And the strong affects through which such a nation is conveyed skews what was once horizontal to the vertical, turning what was once a politics "focused on horizontal issues such as income, class, and economic need" into one that is "focused on vertical issues such as religiosity, anti-elitism, and law and order" (Chafe 367). The study of strong nationalisms, I wager, shows how this discourse led America into the darkness of the present moment, where it worrisomely remains. And if my reading of strong nationalisms proves meaningful, it will be because theories of affect can help us understand much in dark times. Nationalism, after all, is a mode of reading. And because it is a form of reading, literary and cultural critics are all the more poised to respond to its impress. As this book is an attempt to shine light on these dark times, it is also a suggestion that critics can not only broaden the circle of "we" but also broaden the work—and worth—of reading.

1

Hawkishness

JOHN STEINBECK'S VIETNAM JOURNALISM

IN A JANUARY 1966 LETTER to Jack Valenti, press secretary for President Lyndon Johnson, John Steinbeck advocated for the development of a napalm grenade to be used in the escalating Vietnam War. "Almost the exact size and weight of a baseball," it would be "the natural weapon for the Americans," Steinbeck wrote, because "there isn't an American boy over 13 who can't peg a baseball from infield to home plate with accuracy" (Steinbeck qtd. in Wells 88). He thought "this weapon would be valuable for cleaning out tunnels and foxholes . . . burning off extra ambush country or free borne sniper fire." It would incapacitate the opponent, for "an enemy with a bit of flame on his clothes or even in front of him is out of combat." And he suggested that dispatching six men armed with sacks of such grenades would "ring an area faster than you could throw a magazine into an automatic." Valenti forwarded Steinbeck's letter to Secretary of Defense Robert McNamara. It went through the echelons of the Defense Department, which determined that other weapons under development would have a similar effect.

The proposal for the napalm grenade is a reminder that John Steinbeck, winner of the Pulitzer Prize in Fiction and recipient of the 1962 Nobel Prize in Literature, was closely affiliated with the Lyndon Johnson administration, so closely that his advice was circulated among the administration's principals and reached the top of the federal bureaucracy. It is also a reminder that Steinbeck subscribed wholeheartedly to its domestic and foreign agendas. Steinbeck was "strongly loyal" and shared "an intellectual agreement" with Johnson: they were both supporters of New Deal–style politics and both subscribed to the domino theory of communist aggression (Barden 158). The proposal also shows that this agreement was not only intellectual but extended to a peculiar and mutually shared affective disposition toward the theater of war and its instruments. The napalm grenade, in Steinbeck's description, never kills people, it "cleans" out tunnels and "rings out" areas; it does not immolate the enemy, it puts a mere "bit of flame" on him. It is not that Steinbeck underappreciated the damage the proposed grenade would do. It was that he saw American victory in the war as so important that the enemy who would be set ablaze by it was not worthy of human description.

The grenade comes with no ethical quandaries: indeed its description is couched in a perverse innocence.[1] The metaphors that accompany it naturalize war as the epitome of national values. As Steinbeck describes it, the napalm grenade is a biological extension of American ability. It is the "natural" weapon for the "American boy" who can toss it effortlessly: by extension, the soldier throwing napalm is as innocent as the pitcher of a middle-class, junior league baseball team. Napalm, a violent explosive, is reduced in his proposal to an instrument of national pastime. Steinbeck's description of the napalm grenade reduces the Vietnam War to a kind of game: he turns Vietnam into an American baseball field. By doing so, war becomes a sport, and Vietnam is no longer Vietnam, but a place where Americans practice a quintessential Americanness.

This worldview and the affective architecture that supports it proved disastrous not only in the field of battle but in the legacy it left in its wake. "In Vietnam we lost not only a war and a subcontinent," Morris Dickstein writes, "we also lost our pervasive confidence that American arms and American aims were linked somehow to justice and morality, not merely for the quest for power" (271). One way to understand this loss is to examine narratives of the Vietnam War in which the link between arms and aims is severed. In the work of Tim O'Brien, for example, protagonists realize that individual morality is superior to national ideology. Through the experience of war, O'Brien's protagonists, as Joseph Darda notes, have "a kind of liberal enlightenment through an encounter with death," which motivates "shaking off ideological constraints" so that the protagonist ultimately "defends, above all else, himself and his own liberal consciousness" (*Empire* 16). And in the work of Michael Herr, as Marguerite Nguyen notes, war evoked a "crisis of representation" that proved "aesthetically generative" as "formal failure bec[ame] formal innovation, and more important, create[d] possibilities for a new kind of political critique, a new kind of political language" (89). Herr's self-proclaimed difficulty in capturing the moral turpitudes of war led him to new rhetorics that expose the fracture between individuals and the governments that conscripted them and, in doing so, defamiliarize not only the war but the common assumptions upon which its politics relied.

Another way to understand this loss, the one I pursue in this chapter, is to examine narratives that strive to solidify the link between arms and aims and, in doing so, support and defend the purpose of making war. For as Tim O'Brien was fighting and Michael Herr was writing, John Steinbeck was also in Vietnam, extoling the virtues of official policy and portraying the war as the manifestation of everything that was right with America.[2] From November 1966 through April 1967, he toured Vietnam, with brief stops in Laos, Thailand and Indonesia. His dispatches from Southeast Asia, his "Letters to Alicia," were published in *Newsday.* The "Letters" column had an audience of over four hundred thousand as *Newsday* had syndication agreements with large newspapers including the *Washington Post, Los Angeles Times,* and *International Herald Tribune:* twenty-nine American and ten foreign newspapers (see Barden in Steinbeck, *Steinbeck in Vietnam* xviii). Yet in the column's very title, Steinbeck reveals the narrowness of his purpose. The column is billed as "Letters" to Alicia Patterson Guggenheim, the recently deceased wife of *Newsday's* publisher, and Steinbeck insists that he is writing "not to someone who is dead, but rather to a living mind and a huge curiosity" (xviii). Yet in practice he was writing not for the sake of curiosity but for the sake of self-confirmation. By naming his column after a dead person, Steinbeck showed that he was writing to someone who could not protest the quality of his observations.

In the "Letters," as Thomas E. Barden notes, Steinbeck "threw himself wholeheartedly into making the best case he could for the war" (157). Concerns were positively framed. American soldiers and South Vietnamese farmers were unquestionably praised. The Vietcong—and protestors at home—were routinely castigated. The tone of the "Letters" is uniformly bellicose: bountiful in its pride of American soldiers ("They are our dearest and our best men and more than that—they are our hope" [155]) and ardent in its disdain of the Vietcong ("a carcinomic nastiness . . . parasitic on the body of the polity" [114]) and outright belligerent toward American war protestors ("if you hear someone celebrating the misunderstood and mistreated V.C., just punch him in the nose for me, will you?" [26]).[3]

The affect that emerges from Steinbeck's writing of the war is not patriotism, the affect of complex, critical, beauteous feelings of "communal American identity" that need not be based on vilification or exclusion but on the imagining of a "project we all can share" (Railton xiv). Instead, what Steinbeck emotes is blunt, snide, and literal. It vilifies and excludes: he is not interested in evoking a shared cause but is instead interested in castigating those who are not pure believers in his project. The emotional brazenness of Steinbeck's "Letters" does not invite studied, scholarly examination. The ugliness of his reading—the simplicity of his worldview, the stereotypes he peddles, the clichés of his diction—are the antithesis of the complex reading necessary to genuinely understand the difficulties of the war he witnessed. Ultimately, it is saddening that such an accomplished writer could be so poor a reader. And it is little wonder that the "Letters" are considered *verboten* among Steinbeck critics, who have attempted to dismiss them as a blemish on an otherwise notable career. As Jackson J. Benson notes, the few critical appraisals of the "Letters" are "for the most part passing reactions to his hawkish views of the war . . . the object of some ridicule or regret, but again, largely in passing" (1009).

This chapter takes seriously the word that Steinbeck critics use only in passing. It does so by reading Steinbeck's "Letters" for their hawkishness, following Lauren Berlant's advice that prose of this tenor uses "the silliest, most banal and erratic logic imaginable to describe important things, like what constitutes intimate relations, political personhood, and national life" (*Queen* 12). I argue that Steinbeck's letters reveal not only the link between arms and aims that would come into question in Vietnam, but also reveals the strong affect that drives the discourse of intervention and escalation more generally. What Steinbeck's "Letters" show us, ultimately, is how hawks read the world to perpetuate aggression. Hawkish reading, as I use the term, is a way of reading the world in a flat, extreme, and totalizing way: hawks are readers who vigilantly scan their world for the proof of their totalizing and tautological theory that the best response to potential aggression is to preempt it with their own.

To do so, hawks employ rhetorical conventions in ways that do not diminish but instead escalate conflict. Steinbeck's "Letters" in particular weaponize the conventions of synecdoche, the rhetorical substituting of a part for the whole. Neither synecdochical reading nor the rhetoric of nationalism necessarily lead to inevitable conflict. Indeed, Kenneth Burke notes that even the name of the nation, the United States, is productively synecdochical as it allowed those who lived during its contentious founding to "accent our nation either as 'The United *States*' or 'The *United* States'": both Jeffersonians who might accent the "State" or Hamiltonians who might accent the "United" could find satisfaction in it, and thus synecdoche made it possible, Burke notes, to "have both wishes at once," (375) which is exactly what synecdoche does at its best. More recently, Gary

Gerstle notes how Barack Obama used his biracial family background to "comprehend the aspirations and frustrations of both Americas and to find a way to bring the two together" (388). And Michael Billig describes how the very banality of nationalist discourse allows for "infinite discursive possibilities" that need not be "confined to simple differentiating stereotypes" (87). Overall, what synecdoche produces an ambiguous, plural space wherein all can find room for themselves and, in the context of national identity, realize, if only diffusely, their shared interest in others with whom they share a nation.

But this is not what a hawk wants synecdoche to do. Instead, hawks weaponize synecdoche to limit it so that it spurs antagonism alone. The inevitable result of hawkish reading is to disable cooperation, betraying the democratic premises of synecdochical rhetoric. In doing so, hawks reveal their disinterest in the nation as a site of "deep, horizontal comradeship" as much as they reveal their interest in using rhetoric to perpetuate demagoguery's thin, vertical antipathy toward any person deemed other (Benedict Anderson 7). Hawkish reading is a reminder of how rhetoric can be used to create feelings that, as Benedict Anderson forewarned in *Imagined Communities,* "make it possible . . . for so many millions of people, not so much to kill, as willingly to die for such limited imaginings" (7).

In this way, Steinbeck's "Letters" shed light on the tenuous link between arms and aims that hawks articulate through synecdochical rhetoric. The very thinness of hawkish reading is what enables the peculiar intensity of its affective attachments. Steinbeck did not, as many writers did, see the Vietnam War as a "a source of literary and political experimentation" (Nudelman 363). Instead, it was for him literal, denotative proof of virtuous American policy. Neither did the war induce in him a feeling of "anticipatory dread" that so pervaded the writing of the period (Nudelman 363). Instead, the war confirmed with confidence his belief in the nation's greatness. What Steinbeck's "Letters" show is how hawkish readers use the generative power of synecdoche to distinctly unregenerate ends: to exclaim but never analyze their mission; to insist upon, but never examine, their beliefs.

To read the "Letters" is to acknowledge that the very banality of hawkish reading—and the "ugly feelings" that unfurl with it—is the point (Ngai, *Ugly Feelings* 3). Steinbeck's reductive generalizations, his few and ultimately hollow depictions of the South Vietnamese people, his in-your-face textual hollering at war protestors: all these reflect the hawk's incitement to read the world in a particular way, a way that sees intervention and escalation as virtues; a way that endorses an intrusive and invasive foreign policy as just and worth the cost of money and life. Hawkish reading may seem repellent, yet its ability to construct narratives that perpetuate a limited vision of the world—and to incite a desire to invade most of it—should never be underestimated. Hawkish reading solicits our attention not only as a particular incitement to read but for its textual expense—and the human casualties it creates.

Hawkishness: A Strong Affect

The use of the word "hawkish" to describe a person who "is inclined to favor hardline or warlike policies" emerged in the nineteenth century, according to the *Oxford English Dictionary*.[4] It draws upon a broader figurative use of the word "hawk" that the *OED* traces to the sixteenth century: a "hawk" is "one who preys on others . . . one who is keen and grasping" of his opponent. The hawk's keen discerning, their grasping read, is not for the sake of intellection but for the sole purpose of predation: the hawk reads not to unpack complexities or revel in ironies, but to scan for prey, to pierce the jugular, to make a kill. Hawks are not interested in illuminating or accommodating as much as in committing and confirming. The hawk reads with a singleness of purpose: to encourage and sustain war.

The way in which the hawk reads is one of strong affect. For example, Silvan Tomkins writes that "the individual who has a strong fear theory" is one for "whom fear is an ever-present threat which must be anticipated and dealt with" (*Affect* 2:322). To consider hawkish reading from the perspective of strong affect is to explore how it manifests what Tomkins calls a "destructive war script," a strong theory of aggression that presumes that war serves as the ideal "vehicle for stretching the energies, will, abilities, and skills of all to a maximum, exposing and confirming hidden reserves and potentialities" (3:491). Hawkish readers see war not in the cost of lives or the burdening of the economy; if anything, these are interpreted as noble losses for a broader and more important cause. And when the necessity for war is not evident, hawkish readers turn to preemption to invent the conflict that they believe will unleash national energy. Hawkish reading is limited: hawks read only insofar as to justify aggression. As a result, hawkish reading parallels other strong theories, such as what Eve Kosofsky Sedgwick characterizes as paranoid reading's "wide reach and rigorous exclusiveness" that always risks "being strongly tautological" (135). Hawkish reading takes a subject and turns it into a target for its predation: it projects its strong theory of the world onto its prey and in doing so gives itself the legitimacy to attack it. The conflict that inevitably emerges is seen by hawks not as the work of tautological reading but as confirmation of what they have anticipated.

Hawks use synecdoche in the service of strong affect to escalate their agenda: to invent the necessity for conflict, to mobilize national energies to support it, and to devalue opponents. Steinbeck's "Letters" show how hawkish readers weaponize the Burkean maxim that "a reduction is a representation" to create a simple, stark world of heroes and villains (507). In reducing the world to stark binaries that produce strong affect, the hawks' use of synecdoche aims to amplify the strength of their position through an ebullient evaluation of their prowess and to amplify the weakness of their opponent through the devaluation of the enemy's legitimacy (see Kahneman and Renshon 92). The hawk's use of synecdoche is thus not intended to capture complex representation but to facilitate combat between adversaries. The hawk is always the hero, and the other is always the villain: even worse, the dove is always the villain as well. Hawkish reading shows, as Burke writes, how "disagreements within a society as to what part should represent the whole and how this representation should be accomplished" are amplified by how hawks use synecdoche in "peculiarly simplificatory" ways (508, 510).

Two particularly "simplificatory" ways stand out in hawkish reading. First is the use of synecdoche to create and support the rationale for intervention. In the context of Vietnam, as Richard Slotkin notes, both the Kennedy and Johnson administrations were imbued with a common "mystique" toward warfare, which they saw as "the supreme expression of American values, in which the society 'as one man' assumes the moral burden of a struggle for justice" and "submerges petty and individual concerns in a collective and patriotic effort" (500). The transitive work of synecdoche is apparent in the hawks' construction of war's "mystique." Hawkish prose seeks to critique what is petty and individual even as it aspires to valorize society's acting as one man: in effect, it seeks to devalue individuals who oppose war as the bearers of "petty concerns" while amplifying those who support war as the embodiment of society as "one man." Hawks' use of synecdoche thus encourages "conservatism, caution, and reluctance to try a new approach" not only at the macroscopic level of foreign policy but also at the microscopic level of narrative (Pilisuk et al. 505).

Second is the use of synecdoche to justify escalation. The purpose of hawkish reading is not to imagine and illuminate. Hawks derive confidence in flat, literal reading. For hawks, the ambiguity that would come from more complex reading only incites hostility: to them "differences unmitigated by a sense of commonality become threats" (Klugman 580). How hawks substitute part for whole gives them the authority to "do" the something that is the waging of war. Hawks' predisposition to conflict leads to a construction of a binary world of "weak men and strong men; the weak men were the skeptics, who sat around contemplating, talking, criticizing; the strong men were doers, the ones who were always tough and always refused to back down" (Logevall 393). Talk, whether by diplomat or by dissenter, only leads to contemplation, which hawks perceive as weakness. "Doing" is a sign of toughness: "thinking" leads to passive contemplation or worse, criticism. Hawks must "do something," regardless of the cost, perhaps even regardless of the outcome, because thought is antithetical to action. Hawkish reading thus encourages intolerance at a time when, as game theorists note, mutual tolerance of ambiguity is the only way to facilitate mutual negotiation (see Pilisuk et al. 505). Instead, hawks' emphasis on "doing" often leads them to invent conflict before it actually occurs. In the context of Vietnam, hawks saw that "the only way to prevent conflict is to stop the aggressor from the moment his intentions are perceived, or even suspected," as Doris Kearns Goodwin noted of Lyndon Johnson's thinking (258). To stop aggression before aggression is perceived requires a "vigilant scanning" that indulges in a mimesis of the worst possible outcome "simply on the ground that it can never be finally ruled out" (Sedgwick 132–133). Such scanning weaponizes reading as a form of vigilance, a patrolling of signs. But because the worst possible outcome can never be ruled out, hawks presume that it is inevitable and see it as their duty to prevent, through aggression, the imagined worst possible outcome before it occurs. For the hawk, preemption is always legitimate, even though preemption blurs the lines between offense and defense. It is a key component to the hawk's strong theory of aggression that, as Johnson told Goodwin, "doing nothing was more dangerous than doing something" (263).

Synecdoche, as the rhetorical construction of representativeness, offers opportunities for calibration and negotiation. As Priscilla Wald
writes, American authors since the nation's inception have understood
that reading themselves into the national narrative—of seeing themselves as parts of a whole—created a "strangely productive" discourse
in which "the consequences and ambiguities of their own participation"
could be staged (3). The relationship between the part and the whole can
be productively probative: by exploring its contours through narratives
in which "identity has become a question rather than a possession,"
such writing could explore, critique and make more inclusive the scope
of what constitutes being an American (302). But for the hawkish reader,
synecdoche does not do this at all. Instead, synecdoche is used to devalue
others, to ennoble oneself, and ultimately to construct a sense of Americanness that is singular if not absolute. The hawks' use of synecdoche thus
reveals what Burke warns are the "tactical errors" of using synecdoche
to describe "social motivations" (510). Perhaps the greatest of these
during the Vietnam War was the hawks' fundamental misreading of their
enemy. Though he did not use the word, Robert McNamara retrospectively
lamented that America's foreign policy in the 1960s rested on the perver-
sion of synecdoche that occurs with hawkish reading. "We equated Ho
Chi Minh not with Marshal Tito but with Fidel Castro," he admitted (33).
McNamara's reading is doubly synecdochical: he not only substitutes a
leader for an entire nation, but he also substitutes three nations for an
entire global ideology. And his reading is doubly incorrect: Ho Chi Minh
was not Fidel Castro, and Vietnam was not an island ninety miles away
from the United States. But hawkish reading deliberately makes them look
the same. And in doing so, hawkish reading justified escalation and intervention and committed hundreds of thousands of soldiers to a war from
which many would not return.

Steinbeck's "Letters" commit similar tactical errors of hawkish reading, importing onto Vietnam's landscape an arsenal of American myths
while pillorying the South Vietnamese as children in need of American
financial aid and moral insight. At the same time, Steinbeck antagonizes
his own fellow Americans at home, particularly the war's protestors, who
are to him without legitimacy because he sees them as refusing to "do
something." What these tactical errors reveal are not only the limits of
hawkish reading but also hawkish reading's perniciousness to the very democracy it claims to protect. Hawks achieve more than war: they achieve

its justification, even when the majority of its people remain uncertain of war's purpose.[5] In their manipulation of synecdochical rhetoric, hawkish readers call for war in the name of democracy abroad, all the while skirting democracy at home. Such misreading leaves in its wake not only the debris of the country whose invasion it justifies. Its weaponization of synecdoche risks inciting demagoguery at home.

Intervention: Americanization through Synecdoche

Hawks import symbols from home and read them into their target abroad. Steinbeck's "Letters" rely upon a simple claim: that if a foreign land looks like ours and the foreign people act as we do, then our mission is their mission. He devoted many of the "Letters" to noting—one might say inventing—similarities between South Vietnam and the United States. He sought to Americanize the nation he was touring, importing American signs onto its landscape and people without regard to the complexities of Vietnamese self-determination. If the South Vietnamese were like us, his "Letters" presume, Americans would feel compelled to intervene. Yet the "Letters" make clear that Steinbeck is not interested in helping the South Vietnamese build their own unique democracy. The "Letters" show how Steinbeck believes, as the Johnson administration did, that the Vietnamese have "no truly national spirit" of their own (Kahin 249). Indeed, hawkish reading depends on this assumption, for otherwise the link between arms and aims would become unaligned.

Steinbeck's depictions reduce Vietnam to a kind of America. Flying over Pleiku, Steinbeck finds that it "looks and feels like the upper panhandle of Texas or southeastern New Mexico, the air sharp and clean, the plain low brushed and undulant . . . just waiting for herds of Brahmas, or wide ranging white Herefords" to graze on them (15). Upon meeting the Degar people—and referring to them by their colonial name, Montagnard—Steinbeck does not describe their way of life but instead his surprise that they "look very like American Indians" (20).[6] Travelling by helicopter, Steinbeck is enamored by how the pilots "ride their vehicles the way a man controls a fine, well-trained quarter horse. They weave along stream beds, rise like swallows to clear trees, they turn and twist and dip like swifts in the evening" (23).[7] The land and people that Steinbeck depicts—one that looks like Texas and is populated by people who look like "American Indians" and patrolled by pilots who ride their helicopters like cowboys on horses—serve to import not just a similar topography but, synecdochically, the iconography of American Manifest Destiny. In the "Letters," the American landscape, both real and mythic, is wedded to Vietnamese geography. By extension, South Vietnam becomes a land in which the American story is engrained in its landscape, a frontier to be put to use through American intervention.

Steinbeck depicts American pilots as if they are frontiersmen. Like good farmers, "each [Forward Air Controller] has a sizable piece of real estate for which he is responsible . . . he gets to know his spread like the back of his hand" such that anything out of place is recognizable (51).[8] The land is the pilot's "spread," his property to cultivate as he may. The foreign country becomes part of the American soldier's anatomy, its landscape as familiar as the synecdochical "back of his hand." As one pilot, Major William E. Masterson (nicknamed "Bat") tells Steinbeck as they take in the view from his O-1 plane (nicknamed a "Bird Dog"): "'Well, I know four people live there. If there were six pairs of pants drying on the bushes, I'd know they had visitors, and maybe V.C. visitors. Look at that place— see those two big crockery pots against the wall? I know those pots. If there were suddenly three or four, I'd investigate'" (51).[9] What impresses Steinbeck (aside from how Masterson's name evokes the mythical American West and how his airplane's name connects war reconnaissance to an American national pastime of hunting) is Masterson's ability to read wholes—the movements of the Vietcong—from such discrete changes. From the number of pots, Masterson is able to detect friend from foe.[10] Pots are synecdoches: their incorrect number are physical proof of enemy presence and, by extension, proof of the necessity to wage war. Steinbeck's "Letters" perform the textual equivalent of the "vigilant scanning" that Masterson does from the air, distinguishing wholes from parts, friends from foes.

The "Letters" valorize the American presence in Vietnam. His depiction of it as a sort of American West makes American military presence there seem inevitable. His doing so is a reminder of how the hawk not only uses synecdoche to show the priority of the American people and its mission but also uses it to make secondary (and at times outright dismiss) the people whose nation the hawk occupies. Steinbeck's prose displays a "stance of indignation and superiority" even toward fellow allies (Logue and Patton 328). The South Vietnamese, as Steinbeck depicts them, are a pitiable people who could only achieve self-determination with American assistance. His depictions of the South Vietnamese people often resort to the typical hawkish ploy of "creating a feeling of obligation, mixed with the sympathy one feels towards the underdog" (320). His description of the opening of "Gadsden Village," a refugee camp constructed in Phu Loi with $21,000 in donations from the residents of Gadsden, Alabama, offers literal proof of an Americanized Vietnam right down to the name. Steinbeck writes admiringly of the "30 new, white, hand-made cement brick houses for 30 families who had been living in mud," noting further that the families built the houses themselves and would soon start "30 more houses . . . you should see those women throw their might on the lever of the hand-powered brick compressor" (9–10).[11] As he depicts it, the American effort in Vietnam was much like the effort of the Works Progress Administration and other agencies of the New Deal: its purpose was to "get one hell of a lot of poor beat-up people out of the mud" (10). (And in this way the South Vietnamese were reduced to a storyworld familiar to Steinbeck: they became "Okies" worthy of beneficence.) Only through American involvement could the South Vietnamese take nothing and make it into something: from the mud would come, if American self-sufficiency was modeled, modern brick houses, cities replete with clinics and schools. What the "Gadsden Village" allows Steinbeck to invent is a Vietnam undergoing its version of American history: the Vietnamese are not victims forced to rebuild due to civil war, but homesteaders building frontier houses for their families. By extension, American charity would further develop Vietnam into a southeast Asian United States: in one "Letter," Steinbeck enthuses over a Johnson administration proposal to dam the Mekong River, which Steinbeck speculates will lead to "a super East Asian Tennessee Valley Authority" (16). The dam, Steinbeck writes, would generate enough electricity to "bring these nations together in peaceful cooperation" (16). The dam would, by its very existence, turn competing nations into states in union, a sort of hydroelectric federalism that would permanently end sectional strife. Parts would become wholes united by a resource and a policy to share it. Steinbeck's evocation of the TVA also serves as a synecdoche to what was missing in South Vietnam: a New Deal for a country undergoing a chaos that to him was not a sign of civil war but the result of improper self-regulation. Only American intervention, he suggests, could help the Vietnamese common men who were, as he put it, nothing more than "poor damned farmers" betrayed by their culture's "caste of soothsayers and demon tamers" (136–137).[12] American intervention would not only reincarnate both Manifest Destiny and the New Deal; it would also modernize a virgin land with a decrepit, primordial polity, bringing it into the (American) twentieth century.

Steinbeck attempts to import the traits of the American "common man" onto what he assumes are its South Vietnamese equivalents. Yet he falters when he encounters actual South Vietnamese people. In the presence of real people, he can only muster a derogatory flattery, a passive-aggressive variant of the devaluation that hawks perform on their enemies. Of the head chaplain of the South Vietnamese Army, he writes, "Giac is what is called a 'clean man' here, and that is a rare animal indeed. It means he has made no deals, political or financial, that he has shown no ambition for increased power or influence, that he is not taking pay or bribes from the bosses, graft from the crooked nor is he putting the bite on the poor. In this confused but self interested polity, these traits make him as unique as Yellowstone National Park and as lonely towering as the Washington Monument" (96).[13] Steinbeck struggles in his description of Giac as he tries to project American qualities onto a South Vietnamese person. Giac, whose name to Steinbeck sounds like the quintessentially American "Jack," is at first different than those who live in a "confused but self interested polity." (The rampant corruption of the South Vietnamese regime is patronizingly dismissed as a "confusion" that can be clarified through the adoption of American enlightened self-interest.) Yet Giac is described through a negation—we learn who Giac is by who he is not—in a way that does not so much depict Giac as much as confirms American stereotypes of Vietnam as a nation barely "removed from a state of deplorable barbarism" and "undemocratic at its core" (Nguyen 12). If anything, through his depiction of Giac, Steinbeck shows the hawkish presumption that South Vietnam is not a society that could act "as one man" to "assume the moral burden of a struggle for justice" (Slotkin 500). Ultimately, Giac serves as a synecdoche, not of what is right, but of what is wrong with Vietnam. Thus as much as Steinbeck's reading attempts to amplify Giac's positive qualities, the synecdoches he deploys reduce Giac to caricature. Giac's lack of corruption is understood not in terms of South Vietnamese life, or even American life, but in terms of two American landmarks. To compare him to Yellowstone is to turn a human into a sort of national park where one can take refuge from the corruptions of the war, and to compare him to the Washington Monument is to turn him into an obelisk that towers over the landscape. Interestingly, Giac is not like Washington the general, but like the Washington Monument; not animate but inanimate, not active but passive.[14] As the equivalent of an American place or object, Giac is never his own person. As monument or as landscape, Giac is never described by Steinbeck as human.

Steinbeck reduces the chaplain's monumental stature to a "merely interesting" item in the landscape, and not the South Vietnamese landscape, but the American landscape (see Ngai, *Our Aesthetic Categories* 112).[15] Steinbeck's reading of Giac performs the textual equivalent of an American foreign policy that turned South Vietnam and its people into a mere "appendage of the United States" (Kahin 323). Indeed, Steinbeck's observations strive to confirm South Vietnamese dependency: in the "Letters," not only is South Vietnam an appendage to the American national body; it is also the child to America the parent. As John F. Kennedy once said in a speech to South Vietnamese officials, "If we are not the parents of little Vietnam, than surely we are the godparents. We presided at its birth, we gave assistance to its life, we have helped shape its future. . . . this is our offspring—we cannot abandon it, we cannot ignore its needs" (618). Hawkish prose constructs South Vietnam as a child who needs American direction and occasional scolding, who needs to abide by American exemplars. And with a hawkish persistence in the "Letters," the more closely he inspects the terrain, the more Steinbeck writes with a tone of parental disdain. The women of Gadsden Village and men such as Giac might be "clean," but Steinbeck insists that, overall, in South Vietnam, "integrity is a strange word with a foreign flavor. There is no way to judge honesty because it has never been tried" (137).[16]

But if this is what hawks think of their ally, one can imagine what they think of their enemy. The Vietcong were depraved by comparison, not only because of their communist beliefs but because to Steinbeck they lack "the will to be clean, to be neat" (75).[17] Touring Rach Kien, Steinbeck fumes at how its schoolhouses were "blasted and torn apart and [their] thick walls cut through for gun ports" by the Vietcong, upset by "the old hospital, a sturdy structure" in "which once there were wards but now are deep in the manure of pigs and ducks" (75).[18] The Vietcong, in Steinbeck's hawkish reasoning, reversed the part-whole relationship: what civilization kept at bay was brought inside by the communists. To him, this was proof that the Vietcong "have no respect for honor or decency. They consider these matters stupid and weak" (12).[19] They are "a single-track, devoted, uncomplicated animal who follows orders unquestionably," yet who, in the heat of the moment, "loses his head" (66).[20] Steinbeck's description of the Vietcong is an example of the "incoherence of Asian racialization" that hawks performed throughout the Vietnam War, in which they depicted the Vietnamese as both suffering from a "lack of self-control" and possessing a demonic "achievement of absolute control" simultaneously (Darda, "Dispatches" 98). This incoherence authorizes Steinbeck to commingle otherwise contradictory depictions of the Vietcong: they were simultaneously destructive individuals and ideological dupes. Playing on the hawkish dichotomy of "weak men" and "strong men," Steinbeck depicts the Vietcong as both stealthy terrorists who on the one hand "crept in the dark" and "slithered silently" into villages and on the other bored entire villages into complacency with political lectures intended to create a "personality cult" (34, 71).[21] The Vietcong are all talk and no substance. By contrast, Americans are "pitching in to help put the town on its feet" while driving "the V.C. into the countryside where they still are—hiding and sniping" (76).[22] Steinbeck is careful throughout the "Letters" to depict American forces as benevolent: he never documents American military destruction but instead writes of how soldiers are "stripped to the waist, sweeping the filth from the schoolroom and painting the desks," restoring what the Vietcong had destroyed (77).[23] Not only are Americans rebuilding the terrain of the underdog; they are fighting against an enemy whose ignoble tactics are to Steinbeck and fellow hawks proof of their immorality.

Steinbeck's depictions of the Vietnamese landscape and its people could be easily dismissed as flat, stereotypical, and outright false. But underneath such thin depictions lurks a connection between arms and aims that is potent and dangerous. As Richard A. Cherwitz notes, Lyndon Johnson adopted a vivid language of an unseen aggressor attacking an innocent country when he asked for the Gulf of Tonkin Resolution to be passed, a rhetoric that, through hawkish vigilant scanning, claimed to "unmask the face of aggression to the rest of the world" (98). He never explained the presence of American ships in the Gulf that led to the conflict—if there was indeed conflict—in the first place. Instead, Johnson, like other hawks, used a rhetoric that creates an "atmosphere of emergency" that justifies preemption and relies upon "romantic impulses" of rescuing the innocent to widen the support for war after intervention begins (99, 97). In doing so, hawks warn that the United States is losing something—if not a broader campaign for democracy abroad, then the toughness and resolve that hawks see as intrinsic to American character at home. What is most dangerous about hawkish reading is how it sets aside the cost of life for the sake of identity. Hawks read in ways that subordinate the amount of blood spilled in battle to their nation's identity as the executor of global willpower: war is not a matter of casualties to them but a matter of morality. To a hawk, military war is also a culture war.

Steinbeck's importing of American traits onto the Vietnamese landscape sought to fuse Vietnam to America in ways that, if hawkish policy were abandoned, would signal not only the loss of American influence abroad but the loss of American morality at home. Throughout the "Letters," Steinbeck insists that the war in Vietnam is ultimately in the United States' best interest, not only as a bulwark against the domino theory—itself a synecdoche that parts can topple wholes—but also as a bulwark against American moral complacency at home.[24] "The job is long and hard," he writes, "and seemingly endless but it must be done. For it's ourselves we are fighting for—ourselves we are defending lest we become so effete, so careless, so confused, and so self-bedizened that we at home go the same way Rach Kien went" (77).[25] What the hawkish reader warns is that if we do not fight, we will lose our culture: here, Steinbeck depicts an America that is vital, pragmatic, clear-minded and unadorned, qualities he insists will be lost if the nation were to seek compromise or withdrawal. Steinbeck's synecdochalization of Vietnam shows how the conflict is not intended to only liberate the Vietnamese: it is to him a war by proxy over American values. By synecdochically inciting strong affect at home, hawks justify military conflict's endlessness and its expenditure of capital and, ultimately, people.[26]

Hawkish readers insist that war is "a national stake far beyond any earlier stakes" that cannot be retreated from, lest the nation itself fall apart (Thomson). Yet this is only half of hawkish readers' rhetorical battle. To stake this gambit means that those at home who oppose the war must be treated with the same reductive enmity as the enemy abroad. This is how hawkish readers come to prey on their own fellow citizens, insisting that the maintenance of the hard line is more important than a diversity of perspectives or democratic deliberation. Such reading shows how hawks are committed to maintaining their strong theory of aggression, at all costs.

Escalation: Hawkish Reading Comes Home

Hawks do more than escalate conflict abroad. They also escalate tensions at home through divisive invective. Steinbeck uses synecdoche both to amplify the stakes of his mission and to devalue those who oppose it. He approaches domestic dissenters with the same predatory lens as he does the enemy abroad: fellow citizens are treated with the hawk's scorn. His devaluation of American protestors lays bare the hawks' disdain for those who do not see war as the manifestation of national identity. And further, the hawks' devaluation lays bare their disdain for the values that they supposedly bring to the foreign place they have invaded—including the freedom to dissent. The hawkish readers' synecdochical depiction of protestors at home reveals the thinness of their commitment to the national values for which they claim to be fighting. The virulence of their attacks shows how hawks read to sustain their tautologies at the expense of their fellow citizens. In effect, the hawks' depiction of home demonstrates the hawks' potential for demagoguery.[27]

The "Letters" seek to dismiss dissent, both foreign and domestic, in one fell swoop. Steinbeck's close alliance with the Johnson administration inevitably furthered his belligerency, as advisers such as Jack Valenti warned that domestically "the doves, the Lynd-liners, and the *Times* are all of a piece" (Valenti qtd. in DeBenedetti 151). Valenti synecdochalizes the antiwar movement as parts of a piece that was "moving like volcanic lava in their demands for one concession after another until the whole game would be lost" (151). Valenti sees dissent as a pollution of parts, bits of lava that will coalesce and eventually destroy the whole, burning away the national landscape, leaving ruin in its wake. (Valenti also saw, as Steinbeck did, that the war was a "game" to be won or lost instead of a military conflict in which, either in victory or defeat, human lives would be lost.) To both men, antiwar protestors of any stripe had in common a treacherous, destructive intent. In seeing them as such, hawks eliminate room for discussion or debate of policy: all protestors are summarily dismissed as foes, parts of the same whole. For hawks, to allow dissent is to induce the domino theory inside their home territory.

Thus Steinbeck scorns those at home in his depictions abroad. In one telling moment, descending via helicopter to help dismantle a cache of Vietcong-held rice, Steinbeck watches as camouflaged American soldiers slowly appeared on the ground to assist. "Out of the undergrowth, thicker than any I have ever seen, faces, or really only eyes, appear. Mottled helmets and fatigues disappear against the background" (24).[28] He notices that their faces, "black or white from sweat and dirt have become a kind of universal reddish grey. Only the eyes are alive and lively. And when we settle and the rotor stops, their mouths open and they are men, and what men" (24).[29] Steinbeck frames the strong affects he feels in this moment as a rhetorical question: "Can you understand the quick glow of pride one feels in just belonging to the same species of men?" (24).[30] Yet Steinbeck does not answer this question. Instead, he writes, "I suppose it is the opposite of the shiver of shame I sometimes feel at home, when I see the dirty clothes, dirty minds, sour smelling wastelings and their ill-favored and barren pad mates. Their shuffling, drag-ass protests that they are conscience-bound not to kill people are a little silly" (24).[31] Yet this is not merely "a little silly" to Steinbeck, for he adds: "Hell, they couldn't hit anybody. I think their main concern is that a one-armed half blind 12-year-old V.C. could knock them off with a bunch of ripe bananas" (24).[32]

The pride of seeing a whole emerge from parts in a foreign and hostile land should be the pinnacle of hawkish reading. Parts—eyes, faces—become whole soldiers: their faces do not show individual distinction but their shared service to the nation. Black or white, in war, they become a "kind of universal" reddish grey, which is itself inseparable from the terrain. As if they grow out of it, American soldiers emerge from the Vietnamese soil: the land is literally Americanized. Steinbeck's prose reveals not only the pride of seeing soldiers emerge from hostile territory: it is also the pride that the premise of hawkish reading has been confirmed. Yet pride is never enough for a hawk because pride is ultimately secondary to their strong theory of aggression. Pride may have a place in a destructive war script, but it is ultimately a small one in comparison to the hawk's main focus, the sustenance of their script, the motive to perpetuate war. This is why Steinbeck's description of his pride in American soldiers at war in Vietnam leads to its opposite, his shame toward the war protestors at home, who are not dirty from combat, but because of dirty clothes that, to him, represent their "dirty minds." The dissenters' physical bodies serve as synecdoches for their wrong political conscience. Thus Steinbeck's pride in the soldiers begins a war of words against those at home and escalates that war through sharp juxtaposition. What is first seen as "a little silly" turns into a sign of utter ineptitude, politically and physically: Steinbeck insists that the protestors are protesting not out of political conviction, but out of moral and physical debility. The protestors are not only cowardly but are also so weak that they could be defeated through some perverse form of slapstick, that they could be "knocked off" by children armed with ripe bananas. Soldiers are "lively"; protestors "shuffle." Soldiers are "men"; protestors are "wastelings."

Steinbeck's "Letters" reveal the depths of a hawkish reader's "ugly feeling." They reveal a writer whose "willingness to reach out and understand 'the big picture' . . . seemed to wither away under the heat of his certainties and his scorn" (Benson 988). Yet more importantly they reveal the hawk's belief that the only way to be an American is to be a hawk. It is not enough for the hawk to assume that the protestor has no value: instead, the protestor is an adversary who must be countered with a "bully's taunt" (Young 419). Steinbeck's use of ad hominem attacks is not the rhetoric of a citizen interested in democratic deliberation but is more akin to the rhetoric of "dangerous demagogues" who seek to dismiss the opposition by depriving opponents of any legitimacy (Mercieca 273). As Richard Slotkin warns, when military figures are portrayed as heroes, they are no longer merely representative of the people but become "empowered to act beyond the expressed or legislated will of the people" such that none of their actions conflict with their "heroic afflatus" (498). The maintenance of democracy becomes secondary to the guarantee that no dissent will scratch the patina of heroism upon which the hawk is dependent. Steinbeck's tautological reading affirms what Richard Rubenstein calls an "imperial circularity," the idea that "we are defending a forward position because our previous position came under attack" (53). When it becomes so important to maintain the image of the military as victorious that those who advise an alternate course are made anathema, democratic deliberation has been truncated. When those who are perceived to threaten heroic afflatus are demonized so that they constitute a "them" that no "we" can be part of, demagoguery is underway. In Steinbeck's depiction of the war protestors, synecdoche is fully weaponized: there is an "us" (Steinbeck and the soldiers) or a "them" (the war protestors) and no other camps but these. The "deep, horizontal comradeship" that defines a democratic nation is replaced by an antipathy toward others manifested in a rhetoric of flat stereotypes (Benedict Anderson 7). Steinbeck insists throughout the "Letters" that "Charlie is a pure son of a bitch," and equally insists that anyone, even fellow Americans, who disagree with the hawkish mission abroad are as well (26).[33] It is not only in its tacit sanctification of American policy but also in its demonization of those who stand in its way, ambiguously or directly, at home or abroad, that hawkish reading preserves its destructive script at all costs, including democracy itself.

Hawkishness, as a strong affect, is always waging war. If it cannot find a nation in which to intervene, it will invent one: if it cannot find a rationale to escalate abroad, it will find a cause to devalue those at home. This is the problem of hawkish reading that Steinbeck's "Letters" help explicate: how fighting war is more important to the hawk than the war's ethics or ends. It takes a flat, thin language to perpetuate affects so intense they make all opponents look alike. And it takes an inflexible, myopic purpose: to create war and to sustain it. To the hawk, there is something noble in the problem, as McNamara internally disclosed in November 1966, that "I see no reasonable way to bring the war to an end soon . . . we must improve our position by getting ourselves into a military posture that we credibly could maintain indefinitely" (Vietnam Study Task Force 82–83). If anything, the hawkish reader finds satisfaction in sustaining war, even when, as McNamara realized, success was "a mere possibility, not a probability" (88). Steinbeck's "Letters" place on public display what McNamara would only disclose in private. They put on display the hawk's attempts to make such an indefinite commitment possible by insisting that the only way to be an American is to endorse endless war.

Conclusion: Where Hawkish Reading Leads

Steinbeck departed Vietnam with a renewed confidence. Nothing he saw changed his mind. Upon returning to the United States, Steinbeck's advice to McNamara was only a variation of administration policy.[34] He suggests demonstrations of force by bombing uninhabited areas near Hanoi, then pausing, and if the Vietcong did not see the pauses as opportunities to open negotiations, to bomb areas closer to the city (see Benson 1014–1016). If only the Vietcong could understand that bombing was not only material but symbolic, a synecdoche of immense American power, Steinbeck presumes, the Vietcong would relent. Publicly to the end, Steinbeck perpetuated the hawkish rhetoric advocated by the administration. But hawkish reading did not articulate how the war should be fought, how resources should be allocated, and above all, it did not anticipate what would occur if the Vietcong did not yield (see Gibbons 53–54). Hawkishness can fashion a war's endless perpetuation, but it cannot create, from its exhilarations and damnations, a strategy from its parts. The Vietnam War revealed how hawkish reading was creative writing, filled with flimsy symbols and melodramatic plots, which might make for fine fiction but had little connection to reality. The hawkishness of Steinbeck's "Letters" reveals how "the attempted insertion of an entire body of American myths into a historical field incapable of receiving it was producing the most dire results" (Myers 144).

The incoherence of hawkish reading was evident to everyone but the hawks themselves. Michael Herr noted the consequences of hawkish reading: "Where we have not been smug, we have been hysterical, and we will pay for all of it" (qtd. in Polsgrove 174). The smugness of hawkishness can be found in Steinbeck's reading of the South Vietnamese as children in need of Western guidance, and the hysteria of hawkishness can be found in Steinbeck's reading of the war's protestors at home. The disastrous consequences of such reading were apparent to Herr, and they were noticed by other writers and by those close to Steinbeck himself. Much like his father, John Steinbeck IV was a hawk, at least initially. But he became one of the Vietnam War's lesser-known critics, responding in his own way to its "anticipatory dread" by noting, in a powerful essay based on his experience as a soldier there, how 83 percent of American soldiers were using drugs, particularly marijuana, to combat it. He writes of Vietnam that "for all intents and purposes that the entire country is stoned" (Steinbeck IV 34). The younger Steinbeck offered the elder Steinbeck a different sort of synecdoche, one that struck back at his father's faith in the Johnson administration and recasts his father's rhetoric of war as a "game." "The game progresses, and the game gets worse . . . There is no final score other than what can be measured in mutual loss," Steinbeck IV writes (60).

Despite such mutually assured loss, hawkish reading persists. It seems that for every foreign conflict there emerges a writer willing to read into that conflict the belief that American intervention can tame it. Such writers will insist that we "'do something' in the face of oppression and violent fanaticism," a face that they may very well have constructed out of an overly simplificatory use of synecdoche (Ryan 691). Such writers might insist that diplomacy is useless and snipe that "our military may simply be too Boy Scoutish for the rougher side of a dirty war," insinuating that anything other than intervention is a sign of childish naivete or lost masculinity (Young 417). And once intervention takes place, these writers will insist that the most destructive weaponry be deployed, couched in language that suggests innocent national pastimes more than the real carnage those weapons will create. These writers will also claim that escalation is the inevitable next step since "only victory gives meaning to the lives lost" and "to stop fighting short of victory is to render meaningless the deaths and maiming suffered thus far" (422). Such writers will engage in invective, derogatory depictions of their opponents both foreign and domestic, as to them ugly feelings are the noblest expression of national identity. Ultimately, their hawkish writing will be "untroubled by shame or guilt" because to them war offers, as Tomkins warns of those who find satisfaction in destructive war scripts, "a promised cure for the psychopathology of everyday life" (*Affect* 3:491). And should defeat occur, they will not question the strong affect of aggression that drove their reading: they will insist instead that intervention was justified, but that the execution of it was wrong.[35] By doing so, hawkish writers will attempt to enact the "unaccountability" that "is the defining or essential feature of the dangerous demagogue" (Mercieca 267).

Steinbeck's "Letters" ultimately reveal how the link between arms and aims was effected through the weaponization of synecdoche. Hawkish reading shows how synecdoche's promise that "a reduction is a representation" (Burke 507) can be used to demagogic ends, for in the hands of hawks it is perverted into a license to demean, invade, and kill. The rhetoric of hawkishness is thin, but its costs are high, not only in how it sustains a conflict abroad but also in the image of the nation it perpetuates at home. The hawkish use of synecdoche does more than make enemies out of those abroad: it further fractures national divides, turning a variety of positions into a battle between "us" and "them." The "Letters" show how a way of reading that takes the nation to war can also work to undermine the nation's ideals and, ultimately, tear the nation apart.

2

Bile

"HIS ETHOS ain't no fuckin' good" (Booth 10). So Wayne C. Booth writes of Hunter S. Thompson in his review of *Fear and Loathing on the Campaign Trail '72*. He does not approve of how the writer eschews objective reporting for subjective experience—"The thesis of *Loathing* is that Hunter Thompson is interesting," he notes—nor does he trust Thompson's subjective experience as revealing any larger truth of the campaign trail (8). Booth laments that "since he tells me many times of when he has gleefully lied and watched his auditors squirm under his deceptions, I must stand back a bit and doubt his deepest claim of all: to tell his feelings as he felt them" (10).[1]

On the one hand, Booth's concern is a typical critical complaint of the New Journalism. Its technique of reporting "events from the inside out" so that reporters could "openly communicate (rather than mask) their own direct engagement with and active participation in the experiences they reported" always came with the possibility that such engagement could be invented and that such participation might be overstated (Staub 22). On the other hand, Booth's criticism is not just of Thompson's ethos, but his pathos. And while this too is a familiar complaint of the New Journalism—as Michael E. Staub writes of Gail Sheehy's 1971 *Panthermania*, it is a frequent New Journalist tactic to embed so many "suspect perspectives" within a narrative that it enables the author to "illustrate how each spoke ill of all the others" (32)—Thompson pushed the problem of pathos to greater extremes. His was not the "suave malice" of Tom Wolfe, whose 1970 essay "Radical Chic" mocks both the pretentious white elites who attended Leonard Bernstein's fundraiser for the Black Panthers and exoticizes the Panthers as oversexed con men (Staub 32). Instead, as Booth notes, Thompson's is a style that ultimately "derives what liveliness it has mainly from a slashing contempt for every institution and almost every person" (8). Thompson is so busy denigrating everyone that he does not even bother to explain the election's sequence of events, "leaving [Thompson] and us in a mindless, desperate present in which everything happens for the first time" (9). Thompson, Booth concludes, is "so hostile to politicians that he just cannot bother to understand them."

Booth's critique of Thompson's ethos offers a clue to the affective dynamics of his work. While I do not subscribe to Booth's lambasting of the New Journalism, my reading of Thompson's nonfiction is quite different from critics who praise him as "a descendant of the trickster tradition of folklore, the vice of medieval drama, the picaro of early prose narratives . . . a self-portrait of the journalist as rogue" (Hellmann, *Fables* 71). This vein of criticism often interprets Thompson's invective as "the visions of a mad seer" whose unusual perspective shines light on otherwise obscured American social dynamics (77). Others interpret Thompson's hostility as the inevitable position of an underdog who "turned away from the 'truth' determined by metropolitan editors and their establishment paymasters" to disperse truths the elite sought to hide (Stephenson 18). Still others see him as a rebel with a cause whose antics are the sign of "a desperate effort to achieve the American Dream on his own ground, since it has failed everywhere else" (Bruce-Novoa 43).

Yet to praise Thompson as a countercultural nihilist is to ignore his fascination with conventional politics. To praise him as a postmodern paragon is to ignore the stark morality that saturates his work. And to praise him for his indulgent pharmacopeia is to ignore the sobering bite of his prose. Instead of dismissing Thompson's ethos as poor or his depiction of the nation as false, I am more interested in the strong affect that resonates within his work, its "cynicism mixed with deep concern" (Bruce-Novoa 49). I call this bilious reading, a mode of reading that, at its core, cannot accept that the nation is a "formal binding together of disparate elements" (Brennan 62). Thus this chapter explores how bilious reading is predicated upon a particularly populist incitement to discourse: a way of reading that hostilely demarcates who counts as "us" and "them" through hyperbole, invective, threats of violence, and ill feeling. It is a way of reading that presumes the nation was at some past time "morally pure and fully unified" but is now lost to corrupt elites, a middle class of "inferiors," and institutions that support the "wrong" people (Müller 19–20). Reading to amplify the difference between "us" and "them," the bilious reader insists that the corrupt, inferior, and wrong be ridiculed, obstructed, and purged from the national scene. The frenetic energy that comes from bilious reading, its delight in incivility and its raising of antisociality to a virtue, offers a reminder of how "the exact referents of 'the people' or 'the elite' don't define populism; what defines it is the conflictual relationship between the two" (Judis 15). This is not to say that all modes of populism are bilious reading but instead to point out that in bilious reading the conflictual relationship between "us" and "them" is so stark that it commingles ideological zealotry with comic absurdity. Thompson reads the nation to incite conflict where it is not immediately apparent and to raise the ante where it is. As such, bilious reading comes with what Ben Anderson calls a "promise of intensity" that sheds moral light and personal conviction upon the mendacious ways of the nation's false representatives ("Affect" 199). What bilious reading promises is a more entertaining, interesting life if its readers subscribe to a world of "us" versus "them."

Yet the life it promises is neither a comprehensive nor a national one. It is particularly evident in Thompson's reading of Joe Edwards's "Freak Power" campaign for mayor of Aspen in 1970 and his own run for sheriff of Aspen shortly thereafter that Thompson's negative energy exceeds the desire to win an election. This excess shows how bilious reading is more interested in textually condemning perceived enemies and unquestionably praising the virtues of perceived fellow readers than in making a comprehensive political movement. Bilious reading engages in populism's us/them antipathies to incite and maintain an antagonism toward whatever the bilious reader defines as the mainstream. Of course, populism is more than bile alone. But bilious reading's antagonism prohibits the coalition-building necessary for even a populist movement to achieve fruition: its satisfaction with invective and derision means that its conception of the past is nostalgic and its conception of the future is virtually non-existent. Thus while biliousness provides a tremendous incitement to read, it does so with an antic, reactive quality that is more interested in maintaining derision than in the imagining of the "deep, horizontal comradeship" that constitutes the nation (Benedict Anderson 7). The bilious reader simply does not want to get along. As a style of imagining the nation, bilious reading is predicated upon the assumption that the sign of true citizenship is the reflexive and chronic display of bad temper—and nothing more.

Thompson's prose reveals bile's brilliance as well as its limitations. As a way of reading parts for wholes that incites discourse, bilious reading produces moments of excitement, humor, and anger. Yet it can also become so rote that other modes of reading remain unconceived. It never gels into a politics of its own: its voice is one that "if asked to explain what it is that makes it count as the people's voice, answers by naming the people's enemies" rather than outlining its reforms or policies (Urbinati 5). Instead of creating new movements, bilious reading can become, as it did for Thompson, an author's shtick, a cultural commodity to be produced and recycled when money was needed. Its insistence on a past time when the world was a pure one guaranteed the readership of a generation convinced of their self-importance in the pages of publications such as *Rolling Stone*, which assured boomers that "the 1960s were over . . . the 1960s would never end" (Hagan 159). And bile can too easily be borrowed to justify the antics of the status quo: the entrepreneurs who profited from the supply-side economics of the Reagan era practiced their own "false populism," using bilious language as a means to position themselves as an "insurgency against old money, chilly elitism, and also the liberal equation of life with suffering that demands amelioration by the 'haves' and the 'have mores'" (see Berlant, "Unfeeling Kerry"). All these point to how bile's attempts to make "rudeness politically useful" can be a literary and political dead end (Marantz 80). Bilious reading is alluring because every conflict it sees is an epic one. But in doing so, something is lost: bilious reading does not facilitate communion, but rather its opposite, the dismissal of a complex conception of "the people." Bilious reading is a reminder that strong affect can make for a lively world, but that it is ultimately a strong nationalism that makes a livable world for "us" *and* "them" impossible.

Bilious Reading

Bile is the "anger, ill temper, peevishness" that reflects an "excess or derangement" of the body (*OED*). It is a fitting description of the affect that saturates Thompson's reading of America and the nation he depicts as a result. To describe how the national body is deranged is to describe negatively the parts that bring it together into a whole, a whole that by such describing is made insipid and incorrect. Bilious readers are peeved if not outraged by the nation they see. Their anger has a particularly excessive cast: the critique that comes from such reading does not sate but rather increases their hostility. Bile is antisocial: its way of reading neither clarifies nor unifies but instead uses synecdoche to magnify the misattunement between the part and the whole to such a degree that the "us" is far away from the "them."

To think of bile as an affect is to draw upon a wide discourse ranging from medieval humoral theory to contemporary feminist rhetorical theory. The Greek physician Galen, for instance, saw bile as both generative—the source of "acuteness and intelligence of the mind"—and degenerative, as those who suffered from it gained acuity through a "simplicity bordering on foolishness" (qtd. in Pearcy 448). Thus it is not only that bile reads an object with an acute edge; it does so in a way that loses, as Galen wrote, "steadiness and solidity" (448). The bilious readers' deployment of synecdoche may be revelatory, but it ultimately shows, in the simplicity of their reduction of the world to us/them, how they lose the relation between the part and the whole. Indeed, in bilious reading, the potential to bring parts together to form new wholes is set aside for the unsteadiness of antisocial invective.

Bile creates moments of insight not based on shared vision but on public derision. Its energy is intense, negative, and ugly. It scans its world for the animus necessary to maintain its oppositional stance. As with any strong theory of reading, bilious reading engages in what Paul Saint-Amour describes as displays of "cartoon vitalism" and "warrior masculinity" (437). From the perspective of contemporary feminist rhetorical theory, bile relies on "profanity, *ad hominem* invective, and hyperbolic imagery of graphic—and often sexualized—violence" (Jane 533). Bilious readers thrive on hard, tough, mean binaries that prove to them that the truth is offensive to the elites they disdain. Nor are they interested in compromise or moderation. Bilious readers demand from others what Emma A. Jane calls "savage agreement" or "bitter dissent" (534): not nuanced interpretation or pragmatic moderation but stark moments of shared viciousness that are used like fuel to sustain a conflictual relationship with their object. Bile takes "what was probably obvious to any adult who was moderately alert" and amplifies it with screaming theatrics through hyperbole and insult (Reynolds 68). As Thompson's frequent collaborator Ralph Steadman writes, "When he made an insult . . . it was deadly. . . . a kind of contempt that no one had ever felt before or mentioned to this person to make them understand how awful they were" (Steadman qtd. in Wenner and Seymour 196–197). It was through insult that Thompson could identify part of a person, turn it into a vulnerability, and then use it hyperbolically to destroy the entirety of that person. Extended to a form of reading an entire nation, bilious reading transforms an imagined community into a ghoulish place where everyone is equally, albeit differently, awful.

The bilious reader makes conflict an art. The energy that comes from such art should not be underestimated. The acuteness of Thompson's tearing down had an exhilarating effect. As *Rolling Stone* editor Charles Perry notes of Thompson's work, "after you read it, life just seemed incredibly dramatic, like you never knew when a pack of pythons might come attack you from the corner" (qtd. in Wenner and Seymour 133). It was an exhilaration through which the national everyday became rife with negative possibility: an attack where it was least expected; an unwanted surprise that one would be forced to negotiate; a nation antagonistically torn between its past ideals and its present terribleness. Only from bilious reading could come the dyad of "fear and loathing" that would be Thompson's claim to fame: a loathing of the present as the sign of ideals gone astray combined with a fear that the nation could only get worse from here. Bilious reading works in Thompson's depiction of Las Vegas in *Fear and Loathing in Las Vegas,* for example, to confirm that there is "a Them, a House which symbolized everything We are against" (Cooper 532). And bilious reading works, as demonstrated in his depiction of political life in *Fear and Loathing on the Campaign Trail '72,* to confirm that the very house that is against us is the one that governs us. Oscillating between fear and loathing, bilious readers slash at everything in their proximity, cutting away ambiguity and plurality to turn the communal into the mendacious, to turn the mainstream into the villainous.

Bilious reading comes with an "energetic antisocialism" that relishes in turning mundane events into high drama (Trask 4). Its willingness to mock, judge, and insult proved particularly effective in a society that, as Ben Anderson notes of the 1970s, was impatient with "the affective bargain of Fordism: economic security for a tolerated boredom" ("Affect" 202). Bile thrived in the counterculture that found the Fordist state to be constricting and its society inauthentic: what bile offered was "a kind of violent fun, linked to the promise of action without impediment or constraint" (209). Bilious reading, in theory, creates a space of "dignity, spontaneity, fulfillment or freedom," a way, through pranks, cajoling, or cursing, to reclaim the nation through "scenes of intensity" infused with "a sense of eventfulness" (199, 212). But in practice, bilious reading's unsteady oversimplification of the nation to an antagonism between "us" and "them," its alignment of violence with fun, marks it as a strong affect more interested in perpetual negativity than the construction of a coherent political movement. While there may be something pleasurable, as Rita Felski writes, in the "channeling of irritation" that bilious reading performs and "the relief of seeing [irritation] acknowledged, cranked up a hundredfold, and vomited out into the world" that it demonstrates on the page, this also suggests that what bilious reading does best is to take the strong affects felt inside oneself and project (if not expel) them (*Hooked* 104). Bilious readers make *their* affect *our* problem. Bile's intent is to "make bad matters worse" (Tomkins, *Affect* 3:115). Bile never reads in a way that suggests compromise or negotiation, for doing so would make bilious readers feel inauthentic and would sate their fun. Instead, biliousness remains awash in negativity. The bilious reader's delight in the "awfulness of our present historical moment" does not come with the desire to reform what they see as wrong with the present, as that would reduce the antisocial energy upon which it feeds (Steinle 157). As Tomkins writes of those who deliberately seek out anger, bilious readers delight in the maintenance of negative affect, "meeting it head on or of creating it rather than turning it down" (*Affect* 3:181). Conflict is not to be resolved but forever perpetuated: this is how bilious reading works to keep alive a closed loop of negative attunement.

While bilious reading separates "us" from "them," it never goes beyond the sustaining of separation. It never unifies. Indeed, bilious reading's "particularly confrontational attitude toward political authority" is performed in such a way that it reveals the reader's "difficulty of identifying that authority" (Cooper 532). Because the bilious reader sees almost everyone as an opponent, there is no deep examination of what makes the opponent an antagonist. Because bilious reading dismisses both people and nations at the level of surface physiognomy (think, for instance, of Thompson's insults or the many graphic illustrations by Steadman that accompany Thompson's prose) it does not necessarily make a deep investigation of who or what it castigates. Going further, the invective of its rhetoric restricts its ability to commune with others. As Daniel Worden argues, Thompson's writing in particular "aspires to a collective good on some level, but, at the same time, [his] forceful, foul-mouthed tone is so distinctive, so stylistically personalized, that it is incapable of being collectivized, of being imagined as the voice of a group rather than the voice of an individual" (83). Bilious readers, in noting the opposition between "us" and "them," never create a wide circle of "we." The conflict from which they derive their violent fun is so simple that only they can be its true citizen.

The world of "us" and "them" that bilious readers want is one of superficial reductions and sharp dichotomies. Bile may borrow from populism's fascination with "us" and "them," but as Ernesto Laclau writes, genuine populism requires a threefold operation: it must first create "an internal antagonistic frontier" that separates elites from "the people"; then it must create a set of demands that make "the emergence of the 'people' possible"; and finally, it must unify the demands of those people into "a stable system of signification" that goes "beyond a feeling of vague solidarity" among each other (74). But this unification bile does not do. Indeed, bilious reading like Thompson's casts so many aside as false representatives that the bilious reader "does not act 'for' and in the name of the whole but in its place" (Urbinati 37). Thompson's biliousness relies on a personal premise that he is the purest of the pure: as Douglas Brinkley notes, Thompson "was never an egalitarian" (qtd. in Wenner and Seymour 381). He may have associated with outcasts and lowlifes, but what his bilious reading confirms is an assumption that "only some of the people are really the people" (Müller 21). And his campaign for sheriff and his reporting on local and national politicos indicate how Thompson not only acted in their name, but desired to act in their place. In these ways, Thompson's way of bilious reading of the nation never allows a "universalistic moment [to] prevail over the particularistic one" (Laclau 203). Populism can build movements. But bilious reading does not help construct or reconstruct them. Instead, it digests, it disassembles the nation without the vision, much less the desire, to reassemble it.

As Rita Felski writes, "identification . . . can also lie in excess and exaggeration; affiliations can form around kernels of antisocial venom and apoplectic spleen" ("Identifying" 103). Yet the identifications of bilious reading are limited to the chosen few who themselves never cohere into an "us." Going further, bilious reading never defines the criteria of its moral purity: any "us" can easily slide into being one of the immoral "them" as needed to maintain the flow of negative affect. Bilious readers may have accomplices, but they do not have allies, which says much about its inevitable political difficulties. Ultimately, bilious reading only offers an "unproblematized negative take on democracy" (Finchelstein 4). Its readings may be vivid and exhilarating, but the depiction of the nation it generates is not so much degenerate as it is ultimately degenerative. It may shock or surprise by exposing the "terrible logic to it all" that explains national decline, but that logic exposes terribleness for the sake of violent fun and without interest in envisioning a truly national community (Thompson qtd. in Torrey and Simonson 182). What proves most worrisome about bilious reading is how it creates an intense nation through the distempered perspective of one citizen.

Aspen, Colorado

The biliousness of Thompson's reading is most evident in how he attempts to turn it into a form of politics itself. In the September 1971 issue of *Rolling Stone,* Thompson writes of his work as campaign manager for Aspen mayoral candidate Joe Edwards. Though Edwards lost the election, Thompson portrays the campaign as an epic "Battle of Aspen," a sign of "Freak Power in the Rockies," a synecdoche for a truer America that is emerging not from the mainstream but from the motley counterculture that had found refuge there. To do so, Thompson reads Aspen and the majority of its citizens through a bilious lens to construct Aspen as a populist, antagonistic frontier. The "backbone of Aspen," Thompson writes, is "mean-spirited, Right-bend shitheads" who gloat that they had never lost an election (*Great Shark Hunt* 159). They want a mayor "who would give them free reign to go out and beat the living shit out of anybody who didn't look like natural material for the Elks' and Eagles' membership drives" (159). And to Thompson the city's left wing is no better: they are "shysters and horsey hypocrites," "political transvestites" who will first run as a "sensible alternative" only to retreat into a discourse of protecting the public from "menacing extremes" (165, 172). Overall, Thompson sees the village as torn between the inauthentic "seasonal blizzard of fat-wallet skiers who keep Aspen rich" and the authentic "freaks, heads, fun-hogs and weird night-people of every description" who live there year-round (160, 155). This latter group has two things in common: a disdain for "narcs and psychedelic hustlers" and the belief that voting is "copping back into the system" (155). To them, "it made more sense in the long run to flee, or even to simply hide" from the establishment than to register to vote: what they need, Thompson insists, is "an unusual candidate . . . or a fireball pitch of some kind" to get them to the polls (155). The only legitimacy, in the face of so many false representatives, according to Thompson, is a candidate who would not construct a new political order but would gain election by demonizing the current one. What would motivate these voters is accessing and enlisting their bile.

Thompson, as campaign manager for Edwards and then as candidate for sheriff, saw himself as working along the same rhetorical lines as populist George Wallace, albeit for a different audience. In a letter to a supporter, Thompson writes that Wallace is "a populist—and so are we" (*Songs* 145). In fact, Thompson sought to present himself as a truer populist than Wallace because his "main trip is anti-Establishment, and we can beat him like a gong on that one" (145). Whereas Wallace could "whip a hall full of beer-drinking factory workers into a frenzy," Thompson sought to rally a more disparate faction of Americans (*Campaign Trail* 253).[2] He sought to "put together a platform that speaks not only for the new eighteen-to-twenty-one vote but also the 11 million or so who turned twenty-one since '68, and also the Rock vote, the Drug vote, the Vet vote, the Hippie vote, the Beatnik vote, [and] the Angry Liberal vote" (*Songs* 143). This medley of synecdoches bypasses traditional party lines—what they have in common is a sense of being outcast or not cast at all, either dismissed from the political order or taken for granted by it—and is thus in conflict with the political mainstream. They were young; they listened to unorthodox music; they were intoxicated; perhaps they had been to Vietnam and saw the horrors there; perhaps they had been to Berkeley and saw the Free Speech Movement vanish; perhaps the Great Society was too much or not enough for them. These groups, Thompson envisions, are parts lacking a whole to unite them. Instead of running "the 'normal' candidates for the worthless losers they are," he suggests instead that running an "honest freak" would be "neither opting out of the system, nor working with it . . . but calling its bluff, using its strength to turn it back on itself" (*Great Shark Hunt* 163). By finding an "honest freak"—a person whose ethics represented American virtue even if their hair, clothing or drug use did not—and running them for office, Thompson sought to give voters a new synecdoche for Aspen to elect and, in doing so, build a movement out of a disaffected populace who, either in victory or defeat, would find "definite satisfaction in knowing that, even if we lost, whoever beat us would never get rid of the scars" (169). The audience Thompson constructs as a whole is reliant on a loose scaffolding of discontents from multiple constituencies, an "us" energized against a "them" through displays of vitalism that one might see in westerns, superhero comic books, or sword-and-sandal films: calling bluffs, taking punches, swinging fists, inflicting scars in the name of a battle against good and evil. It is an audience constructed not from mutual dialogue but from the savage agreement that those in power are not to be worked with but worked against: condemned, harassed, and expelled.

Even though Edwards lost the election, Thompson writes of the "Battle of Aspen" as if it were a victory. He insists that he "had changed the whole structure of Aspen's politics. The Old Guard was doomed, the liberals were terrorized and the Underground had emerged, with terrible suddenness, on a very serious power trip" (*Great Shark Hunt* 158). And in his own campaign for sheriff later that year, he promises to unleash a terrible suddenness into Aspen's everyday life. In his campaign, Thompson displays the populist's "undisguised—indeed, an enthusiastic—politics of partiality" (Urbinati 4). He promises that if he is elected sheriff, he will not use this position of law and order for everyone but instead will "disfigure the rule of law" to benefit those whom he sees as the city's true representatives (4). In effect, the sheriff would be instrumental in turning bile into policy. Those who oppose him "should be fucked, broken, and driven across the land" (*Great Shark Hunt* 173). As the sheriff cannot do this legally, Thompson promises not to hesitate to "set up a tar-vat, scum-drain or gravel-pit" to threaten the city's inauthentic elites (175). Thompson's conception of the role of sheriff proves to be one of a law-and-order figure with a "cartoon vitalism": the return of the stocks, the digging of moats, the herding of the elite like cattle, the tar and feathering of the insiders-now-outsiders. He promises to punish with "overwhelming zeal" the "greedfreaks" and "kill-freaks" who committed "land-rape" (174). He will use his authority, he writes, to "fuck the tourists, dead-end the highway, zone the greedheads out of existence, and in general create a town where people could live like human beings, instead of slaves to some bogus sense of progress that is driving us all mad" (160).

It is Thompson's enthusiasm for the dehumanization of those deemed impure—they are to be humiliated, tortured, driven out of town—that shows the full register of bile's churning. It is accomplished through an ever-increasing violence, at times sexual, but always physical, that expands from an individual to a class of people to an entire "sense of progress" that is phony and is, whether or not its false representatives know it, "driving us all mad" (*Great Shark Hunt* 160). The only way to remedy this, Thompson ventures, is to expel the bad whole. To accomplish this, he inverts the popular discourse of the subcultural "freak" to include those motivated by gentrification, urbanization, and profit. Similarly, he inverts the role of sheriff from the agent who upholds the social order to the agent who disrupts it. It would be his task to rename the city, sod its streets, sell its dope, and set its speculators, landlords and tourists into a state of permanent flight. Not only would automobiles be banned from downtown, but the streets would be turned into "grassy malls where everybody, even freaks, could do whatever's right" (160). The police would be reduced to serving as "trash collectors and maintenance men for a fleet of municipal bicycles" (160). They would be unarmed; they would not enforce drug laws but instead would "punish dishonest dope dealers" by putting them in stocks on the courthouse lawn (173). And in an especially bilious move, the name of the city itself would be changed to "Fat City," which would permanently desynecdochalize Aspen's associations with elitism, wealth, and privilege. Thompson proposes to change the city's textual physiognomy, making it unattractive to investors and unhealthy to the national body, who would leave it alone for its true denizens to enjoy.

Thompson's platform points to the problems inherent in any city in the second half of the twentieth century: the fragmenting of the social landscape by new highways, the rise of suburbs, exurbs, and resorts that sold a caricatured regionality to naive travelers, and the rise of "law and order" style policing with distinct racial, economic, and cultural biases. While Thompson's bilious reading points with Galenic acuteness to these problems, his solution is indeed "simplicity bordering on foolishness" (Pearcy 448). His proposed means of reforming these ills is as hyperbolic as it is authoritarian. His bilious invective encourages him to forget that the punitive, punishing way he would rid the town of the elite only mirrors that desired by the town's conservative backbone: instead of the "mayor who would give them free reign to go out and beat the living shit out of anybody who didn't look like natural material for the Elks' and Eagles' membership drives," it would be the sheriff who would be putting to the stocks and ensnaring in moats those who did not subscribe to the counterculture (Thompson, *Great Shark Hunt* 159). And while it may have been in jest, Thompson's platform is a reminder of how the populist presumption that most of the people are not "the people" can easily veer into the synecdoche of a sole glorious leader who is authorized to attack "them"—in this case, almost everyone—in "our" name. The imagined community of Aspen that Thompson offers may be purer, but it would be smaller and dependent upon one figure—the sheriff—with the law in his own hands. It would not be democracy, but government by bile.

Thompson's platform can be taken as the antics of a writer who relishes controversy for its own sake.[3] He concludes the "Battle of Aspen" by writing that "it will make no difference which label I adopt; the die is already cast in my race—and the only remaining question is how many Freaks, heads, criminals, anarchists, beatniks, poachers, Wobblies, bikers and Persons of Weird Persuasion will come out of their holes and vote for me" (*Great Shark Hunt* 172). And it is worth noting that many did—Thompson won 46 percent of the vote.[4] Yet even this is telling: a coalition of weird people does not make a majority. The vote offers proof that bilious reading does not allow for the construction of an imagined community: it marshals a shared sense of antipathy but not a sense of solidarity from which "a stable system of signification" can emerge (Laclau 74). When a reader antagonistically defines "themselves first by what they were not," when they define themselves through their bile, the culture that comes from such definition is "an inherently unstable collection of attitudes, tendencies, postures, gestures, 'lifestyles,' ideals, visions, hedonistic pleasures, moralisms, negations, and affirmations" (Braunstein and Doyle 10). Thompson's campaign in Aspen shows that there is no guarantee that those who are yoked together by shared disaffection develop mutual political affection. That Thompson presumed such a bilious group would cohere and become a movement through antisocial energy alone, much less that he could be elected as its representative, shows how bilious reading attempts to construct a political strategy through a peculiarly intense yet narrow vision of the world.

The Presidential Campaign Trail

Thompson was not the only candidate interested in harnessing the energies of the counterculture. A similar rhetoric can be heard nationally in the initial phases of George McGovern's 1972 presidential campaign. The South Dakota senator assailed the center as the "establishment," "an empty, decaying void that commands neither [Americans'] confidence nor their love. It is the establishment center that has led us into the stupidest and cruelest war in all history . . . devouring two out of our three tax dollars . . . inflates our economy, picks our pockets, and starves other areas of our national life" (qtd. in Miroff 126–127). But even the McGovern campaign became the perfect opportunity for the bilious reader to cry foul. As it inevitably moved, sometimes by force, to the political center after the convention, the McGovern campaign was destined to be torn between "idealistic convictions about equality and peace . . . and practical calculations of how to win elections in a country whose majority evidently did not share such convictions" (Miroff 3). Such a dilemma within the Democratic Party, its lack of resolution, and the ever-lurking presence of President Nixon and his adherents formed an ideal opportunity for Thompson to take his bilious reading beyond the confines of Aspen. His bilious reading found national scale: reporting on the 1972 presidential campaign gave Thompson the opportunity to confirm what he saw locally and extrapolate it into a narrative of national decline.

As Natasha Zaretsky writes, "The standard vision of national decline is premised on the belief that the effects of time on the nation are the same as its effects on the human body: decay, degeneration, and eventual collapse" (145). This vision was synecdochically at work in Thompson's depiction of the nation's politicos and their effects on the landscape. The campaign trail offered a steady stream of figures to be insulted as false representatives. The political was made personal through synecdoches that made moral corruption evident in the surface physiognomy of their bodies. Chicago Mayor Richard Daley looks "like a potato with mange" (Thompson, *Campaign Trail* 234). Hubert Humphrey speaks like "an eighty-year-old woman who just discovered speed" (140). In Thompson's critiques of not only their mental acuity but also their physical stamina, the timbre of their voice, their masculinity, and ultimately their humanity, leaders are depicted as "senile leeches" feeding on the national body (109). As Thompson traveled with the McGovern campaign throughout the election, it seemed that wherever these elite "leeches" went, the nation died a little. The effect of their parasitic feeding was evident, Thompson notes, in the topography of the campaign trail. Looking out the window of his Milwaukee hotel room, he observes, "Dawn is struggling up through the polluted mist on Lake Michigan . . . a giant body of water full of poison" (119). At Miami Beach, where both party conventions were held, "an unnatural number of ravens have been seen in the city recently," making "horrible croaking sounds" and defecating everywhere (231). Death and its signs are evident in the landscape: the water and air are impure, and the few remaining animals prove the sign of bad omens to come. Wherever politicos went, decay ensued. In depictions like these Thompson asserts that the political elite are toxic to the national body.

In a nation run by elite monsters, genuine political conviction was simply not possible. Democratic candidate George McGovern is portrayed as a sort of bumbling idealist: Thompson's encounters with McGovern cast the candidate as an outsider who shows up in utterly banal places—his first conversation with him takes place as they stand at a bathroom urinal. At one event for the candidate, Thompson does not even realize that McGovern is standing next to him and calling his name: "I realized that the voice that had been yelling 'Sheriff'—belonged to George McGovern" (*Campaign Trail* 132). And even at the height of McGovern's popularity, Thompson finds him alone and aloof at a campaign stop smorgasbord, dressed in an inauspicious "tan gabardine suit" and "quietly loading his plate with carrots & salami" (222). The candidate seems incidental to the whirlwind that surrounds him. It is a biting synecdoche of his presidential campaign that Thompson writes of McGovern that "nobody in the room even knew he was there" (223). Thompson contrasts the overall dull predictability of the campaign trail with the voices of those he sees as the last holders of the American Dream, who are not presidential candidates or fellow politicos but "the hustler, the activist, the radical and the drug fiend" who "possess rebellious individuality within" the system (Worden 70). Picking up two hitchhikers on his way to Washington, DC, Thompson tells them that his goal is to "check out the people and find out if they're *all* swine" (*Campaign Trail* 18, emphasis in original). In a moment of savage agreement, his wanderlustful passengers can't see it any other way: "Those bastards wouldn't even *be* there if they weren't rotten," they tell him (18, emphasis in original). They understand, as Thompson does, that elections are nothing more than "stinking double-downer sideshows" in which people could not vote for something they believe in but "that old familiar choice between the lesser of two evils" (41). Scenes like these work throughout *Campaign Trail* not only to confirm Thompson's reading of the elite as ill, deranged, and barely human, but also to show how presidential campaigns bring people together—he finds few with faith in the political process—through mutually shared disaffection.

"The name or even the Party Affiliation of the next President won't make any difference at all, except on the surface," Thompson writes (*Campaign Trail* 74). Yet this populist assumption blurred important distinctions: once everything is rendered equally corrupt and every campaign unhopeful ("a sprawling, hyper-tense boredom"), it is hard for Thompson to discern key differences among the candidates (74). The bilious reader forgets that not all is bile, that not everyone is conspiring, that even in politics, there are improvisations.[5] And because he finds every part in his purview to be fuel for his bile, he also loses a broader perspective: as much as Thompson sees chicanery within the Democratic Party, he catches no trace of the sabotage being performed by Nixon's "nasty operatives" who forged the "Canuck Letter" that ultimately brought down the Muskie campaign, interfered with the Wallace campaign, hired actors to play extremists at the convention, and, emboldened by these successes and with increasing paranoia, attempted to steal Daniel Ellsberg's medical history and broke into Watergate (see Slocum-Schaffer 20–24). Thompson's perspective on the 1972 presidential election shows how, in the acuteness through which he derives the whole only from the parts in his sight, the bilious reader loses sight of the actual whole. Its absurdity may prove entertaining, but its oversimplistic foolishness becomes evident on further inspection.

Of the 1972 presidential election, Thompson's bile would make anyone's victory a pyrrhic one, including his own. Of the gambles he made with fellow journalists on the campaign trail, he notes that "I won all my bets—I made no money" (*Campaign Trail* 480). Reflecting on the outcome of the race—an enormous win for Nixon—he concludes that "This may be the year when we finally come face to face with ourselves; finally just lay back and say it—that we are a nation of 220 million used car salesmen with all the money we need to buy guns, and no qualms at all about killing anybody in the world who tries to make us uncomfortable" (389). The election exemplifies to him that America finds righteousness in the marking up of secondhand wares for even higher profits, that the average American is more interested in ripping off their neighbors than in embracing them. Even worse—with the bilious reader it is always worse—Nixon's election showed to Thompson how any deviation from this mendacious way of life would be met with devastating hostility: anyone who made the establishment uncomfortable would be quickly destroyed. In its reelection of Nixon, the nation demonstrates to Thompson that its everyday people were like its elites, "inclined to protect Their Own" and uninterested in "who actually wins; the only thing that matters is the point-spread" (105, 38). Thus when he asks at the end of the book, "How low do you have to stoop in this country to be President?" (389), there is no need for him to answer because he has already answered it. The campaign, from its beginning to its end, confirms to him the nation's low stoop, and if the campaign is a contest for who will serve as a synecdoche for the nation, the campaign proves the nation's fullest departure from its ideals.

Those ideals went mostly unspoken. *Campaign Trail* ends with Thompson leafing through the Sunday papers: he comes across a full-page advertisement from McDonald's ("one of Nixon's big contributors") with a lengthy quote: "Nothing in the world can take the place of persistence. Talent will not: nothing is more common than unsuccessful men with talent. Genius will not: unrewarded genius is almost a proverb. Education alone will not: the world is full of educated derelicts. Persistence and determination alone are omnipotent" (481). This quote has often been attributed to Calvin Coolidge, but its source is an 1881 book of spiritual guidance for young people by Theodore Thornton Munger entitled *On the Threshold*. Thompson reads the advertisement several times "before I grasped the full meaning" (481). But what that meaning is he does not say.

On the one hand, the sermon seeks to explicate the moral value of persistence, a distinctly American ideal that as long as one works toward a goal, it will be achieved regardless of other factors. Yet the way in which Thompson presents it, at the conclusion of a narrative of an exhausting and embittering presidential campaign, also offers a manual of bilious reading. The talented, the educated, the genius—the true representatives of the nation—have been cast aside by the inauthentic persistent—the talentless, the depraved, the imbecilic elite. In silence, Thompson suggests a final time that the moral world is now long past and the present has been emptied of its ethics: the noble words of past leaders have been appropriated by a global fast-food chain, and their original intention, to guide character, has become pablum to those with no morals at all, more interested in selling hamburgers that taste alike everywhere in the country to those dumb enough to think that consistency of taste is the same as quality. Indeed, their very consumption of what the elite peddles as national sustenance confirms to Thompson that America is an unhealthy, dying country.

Thompson finishes his paper, and "around midnight when the rain stopped, I put on my special Miami Beach nightshirt and walked several blocks down La Cienega Boulevard to the Loser's Club" (*Campaign Trail* 481). With winners like these, one wants to be the loser: to be a winner would be to be a false representative of the country; to be a winner would mean having no bile to discourse. It is only as an outcast that Thompson has the authority to depict the conflict between "us" and "them" in his distinctly bilious way. And in his retreat to the "Loser's Club," Thompson leaves us so he may be with who he sees as the nation's true representatives.

Plains, Georgia

Thompson's hatred of Richard Nixon is legendary. Of the 1969 presidential inauguration, Thompson notes that wherever Nixon went, people in Washington, DC, threw garbage, but the worst smell in the capital emanates from Nixon's "armored hearse" as it travels down Pennsylvania Avenue (*Campaign Trail* 71). The victory was itself proof to Thompson that Nixon is a "cheapjack hustler" who embodies "everybody's worst fears about the future of the Republic" (46, 70). The Watergate scandal that was revealed soon after his second election was a confirmation to Thompson, given his decades-long insistence that Nixon was a synecdoche for everything wrong with the nation: the revelation of the president's illegal behavior did not surprise him.

But what is curious—and perhaps most revealing about bilious reading—is Thompson's intense affection for Jimmy Carter. On the one hand, Carter is to him the only candidate who presented a break from the "gloom, pessimism, and a sort of aggressive neutrality" between the Kennedy and McGovern camps that emerged after the 1972 election (Thompson, *Songs* 173). On the other hand, what Thompson sees in Carter—reads into Carter—is a populism of its own bilious nature. Thompson's depiction of Carter in a 1976 *Rolling Stone* article reveals the extent that he tries to fit Carter into his bilious reading, how he depicts Carter as representative of non-elite Americans while instilling in him a populist "cartoon vitalism" (Saint-Amour 437). According to Thompson, Carter "could pass for a Fuller Brush man on any street in America" (*Great Shark Hunt* 471). Yet simultaneously, Thompson extols Carter's very ordinariness as a sign of his hostility toward the elite. Carter's "Law Day" speech, given at the University of Georgia in 1974, is that of "an angry agrarian populist, extremely precise in its judgements and laced with some of the most original, brilliant, and occasionally bizarre political metaphors anybody in that room will ever be likely to hear" (477). His enthusiastic reading of Carter's speech shows how bilious readers lose their "steadiness and solidity" in the presence of an ally (Pearcy 448). In his support of Carter, Thompson demonstrates the "savage agreement" in which bilious readers celebrate a kindred spirit (Jane 534).

Thompson was not so interested in Carter's morality—he writes that if Carter ever attempts to "mention anything to me about bringing Jesus into my life," he will dose him with LSD—as he is in the candidate's willingness to castigate those he sees as immoral (*Great Shark Hunt* 486). In this, Thompson oversimplifies: he seems to have selectively forgot that Carter had himself been a member of the military, had been a business-man, and had worked his way up the ladder of state government—not exactly countercultural or populist activities. The Carter that Thomp-son depicts is not a farmer or an engineer or a governor or a candidate but a crusader, a practitioner of strong affect. Thompson describes the Carter campaign as having an "awesome" populist intensity (481). That "an almost totally unknown ex-governor of Georgia with no national reputation, no power base in the Democratic party and not the slightest reluctance to tell . . . anyone who asks that 'the most important thing in my life is Jesus Christ'" could become the presidential nominee fascinates him (481–82). His rise recalls to Thompson the political ideals of the pre-vious decade: for Thompson, Carter is the reenactment of "the first wild days of the [Free Speech Movement]" (485). This time around, he feels assured, the electorate will partake in a "great leap of faith" and vote for Carter (452). The alignment of the staid Carter with the wild days of the 1960s, the construction of Carter as the sign of yet another great awaken-ing, is a conflation that can only take place through a bilious oversimpli-fication. Thompson reads into Carter's speech and his candidacy a bilious temper while setting aside the evangelical morality that led the candi-date to deliver such jeremiads. Thompson portrays Carter as a populist in the George Wallace tradition (one might say a populist in the Hunter S. Thompson tradition). Yet the distance between Thompson's reading and Carter's politics shows a use of synecdoche that borders on foolishness. It is what happens when a part is subsumed by savage agreement into a bilious reader's whole.

Carter himself is a man with a cause and a commitment to scripture. But Thompson's Carter is a harbinger of antisocial energy: he is a pissed-off populist, and nothing more. This misreading is evident in Thompson's depiction of Carter's "Law Day" speech at the University of Georgia Law School in May 1974. The "Law Day" speech begins by Carter identifying those from whom he had learned "the proper application of criminal jus-tice and the system of equities," not from lawyers but from the philoso-pher Reinhold Niebuhr, and how he came to understand "the dynamism of change in modern society" not from reading academic treatises but from listening to "a poet named Bob Dylan" (*Great Shark Hunt* 476–77). (Indeed, Carter's early presidential campaign material was littered with quotes from Niebuhr—"The sad duty of politics is to establish justice in a sinful world"—and Dylan's "Song to Woody," a lament that the nation "looks like it's a-dyin' an' it's hardly been born") (Carter 7). What piques Thompson's interest in Carter is that he sees the nation through a highly moral lens and that he speaks of justice not just in a legal sense but as a remedy to a world of sin, a nation to be built upon individual duty rather than mendacious conformities. (That he quotes Bob Dylan, subcultural paragon of the 1960s, likely helps as well.) But what impresses Thompson the most is Carter's willingness to be in direct conflict with the elites in his audience. Carter has the audacity to ask a room full of politicos to "search their heart and soul" to ask, "What can we do to restore equity and justice or to preserve it or to enhance it in this society?" (Thompson, *Great Shark Hunt* 491). Suggesting that the presidential candidate is a verbal pistol, Thompson intuits that Carter sees the speech as an opportunity "to unload" on the elites, "whether the audience liked it or not" (475). Thompson is delighted that Carter's genteel audience is described by the candidate himself, in their presence, as "running dogs of the status quo" (475). Carter not so subtly insults those in front of him by saying that "a black pencil salesman . . . could make a better judgement about who ought to be sheriff than two highly educated professors at Georgia Southwestern College" (see 491). From Thompson's perspective, Carter "railed and bitched about a system of criminal justice that allows the rich and the privileged to escape punishment for their crimes and sends poor people to prison because they can't afford to bribe a judge" (477). As he listens to Carter, Thompson inserts invective into the candidate's speech, using words that the then-governor certainly would not have in public. In effect, Thompson's depiction of Carter is that of a populist—a true representative of "us"—willing to chasten "them."

Yet Thompson's reading of Carter's "Law Day" speech only makes sense if one listens selectively for a bilious tone. Thompson's reading is counter to most historical accounts of Carter's speechmaking. Most have found that Carter "made for uninspiring oratory" because he "distrusted rhetoric altogether . . . endlessly frustrating his own speechwriters" (Schulman 123). As Bruce Schulman notes, voters at first "found Carter's bland style and lack of ideological vigor reassuring" (123). His blandness attracted a diverse audience and allowed him to campaign on a loose sense of moral rightness based on "deliberate ambiguity": instead of policy, he offered "love and compassion and honesty—things nobody could disagree with" (Sandbrook 150). Yet as much as Carter practiced deliberate ambiguity, he also called upon his audience to practice a politics of purity—and he would promise to do so if he were elected to the office that synecdochically represents American democracy. "Carter believed that the presidency should be above petty politicking, negotiation, and even compromise. His was a moral vision for the office, not a political one" (Stanley 44). This vision led to both a naivete about the office itself (Carter's populist vision demanded that he have no "knowledge of the Washington scene") and to a disrespect toward those seen as less moral (Carter's barely hidden "contempt for the Congress"), both of which were key components of his administration's failure to achieve its mission (Slocum-Schaffer 64). The president lost advisers as they came to realize that he saw himself (much as Thompson saw himself) in place of the people instead of representing them: as one told him, "I am not sure what you believe in, other than yourself" (Shrum 69). Carter would "refuse to budge on some element of an issue for the sake of the larger victory": by insisting that every part be pure, he in effect made those victories so few that he lost allies within the government and the confidence of those who elected him in the first place (Slocum-Schaffer 72). Indeed, it would be Carter's biliousness that ultimately undid him: as Robert M. Collins notes of Carter's infamous "Malaise Speech," what stood out was the president's explanation of American "adversity in a profoundly pessimistic formulation" (24). Turning a material problem into a moral problem, Carter insisted that the energy crisis was a "crisis of the American spirit" (24). And in admonishing the people he was elected to represent as those who created the crisis, Carter turned blame inward, casting the entire nation as an environmentally wasteful and morally corrupt "them." In effect, Carter severed the synecdochical bonds between a president and the people. The "Malaise Speech" shows how bilious readers have a tendency, as then vice president Walter Mondale would later write, of turning "sugar into shit" (qtd. in Collins 25).

Both Thompson's oeuvre and Carter's administration demonstrate how an imagined community is not possible through a purely "moralistic imagination of politics" (Müller 19–20). As much as bile produces a closed loop of negative attunement, it also produces a closed circle of fellow moral purists who may share savage agreement with each other but never translate it successfully into policy. (We might sense already the closed loop that comes from bilious reading: it was repetitions on a theme that led to Thompson's several titles, from 1970s Las Vegas to 1980s Ronald Reagan, of "Fear and Loathing.")[6] Of course, there will always be an audience for bile; if for entertainment value alone readers will enjoy its use of invective. Others may find its tactics of "authenticity over civility" and its displays of "strategic acts of incivility" can both "bring attention to your point of view" and demonstrate virtue (Cmiel 269). But in Thompson's depictions of Aspen, the 1972 presidential election, Jimmy Carter's run for the White House, and the many "Fear and Loathing" articles that followed for the next thirty-five years, this bilious reader, through his "simplicity bordering on foolishness" and his losing of "steadiness and solidity" in his synecdochical depiction of the nation, regurgitated ugly feeling in perpetuity (Pearcy 448). By sticking to his bile and recasting it over and over again, the bilious reader proves right just enough of the time for his interpretation to have some credence, no matter how flawed the majority of his readings are. Thompson did not get to his conclusions through reasonable intellection but through strong affect. As a result, of all the incitements to discourse, it seems that bilious reading is what gets to the right conclusions through the most embittered of means.

Conclusion: Bilious Reading and the American Nightmare

As Joel Best writes, "the American Dream is best understood as a straw figure . . . rarely invoked with complacency, it is almost always framed in terms of anxiety or critique" (63). The phrase often detracts from a more honest exploration of the nation's ambivalent image, substituting complex politics for scapegoats that demonstrate *who* is wrong in place of any discussion of how to achieve *what* is right. Seldom does the discourse of the "American Dream" evoke complexity: by its nature it incites an us/them interpretation that is idealistic to some and idolatrous to others.[7] The same strong nationalism applies to those who discourse on the "American Nightmare." In June 1966, Thompson pitched to *The Nation* editor Carey McWilliams a book on "the fate of California" (*Proud Highway* 573). It would be "a microcosm of American history. The destruction of California is the logical climax to the Westward Movement" (573). In California, a particular type of story of America could be told, one that Thompson sees "as logical as mathematics": an equation including "the redwoods, the freeways, the dope laws, race riots, water pollution, smog, the [Free Speech Movement], and now Governor Reagan." Each of these pieces coalesce into an unpleasant whole that shows Thompson how "California is the end, in every way, of Lincoln's idea that America was 'the last best hope of man.' . . . California is the ultimate flower of the American Dream, a nightmare of failed possibilities" (573).[8]

Strong affect can be detected in the letter's extremity: Thompson is uninterested in depicting rough stitches in an otherwise smooth fabric. Instead, he proposes to write a narrative of destruction, congestion, regulation, deforestation, pollution, disorder, restrictions on liberty, and neoconservatism as the "logical climax" of the American project. California is "the end" and "the end, in every way" of the nation: it is not just an example, but "the ultimate flower" that would never germinate. Thompson seeks to depict a nation that was not a site of hope, but a site of hopelessness: not a dream, but a "nightmare." And that he sees this nightmare as "logical as mathematics" is not so much a quantitative claim but a qualitative, ultimately cynical one. Thompson casts blame upon every part of the whole: it is not just polluters and junkies and Ronald Reagan who contribute to this nightmare, but environmentalists, racial activists, even the Free Speech Movement at Berkeley. Everyone is to blame for the nation's downfall—left, right, or center—each is a contributor to the nation's "failed possibilities" (Thompson, *Proud Highway* 573). Each had, Thompson writes, betrayed the ideals of Lincoln, and in doing so, they betrayed the representative for what he considered a moral American public life. Thompson uses the rhetoric of synecdoche to produce a nation that is far from its dreams and is actively working to create a national "fate" of disarray and disaster (573).

Thompson would never write the book he pitched to McWilliams. Yet its trajectory can be seen in his writing of Aspen, the 1972 primaries, and the rise of Jimmy Carter, as well as through his more canonical works. In *Fear and Loathing in Las Vegas*, for example, Thompson offers himself as the true representative who had lived the dream and was now living its nightmare in perpetuity, a man who had seen Eden and now lived east of it. Just one year after the beginning of the 1970s, Thompson laments that "the middle sixties was a very special time to be a part of," that American life had culminated the decade before with "a long fine flash" (*Las Vegas* 66–67). Recalling how he sped across the Bay Bridge on his motorcycle, Thompson describes the mid-1960s as a time in which he was "absolutely certain that no matter which way I went I would come to a place where people were just as high and wild as I was" (67). This moment of absolute certainty is a populist's dream, a nation where "we" are surrounded by those exactly like "us" wherever we look. Thompson notes the exhilaration that comes with such certainty: "There was a fantastic universal sense that whatever we were doing was *right,* that we were winning" (68, emphasis in original). It is not just that the 1960s are a "special" time, but that they are special because the "we" Thompson imagines himself representing has won out over the "them": he is no longer one person, but "universal" and "right." His part has become the whole and he is authorized to speak in its place. But from such an Eden one can only face expulsion. Now, Thompson mourns, "you can almost *see* the high-water mark—that place where the wave finally broke and rolled back" (68, emphasis in original). Thompson depicts the perverse, distorted world that comes when the wave rolled back in "The Kentucky Derby Is Decadent and Depraved." The Derby is a "pretentious mix of booze, failed dreams and a terminal identity crisis; the inevitable result of too much inbreeding in a closed and ignorant culture" (Thompson, *Great Shark Hunt* 31). The Derby, as Thompson biliously reads it, is not the fulfillment of the American Dream nor a tradition anyone should take pride in, but a drama of "failed dreams," a celebration not of a thriving regional identity but of the nation's "terminal identity crisis." The Derby is to Thompson a synecdoche for "the whole doomed atavistic culture" of post-1960s America (34). Traditions such as the Derby do not show a thriving democracy but one that is unregenerate. Underneath its "stylish southern sag," the national body is nothing more than a "puffy, drink-ravaged, disease-ridden caricature" of a promising life unfulfilled (34, 37).

As Florian Keller writes, "The American Dream . . . is the public discourse that provides each American subject with the coordinates for his or her desire" (53). Yet the desire the Dream activates is not always inviting or magnanimous. Thompson's desires were not inclusive or democratic: they sought to wall off the Dream for the benefits of its few— to him, very few—true representatives. Thompson's bilious incitement to discourse is thus generative in how it magnifies the part to represent the whole, but ultimately degenerative in how it magnifies not for the sake of unity but for the sake of derision and dismissal. It is a peculiar use of synecdoche's premises to create the opposite of its rhetoric. Thompson's bilious reading throughout his career, in both normalizing the subculture and indicting the mainstream, showed that, according to its logic, there was very narrow space for the real American to exist, for bilious reading winnows the space of the nation to one in which the reader is the only exemplar. It is space that bilious readers must endlessly defend by going on the offensive: in their discourse, events change just enough to index new names and places as parts for the national nightmare it insists one can never be awoken from. It may yield an antic and exhilarating observation of the country, but biliousness is a one-note nationalism. The bilious reader, as Silvan Tomkins notes, "keeps his rage endlessly alive as he replays the scene now made increasingly intolerable through the large numbers of rehearsals which culminate as though there had been multiple offenses" (*Affect* 3:207). Bilious reading is always glad to relitigate the past on its populist terms, and the present serves exclusively to perpetuate a steady flow of material upon which bilious readers can continue their state of permanent negative attunement. What Thompson's writing shows is how bile is a strong nationalism: for all its moralizing and condemning, for all its insulting and its invective, its use of synecdoche is meant to conclude that the nation is beyond redemption unless hostility is substituted for sobriety, populism for democracy, "the people" for all the people. This false choice gave Thompson his claim to national fame, both literary and political, even as he reduced the nation to something unworthy of our imagining.

3

Futility

"A PIECE of nonsense in the literal meaning of the word" is how critic Jonathan Yardley describes James Baldwin's 1985 book *The Evidence of Things Not Seen:* "It makes no sense at all" (243). Yardley, like many reviewers, was taken aback by Baldwin's biting depiction of the United States: he could not understand Baldwin's persistent assertion that America remained unchanged since the 1960s and that the nation's lack of change was a sign of both national and global peril. "In three decades have we made any progress toward a more egalitarian society? Of course we have," Yardley responds with a confidence that rejects outright Baldwin's thesis (243).[1]

How readers answer Yardley's question says much about how they read Baldwin's book. And how they answer also says much about their own perception of the nation. To critics such as Yardley, George Shulman asks in response, "How does one digest the bloody, hysterical termination of the second American Reconstruction by a repressive regime invoking 'law and order?'" (165). From his perspective, it is impossible for Baldwin to *not* become "disillusioned and radicalized by the assassinations of Malcolm X, King, and Black Panther leaders, by the failure of the civil rights movement in the North, by invasive spying on political opposition, by the violence linking the Vietnam War to the repression of Black and student radicalism, and by the ascendancy of white backlash, an emerging Republican majority, and the election of Nixon twice" (165). Whatever "progress" was made in the 1960s was abated by the resurgence of white conservatism in the 1970s and annulled by the dismantling of Great Society programs in the 1980s. George Shulman—and James Baldwin—would certainly have answered Yardley's question with a definitive "no."

Perhaps it is because of the intense questions Baldwin's book raises that *Evidence* has received little critical notice. Perhaps too it is not only the questions but also the voice and tone of Baldwin's prose in his answering of them that has sparked fiery but few responses. This chapter aims to correct this critical absence by reframing what some critics take to be nonsense as a certain type of sense about the nation, a sense of what America is not and cannot become, and the candor of conviction that follows when it is realized that the nation will never fundamentally change. *Evidence* is the product of an author who wrestled with the nation throughout his career and ultimately found it no longer worth his fighting for. The reading that emerges from this perspective is not the work of an author so exhausted by his own celebrity that he could only muster a "truculent belligerence" toward America, as one critic wrote, but of a reader who has seen through us and, in doing so, gives up on America as a source of "us" altogether (see Lowe 54). What makes sense about Baldwin's *Evidence*, ultimately, is the futility that drives his reading of the nation.

Thus in this chapter, I explore how Baldwin's *Evidence* is an example of what I call futile reading: an incitement to discourse that reads parts to depict a whole beyond reform. Through its use of synecdoche, futile reading seals off any ambiguity that may defamiliarize or engender a new reading of the nation: what it depicts is terminal. It is a mode of reading that has realized that any "turn to repair is entangled with the very history and practices of neoliberal empire and the settler colonial state" and that to repair is to remain complicit in repairing what will endeavor to destroy you (Stuelke 17). Thus futility is a mode of reading driven by a certainty that progress is not possible. Futile reading is not melancholic and reparative but definitive and conclusive: it shows a history without progress, a community without possibility, a nation without redemption. The only way for a better future, the futile reader concludes, is to exit the nation altogether.

Throughout his career James Baldwin was a synecdochical reader who sought "to shift the fundamental narrative by which part and whole mediate their histories and conceive their possibilities" (Shulman 167). It was through synecdoche that Baldwin could foresee, in an inconclusive present, the potential for progress. But such reading was inevitably and repeatedly frustrated by the resistance of the nation to walk away from the injustices of class and race. The "New South" was no different than the "Old South," Baldwin would conclude in *Evidence*: America in the aftermath of the civil rights movement stubbornly remained the nation that it was prior to it, and the election of Ronald Reagan to the presidency codified a retreat from the fight for equality. Baldwin's use of synecdoche thus pivoted away from the promotion of American exceptionalism that formed much of his earlier writing, toward a resignation that the American project could not be fulfilled. He no longer saw the promise of an inconclusive present but instead saw conclusively a futureless nation.

Futility may well be the bleakest of strong nationalisms. Baldwin's futility—the opposite of futurity, the antithesis of American exceptionalism—is a demonstration of what Albert O. Hirschman calls "exit." By reading the nation as futile, Baldwin exited its orbit, giving his rationale to refuse communion with "us." And just as loyalty—"my country right or wrong"—is a strong nationalism, so is exit. Exit does not insist that all nationalisms are inadequate: importantly, futile readers who exit explicitly state in the act of their exit that *our* nationalism is inadequate for *them*. In their exit, futile readers reject the belief that America can be the "we" of its ideals. To engage in futile reading is to ultimately come to the definitive conclusion that there is no possibility for national reform. There is no way to live in America now—or ever.

Baldwin's futility emerges in the evolution of his two accounts of the Atlanta child murders of 1979–81, which share the same title, *The Evidence of Things Not Seen*. First published as an essay in *Playboy* in 1981, then in book-length form four years later, both narratives aspire to illuminate that which is not immediately visible about the murders and subsequent trial. But the America these two narratives give evidence of differs starkly. The *Playboy* essay is a narrative of futurity, a call to action for Americans to unite and protect children because they are the part that can redeem the national whole. The book, by contrast, is a narrative of futility, one in which the questionable justice of the trial exposes the permanent fractures of race relations in the nation, a national whole that will never change. As a narrative of futile reading, the book tells much about the nation that its denizens would much rather leave unexamined, a book of synecdoches with such scope that they indict every tendril of the American project.

The Atlanta Murders

What is today called the "Atlanta murders" is an event only visible in retrospect. In July 1980, Atlanta Mayor Maynard Jackson authorized a task force to investigate a surge in child murder—a child homicide rate of one per year had surged to as many as three per month (see Hobson 107). The task force found that the only commonality among the murders was the victim's economic class and their race: African American boys (though eventually two girls would be added to the investigation) as young as four (and men as old as twenty-eight), from July 1979 until May 1981, were found shot, asphyxiated, or stabbed to death. Under the guise that one of the murders may have been an out-of-state kidnapping, the task force contacted the FBI, which saw the city as a test site for its theories of criminal profiling. An FBI agent soon announced that four "children had been killed by their own families because they had been considered 'nuisances'" (Lopez 226). When this announcement proved untrue, the task force insisted that the children were "hustlers and runaways" who could have avoided their deaths if they lived middle-class lives in dual-parent families (Hobson 97). And when this announcement proved unpopular, the FBI, in an event that would trigger outrage upon its discovery, sent white agents "posing as workmen" into the area, "offering a child five dollars to come with him to do some job" (Douglas 203). Each announcement, reaction, and subsequent official response to the reaction exacerbated racial tension—and had the effect of blaming the very audiences who had appealed to investigators for the rescue of their children.

The murders occurred in the wake of explosive yet uneven economic growth in Atlanta. As Maurice J. Hobson writes, by 1972, "Atlanta ranked among the most prosperous cities in the United States" (95). Yet the majority of its African American population remained poor and were increasingly discontent with their continuing disempowerment. Atlanta's municipal politics were a "tightrope" between the white business elite and a Black constituency increasingly torn between an "old guard" of political kingmakers and a public who wanted substantive reform (94–95). The election of Maynard Jackson as mayor in 1974 proved a watershed moment—the first Black mayor of a southern metropolis—but it was also a moment of high, ultimately unrealizable, expectations. "Many had believed that Jackson's election would remedy some of the numerous problems experienced by Atlanta's poor and black populations" (95). The murders occurred at the same time as it became apparent remedies were not forthcoming, and frustration with Jackson's inability to address such problems was increasingly public, putting on display first the disorganized, insular nature of the city's police force and then ultimately the tactics of a mayor more attentive to elites and more distant from citizens than his rhetoric depicted.

The murders also occurred in the midst of a national moral panic, a backlash to the rise of feminism and gay rights. "Launched in the name of child protection," this panic gave "new life to old themes of predation, despoliation, and contagion" (Lancaster 41). Underneath the familiar world lurked sinister forces out to destroy children. A "satanic ritual abuse" scare emerged late in the decade in which "McDonald's magnate Ray Croc was rumored to have been a satanist; Procter and Gamble's arcane logo was rumored to be an occult symbol; and various rock bands were imagined to be winning converts to Satan by embedding secret, coded messages in their songs" (47). The spreaders of moral panic, from journalists to politicians to preachers, insisted that the symbols of a supposedly banal consumer culture hid a sinister whole, and suggested that if these signs could be read for the evil they synecdochically concealed, children could be protected from their diabolical influence. Further, they insisted that to not read the world for these evil signs would mean the loss of children's innocence if not their lives: a 1975 *Time* article estimated that more than a hundred thousand "American boys" were engaged in prostitution (43). Thus the moral panic of the period asserted that childhood was not only a period of innocence but was a proxy for a nation under attack by otherwise invisible forces.

As the murders became an incessant feature of Atlanta daily life, speculation abounded, so much so that it was difficult to ascertain its source. Martin Amis documents how the presence of a Bible at one of the murder scenes led to the circulation of a "Cult Theory" in which children were being sacrificed in the name of "some voodoo brotherhood": there was also a "Disturbed Female Theory" in which the culprit was a "failed mother or childless woman acting out a complicated revenge on the living world" (18). And as Joseph Vogel notes, television networks throughout 1981 ran stories circulating a theory that the murderer was a male "black homosexual," based on the premise that some of the victims were dressed only in their underwear (a theory that forgets that two of

the victims were females and that none of the victims had injuries suggesting sexual assault) (120).[2] With each theory came the identification of
a motive but not a suspect, a scheme but not a villain, of a whole without
the crucial part to validate it.[3]

The Atlanta murders were a synecdochical morass that challenged the
concept of plot. Who was the culprit and why was he—or she—murdering?
The authorities who could answer these questions were in conflict with
each other: their explanations lacked the "idea of boundedness, demar-
cation, the drawing of lines to mark off and order" the narrative of the
situation (Peter Brooks 12). And as a crisis of plot, the word's more sinister
definitions percolated to the surface, that of "a secret plan to accomplish
a hostile or illegal purpose" (12). The audacity of the murders compelled
theorization, yet there was little and conflicting evidence to support
any theory. And the murders' multiyear lack of resolution encouraged
interpretation, if only to make them representative of something rather
than the nothing that authorities offered.

When plot fails, strong affects surge. When an order of events cannot be conclusively established, feelings of unease, paranoia, and rage
become the only means of reading. A variety of competing strong nationalisms surfaced as the investigation stalled. The Ku Klux Klan was
investigated and dismissed by both Atlanta and FBI officials. One Atlanta
community initiated a "Ron Carter Patrol," named after a murdered Black
Panther, in which "adult residents carried firearms . . . and teenagers carried baseball bats to secure their housing project from suspected killers"
(Hobson 117). The Nation of Islam offered evidence to comic and activist Dick Gregory that the murders were orchestrated by the Centers for
Disease Control in order to harvest Interferon, claimed to cure cancer
in white people, from the genitals of prepubescent Black male children
(127). As these theories abounded, it became entirely unclear who could
be trusted: "On the streets, the killer was referred to as 'the Man,' a term
that was also applied to the police" (99). In Atlanta, it was no longer clear
what this particular synecdoche meant—the nickname for the lawless
the same for the law, the moniker of the violator the same as the pro-
tector. "The Man" could kill you, and if he did, the chance of his ever
coming to justice was slim to nil, or "The Man" could send you, based
on the color of your skin, to prison for a crime you did not commit. Atlanta became a city in which "we" are under attack by a "them" that is
everywhere, from both authorities and criminals, a world in which "we"

have no space to live metaphorically—or literally. The murders "forced the country and the world to question Atlanta's aspirations to be viewed as the new, highly touted 'Black Mecca,' a city that represented the highest educational, political, and economic aspirations for Black Americans" (130). By extension, the murders also reawakened a discussion of race and its centrality in American life. It challenged an unspoken narrative that assumed America had become moderate if not tolerant after the tumult of the 1960s. And it showcased the continually fraught nature of Black striving: how, time and time again, what was supposed to bring freedom was manipulated to perpetuate racial inequity.

In May 1981, through sheer chance, twenty-three-year-old Wayne Bertram Williams was pulled over and questioned after he drove across the James Jackson Memorial Bridge and a large splash was heard in the water underneath: the body of twenty-seven-year-old Nathaniel Cater was discovered in the water two days later. Williams had no alibi. Three polygraph examinations revealed signs of dishonesty, and he engaged in several public eccentricities, including distributing his résumé at a press conference he hosted outside his family's house shortly after his release from initial investigation. Eventually, Williams would be tried for two murders: Cater's and that of twenty-one-year-old Jimmy Ray Payne, whose case was added as Williams was on trial for Cater's murder, the prosecution exploiting a state law that permitted it "to include evidence from other cases if it helped to establish a pattern" (Hobson 125). In effect, prosecutors asked the jury to presume that as long as two murders could be proven conclusive, then Williams would be guilty of all the murders, even if he had not been charged with them. And patterns would indeed garner Williams's conviction: fibers from a violet and green bedspread found on the bodies, animal hairs consistent with that of Williams's dog, debris that matched the Williams family station wagon. The prosecution never sought to expose a corpus delicti or provide a mens rea that incited him to serial killing. As Chet Dettlinger notes, "No one would testify that Wayne Williams threw a body into the water. No one would testify that Wayne Williams even stopped on the bridge" (324). Instead, the jury was asked to make sense of the murders through an assumption of transitivity. There is likely no more morbid an example of synecdoche at work than one that establishes the responsibility for murder.

Williams was found guilty for both murders and sentenced to life imprisonment. The Atlanta police disbanded its task force. Yet even those who assisted the prosecution harbor doubt that Williams committed all of the murders on the task force's list, which had swelled to thirty by the time he was arrested. John Douglas, at the time the FBI's major profiler of mass murderers, speculates that Williams was "the killer of eleven young men in Atlanta," but that there "isn't a single offender and the truth isn't pleasant" (222–23). Chet Dettlinger notes that sixty-three other "unsolved Atlanta-area killings of blacks who fit the arbitrary age, sex, race, and cause-of-death parameters that the authorities used for The List" to tie the murders to Williams were not added to it and were thus never investigated or prosecuted (44).

"Perhaps, then, the Killings in Atlanta are over, while the killings in Atlanta go on," Martin Amis wrote at the conclusion of the trial (22). Amis's capitalization shrewdly works to differentiate how the Killings, as a synecdoche, came to an end, even as child murder persisted as a problem, albeit no longer organized as a site of synecdochical reading that could galvanize public attention and elicit official response. The murders continued but without "The List" or the narrative that would bring those murders to justice. And that the "Killings" were considered "over" masked the social problem of child murder in the city. The millions of dollars of public and private money spent to keep children off the streets during the murders did not stop the crimes from being committed: the bounties offered for the murderer did not bring forth any suspects. Donations to the victims' families were at times misdirected: as Maurice J. Hobson notes, almost $140,000 put into trust for the families remained undistributed even thirty-two years after the murders were committed (130). Above all, the arrest, trial, and imprisonment of Williams did not answer the local questions, much less resolve the national issues, that the murders raised: it did nothing to abate the moral panic that would continue throughout the 1980s, did nothing to restore the reputation of Atlanta as a "city too busy to hate," and did nothing to counter a narrative with international spread that urban America was unsafe and that the entire nation was racked with perverse violence. It reminded both Atlantans and Americans that Black life in the United States was one of "promise and letdown," that even gruesome events such as serial murder were part of a broader cycle of "repetitive events and remarkably nonrising plot structure" that left its denizens trapped and deprived of a future any different from their past (Stockton 76, 75). This too would be James Baldwin's ultimate conclusion, though he first tried to salvage the murders' non-rising structure with a promising, future-oriented ending and turn the repetitive events of serial murder into a national call for action.

The Future Nation

The Atlanta murders evoked a broad commentary that connected the child to the future of the nation. "Any nation that does not operate on a children-first basis is being suicidal," the mother of victim Yusef Bell said at a rally held at the Lincoln Memorial in May 1981 (qtd. in Hobson 103). Part of Camille Bell's plea for additional police resources and federal funding was an insistence that the Atlanta murders were not just locally (or personally, in her case) harmful, but that they were harmful to the entire nation because they threatened its future. In doing so, Bell synec-dochically appealed to strong nationalist affect. As Sara Ahmed writes, "National love places its hopes in the next generation; the postponement of the ideal sustains the fantasy that return is possible" (*Cultural Politics* 131). Strong nationalists assume that children, in the future the national-ists have made for them, will become the concrete manifestation of their ideals. Children will, in a way the strong nationalist cannot, "achieve our country" (Shulman 155).

The nature of Bell's plea, while genuinely heartfelt, also fit well within the political turn of the 1980s. Natasha Zaretsky notes that "the family served as a symbol for the nation itself" as the nation adjusted to civil and women's rights, defeat in Vietnam, and a shift in national population to the South and the West (4). American politicians at the highest levels verbalized that what "served as a link between generations" was a "confidence in the future" that was discernable in "a faith that the days of our children would be better than our own" (Jimmy Carter qtd. in Zaretsky 218). At the same time, the rhetoric of family also served the political fringe to perpetuate the moral panic that reasserted the hetero-sexual family as the conduit for national ideals. In the formation of the Moral Majority and its subsequent rise to national power through Ronald Reagan, the figure of the child was used to criticize a weak nationalist conception of the nation as a diverse plurality of people. In particular, strong nationalists would come to use the figure of the child to override weak nationalism's conception of the nation as an imagined community of the "deep, horizontal comradeship" that constitutes all its members (Benedict Anderson 7). They would instead refute any comradeship that did not place the child as the "perpetual horizon of every acknowledged politics, that fantasmatic beneficiary of every political intervention" (Edel-man 3). It is in this way that strong nationalists use the child as a figure that "shapes the logic within which the political itself must be thought" (2). For conservatives and other strong nationalists, the child synecdochi-cally creates a nation of flexible absolutes that are beyond question.

Baldwin's *Playboy* essay on the Atlanta murders, "The Evidence of Things Not Seen," is a reflection on Black futurity. It is not only a con-demnation of the murderer of children but also a call for African Ameri-cans and ultimately all Americans to rally together to achieve a particular type of future. Much like Bell's plea at the Lincoln Memorial, "Evidence" calls upon the figure of the child as the figure of the nation's future. Baldwin begins "Evidence" by writing of Atlanta: "I have friends there, people whom I love. I cannot read the news reports without thinking of those people and wondering what is happening to them. Most of them have children" ("Evidence" 140). It is through the perspective as a writer and as a friend of the family (and therefore a friend of the concept of family) that Baldwin writes his essay—as one, while not directly affected by the murders, who is connected to them by way of his friends who have children. "I have handled a great many children," Baldwin continues, "washed them, spanked them, put them on the toilet, tied ribbons in their hair." This love of children, evoked through everyday parental tasks, is juxtaposed by Baldwin against his inability to fathom—as he assumes the murderer does—"a child as a sexual object." In effect, Baldwin writes from the perspective as the carer of children: he writes from the perspective of a parent by proxy. In doing so, Baldwin aligns himself (and by extension, the Black homosexual community) with those who nurture children, not those who abuse them. In contrast to a vehement conservative discourse championed by Pat Robertson, Anita Bryant, and Phyllis Schlafly, who saw homosexuals, as Jerry Falwell told a Miami audience in 1977, "as folks who would just soon kill you as look at you" (qtd. in Lancaster 42), Bald-win tacitly refutes the "Black Homosexual" thesis that circulated through-out Atlanta in 1981, insisting that to be homosexual is not the same as to be a murderer. And by further proxy, readers are interpellated as fellow parents or friends of people with children: even second or third hand, a relation with others through the central figure of the child. This figure, Baldwin writes, is a tabula rasa. "Children have no defenses. . . . A child believes everything; he has no choice" ("Evidence" 140). It is the funda-mental helplessness of children—the helplessness of those who bear the future of the nation—that drives Baldwin's analysis. The person or per-sons committing the crime are not only destroying individual children, they are polluting the national ideal of childhood itself. "Now, somewhere in Atlanta," Baldwin writes, "some desperate person who must certainly once have been such a child is seducing children to death." Baldwin writes of the murderer as a child gone astray, not only in his corporeal destructiveness but also in his botched use of an adult strategy—seduction—to perpetuate it. The problem, as Baldwin articulates it in the *Playboy* essay, is that Atlanta's child victims are trapped "between poverty and puberty," an economic class and a period of life in which they have little choice but to do what anyone richer and older tells them. And he suggests that the murderer knows this as well. "Someone—consider this—gets a bright black boy, a child into his car. He knows that the child imagines, as all children do, that he knows the score, that he can get out of any trap. But no child knows that death is real" ("Evidence" 142). It is this innocence—a synecdoche for childhood itself—that the murderer exploits.

"Human life, and especially a child's life, is our most important gift, our only real responsibility, and is more sacred than any temple or doctrine, anywhere," Baldwin continues ("Evidence" 142). He insists that what taints this gift, breaks this responsibility, is the class dynamics of Atlanta and, more specifically, the alliance between its Black middle class and white business owners. Baldwin sees the Atlanta of the early 1980s much as he saw it twenty years before: its corporate veneer could not obscure what he first described in his 1959 essay "Nobody Knows My Name" as a "sensual, languid, and private" city that every evening reenacted the days of slavery in which the "ruder, more erotic beauty" of Black life was constrained and made subservient to "the master who had coupled with his slave," a city that "brings what was done in the dark to light" (*Collected Essays* 204). Atlanta, as he saw it then, was the base eros of a racist past that all Americans should condemn and replace with a new "standard of human freedom" (208). This would demand that "everyone who loves this country [take] a hard look at himself," and Baldwin warned that "if we are not capable of this examination, we may yet become one of the most distinguished and monumental failures in the history of nations."

What Baldwin had written of Atlanta twenty years before he sees now being played out in its most perverse form. The murders prove the "monumental failure" of which he had warned (*Collected Essays* 208). The murders prove to him that the "hard look" had not happened. The victims of the murders are to him "the heirs of the distilled and dreadful bitterness of the blood-soaked and sovereign state of Georgia" ("Evidence" 142). As children they not only inherit the past but are made to account for it with their lives. "The New South. Do not come down here looking for it," he writes: "Forget everything you may have heard, or may wish to believe, concerning the New South" (142). Whatever its metropolitan pretense as a "Black Mecca," Atlanta has not changed, and by synecdochical extension, neither has America. Indeed, the opposite has occurred: the "white city fathers" and "black middle class saw eye to eye on one thing, which was that desegregation had to be accomplished with a minimum of drama and a maximum of style" (310). Baldwin sees this concretely manifested in the architecture of the city. He describes the Atlanta Omni complex as "a kind of frozen, enclosed suburb" across from "a sprawling, poor-black neighborhood called Vine City" (316). It is a "galaxy of shop-windows selling clothes that your momma and poppa can't afford to buy": while the complex entices tourists, it offers no home for locals, especially those who do not want to be turned "into a new serving class" for those with wealth (316). The Omni is for Baldwin a synecdoche of a gentrified South that attempts to cloak its old ways behind an impersonal, modern façade. Its architecture, with "squares, tubes, vials and bubbles" that "assault the patient sky," is the twentieth-century equivalent of the lawn of the plantation owner's Big House: the tourists who consume at its bars, shops, and restaurants perform the contemporary equivalent of those who "trample Miss Scarlett's lawn and climb her steps and pose before the columns" of the fictional Tara in *Gone with the Wind* (308). Not only are the city of Atlanta and the state of Georgia complicit in the moral blindness that perpetuates the murders; so too are the tourists and conventioneers from across America who stay at the Omni, eat its food, and buy at its shops. The architecture may have changed, but Atlanta remains fetishized as a beacon of the "South" in the worst sense of the word.

The "unseen" thing for which the murders give evidence is the willingness of Americans to conspire against other races—or their own race—to ignore the realities of economic class in the nation. Baldwin uses the *Playboy* essay to lambast the followers of Martin Luther King Jr. who turned to the Republican Party in the 1980 presidential election, lamenting, "It is difficult to make bricks without straw" ("Evidence" 312). To him, the rise of Reagan is a sign of how taboo the subject of class is in early 1980s America. "When the word class, which is a mystery, is preceded by the word black, which is anathema, Americans simply become spiritual basket cases and head for the nearest cliff, needle, swastika, or cowboy," he writes (310). Americans, as Baldwin sees them, are more willing to destroy or drug themselves on the one hand, or adopt right-wing ideologies or become vigilantes on the other hand, rather than address realities at the intersection of race and class. He commingles the figure of American exceptionalism (the cowboy) with the figure of fascism (the swastika) and the figure of abuse (the needle) with the figure of suicide (the cliff). Thus the entire American mythology, Baldwin asserts, is designed to deny the realities of race and class and offers, from the frontiersman to the junkie, a well of images that obscure such denial.

Most devastatingly, Baldwin insists that African Americans themselves are complicit in this: the Atlanta murders ultimately "revealed relationships among black people" ("Evidence" 314). Baldwin depicts African American society as a family gone so haywire that it would kill its own children:

> Whoever is murdering the children must, on the evidence, be dark enough to go unnoticed, is someone who has been driven mad by the double inheritance of the house nigger and the field nigger, of genuine bondage and promised freedom; who is both the son of the white master and blood brother to the black castrated corpse; brother and pimp and nephew to the high-yellow or chocolate or ebony whore; nephew and foster son and occasional lover to that dispenser of milk and pancakes, Aunt Jemima; mercilessly pursued and bewildered sexual object and ruthlessly helpless sexual aggressor, hippie, drug dealer and thug; dog soldier and violently chaste, repressed and repentant soldier in the army of the Lord. (314)[4]

There is an entire history of Black America in this passage, an entire history whose parts coalesce into the sole figure of the murderer. Each part works to complete the whole, a whole born out of false promises, of discordant consciousnesses, of social hypocrisies, of living in a world, past and present, that keeps one unequal in perpetuity. One might be of the house or of the field, but either way, one remains a slave; one might be free legally but is subject to the whims of oversexed or violent whites who either lust over you or hate you, likely both simultaneously. And if you are not one of them, a relative likely is, and thus you walk in their shoes of being both sinner and savior, feeder and fed. This is a world that works hard to produce a person who feels like a nonperson—and the only way to survive in it is to turn on one's self or turn on others.

Baldwin insists that the murderer must be mad even as he outlines the circumstance that might drive anyone mad—the hopeless intersection of race and class in America. Torn between what he is promised and what he has received, torn between accommodation and liberation, and torn between those who exoticize him and render him mundane, the murderer is "dark enough to go unnoticed" at the cost of both his own and other's demise. Yet as Baldwin writes of him, the murderer is also a member of our family, possibly a brother in the genetic sense or in the social sense (or as Baldwin interweaves, possibly both). The hypocrisies of the past and the stigmas of the present collide in this figure, a Black everyman who is both a preacher and a pusher.

Baldwin's inventory synecdochically evokes not only the murderer but the depth and breadth of the problem the Atlanta murders expose. For him, the problem of race is a source of shame, a shame from which a call to action can be raised. As Sara Ahmed writes, "shame 'makes' the nation in the witnessing of past injustice, a witnessing that involves feeling shame, as it exposes the failure of the nation to live up to its ideals. But this exposure is temporary and becomes the ground for national recovery" (*Cultural Politics* 109). Thus when Baldwin concludes that the murderer is, "in short, what our history has made us, and we must take our children out of his hands," he is also quick to state that "we had never acquiesced in the slaughter of our children before" ("Evidence" 312). Baldwin converts the figure of the child as a victim into a figure of political resistance, a position from which parents and by proxy the nation cannot acquiesce. By pointing to the murders as a source of shame, Baldwin evokes a new "we" who can reclaim the child, a new "we" that seizes the child as synecdoche away from Reagan and Falwell, the neoconservatives and practitioners of moral panic. In effect, the shame Baldwin asks readers to feel about the murders is meant to bring to light the intersection of race and class in Atlanta and in America, to show that this site of shame can be the source of a new national beginning. Playing on the figure of the child, Baldwin insists that to care for children now is also to do something for future generations, noting that "if the father is irrecoverable, then the son is lost" (316). His call to action is a call to recognize ourselves as a nation lest our progeny and our legacy be further victimized.

The call to action in "Evidence" is universalizing. Baldwin writes that "for every black corpse, there is a white one, or an equivalent actual and moral disaster" ("Evidence" 142). The somewhat awkward phrasing of this statement indicates how Baldwin attempts to synecdochically stretch the murders in Atlanta so they become the expression of a national problem, to universalize not only a nation of children but a nation of citizens to whom all such a tragedy could happen. If it could happen to "them," it could happen to all of "us": in this way, Baldwin's call to action fits into the tradition of his writing that frames African American issues as American issues. But it is ultimately the limitation of this synecdochical strategy that is seen in "Evidence" as well. As Cheryl A. Wall writes, Baldwin engaged in a "strategic American exceptionalism" throughout most of his career (36). He was careful to demarcate the government from the nation, as in a 1963 speech when he said that "a government and a nation are not synonymous. We can change the government, and we will" (*Cross* 51). By pointing to a national ideal that was more democratic than its actual government, Baldwin could insist that the premise of the nation was something greater than what its current government practiced and thus place civil rights at the core of the national project even when the government refused to acknowledge its necessity. It was not that the government was faulty: its representatives need only be replaced by better exemplars of national values. Thus even if present circumstances were unjust, its ideals could still eventually ring true. An essay from 1963 performs a similar yoking of parts: that "if Mr. Kennedy is the President of this country, and it is his country, and if Senator Eastland can be responsible in this country, and it is his country—well, it's my country too. And that means that it's your country, too" (11). This use of synecdoche, this way of saying that all are part of the nation, allowed Baldwin to "undermine white supremacy without denying the humanity of either white or black people" (Balfour 16). The *Playboy* essay is careful to perform a similar synecdochical pivot as it moves from Baldwin as parent by proxy, to the parents of the victims, to all parents in the nation. In doing so, he insists that what is happening in Atlanta is not just the murder of people, but the murder of a national future.

The *Playboy* essay ends with a direct call to action: "I think we better take it from here" ("Evidence" 316). This call to action is the incitement for a "we" to cohere in a collective effort toward ending the murders and bringing the murderer to justice. And to refer to this as an ambiguous "it" synecdochically makes the event encompass not only the murders but the race and class dynamics he condemns throughout the essay. It is a call to action that harkens back to the climactic conclusion of "Down at the Cross," the concluding essay of *The Fire Next Time*, in which Baldwin's "we" is explicitly defined as the "relatively conscious whites and relatively conscious blacks" who "must, like lovers, insist on, or create, the consciousness of others" (*Collected Essays* 346). If this could be done, this "handful" of conscious, loving Americans could "end the racial nightmare, and achieve our country, and change the world" (346–47). And for Baldwin to suggest in "Evidence" that "we better take it from here" is not only a rejection of inept local and federal police, of a city and state anchored to the worst of its pasts. It is a call for all Americans who love their children to act like the "relatively conscious" loving Americans he wrote of years before, not just to protect their children but to fulfill the promise of equality promulgated years before in the name of a national future.

By ending "Evidence" with a call to action, the essay attempts to take the moment Camille Bell deemed a national suicide and turn it into a source of national life. It is an essay that carefully plays with the tempo of time, turning the "not-yet" of racial discrimination into a "could-be" moment of political hope (Corrigan xviii, 10). As Ben Anderson notes, hope is often a response to a "set of diminishments within the present" ("Becoming" 742). Hope arises out of diminishment with the incredible suggestion that in the future what has been diminished will be restored, not only restored to its previous state, but further strengthened such that those diminishments will never recur again. In effect, "we better take it from here" elicits a future, not only in terms of collective agency in the present but also the actualization of the future that the child as a figure incites. Baldwin, much as he does in his writing and speeches throughout the 1960s, sees Atlanta of 1979–81 as an opportunity to make concrete the nation as exceptional. By taking charge, "taking it from here," Baldwin attempts to salvage a narrative from the unnarratable chaos of the Atlanta murders. In doing so, he attempts to emplot a past, a present, and a future, not only through the figure of the child but of the imagined nation that will emerge once those children are out of harm. Staying close to a premise that "the Atlanta tragedy was a story of the world of sad children being forced to grow up much too fast. . . . mostly young boys being pushed—and sometimes pulled—into dubious manhood," he affirms a place for the city's children (Headley 27). And in consistently connecting the figure of the child to the figure of the nation, Baldwin aspires to turn chaos into opportunity, not only for the children of Atlanta but the children of all races and classes in the nation.

In "Evidence," Baldwin emplots the hope that once the murders cease and the murderer is imprisoned, social liberation will inevitably follow. But this is more the effect of believing that the world will follow one's rhetoric than an assessment of what could realistically occur. It is also a conclusion desperately desired by the prospective publisher of Baldwin's essay. As his commissioning editor at *Playboy* notes, the magazine first and foremost wanted an essay that identified "who was killing the children" (Lowe 54). The magazine also made it a priority to publish on the murders only if they could get the perspective of someone who would sell: the commissioning editor had been told by management that "unless you can get somebody whose name we can put on the cover," *Playboy* was not interested in the topic appearing in their magazine. Thus not only did the magazine want something simple in its conclusions; they wanted it only for the sake that Baldwin, as a celebrity, was writing it. All said, "Evidence" was written for a publication that wanted to publish easy answers; it was written for an audience that cared so little about the murders that they would only be motivated to read about them if it fit the frame of what they expected a "James Baldwin" essay to be.

Yet Baldwin was interested in something fundamentally different than what *Playboy* expected. After completing the essay, Baldwin told the commissioning editor that there was something lingering in Atlanta that he was "not sure I have the strength to answer," something not about who was killing the children, but "how the children happened to be out there, waiting to be murdered" (qtd. in Lowe 54). The book-length version of the essay shows that to fully answer the "how" question, Baldwin had to expand his synecdochical scope and in doing so would come to conclusions that were the opposite of what the public had come to expect from "James Baldwin." This unexpected voice would be the antithesis of the strategically exceptionalist narrative Baldwin crafted throughout his career, and it would incite an equally strong nationalism, not one that promised progress but one that proved thoroughly dismissive of Americans as arbiters of positive social change. It would be a reading of America entirely deprived of hope in the nation itself.

Futility: Neither Pessimism nor Dread

The word "futility" comes from the Latin word *fundĕre*, "to pour out" (*OED*). Futile reading is a kind of pouring, the emptying out of the contained from the container, the emptying out of one's connection to an object. If futurity fills the object with an anticipatory space of hope, a space where the "not-yet" is turned into the "could-be," then futility empties the object not only of anticipation but of relevance altogether. Futility is the space where the "not-yet" becomes "never." To see something as futile is to sever ourselves from it with a definitive conclusion: this does not represent "us." In its being poured out, much like how in the affect of disgust "the expulsion itself becomes the 'truth' of the reading of the object" (Ahmed, *Cultural Politics* 87), the futile reader aims to expose the object's untrustworthy construction, to entirely expel its validity.

As Albert O. Hirschman writes, futility is an incitement to read that concludes that "any alleged change is, was, or will be largely surface, façade, cosmetic, hence illusory, as the 'deep' structures of society remain wholly untouched" (*Rhetoric* 43). Thus futility is a way of reading that does not examine the potential for change in its object but instead examines how the object can never be anything more than what it is in the present. It is a reading that does not look for gradations or ambiguities. Instead, futility reads to expose the façade, to purge the illusion that the object will ever change. Futile reading coldly closes down any sign of hope: nothing at the periphery can change the core, no part can ever alter the corrupt whole. Futile readers see the object as "impotent to modify" (72). Their reading serves to leave "the promoters of change humiliated, demoralized, in doubt about the meaning and true motive of their endeavors" (45). If, as Eugene Thacker writes, "the ultimatum is the core of pessimist thinking" (32), it can be similarly argued that the ultimatum to exit is the core of futile reading. In its pouring out, futility goes beyond its object to lambast the audience of believers in the object's potential to change. In doing so, futile readers become as uninterested in "us" as they are in the object they have cast aside. In futile reading, there is no "call to action" because futile readers are certain that any such call will be in vain.

Futility is a strong affect. While it may be tempting to see it as synonymous with adjacent affects such as pessimism and dread, futility is far more reactionary and monopolizing. If pessimism is defined as "the conviction that the culture of a nation, a civilization or humanity itself is in an irreversible process of decline" (Bennett 1), pessimism nonetheless allows some chance, though a minor one, that decline can be remedied. Pessimism, as an incitement to read, Joshua Foa Dienstag notes, comes to plural conclusions: pessimists either resign themselves or find value in the world despite their resignation (see 40). Futile reading, by contrast, is an incitement that comes to only one conclusion: that the end point has been reached. Pessimism may be suggestive, but futility is a conviction.[5]

Futility goes where pessimism will not tread. It defects from the melancholy that affects a pessimistic relationship with the object. If pessimism, especially the variant described by Frank B. Wilderson III as "afropessimism," involves the "ontological foundation" of Black life resting upon "the condition of being owned and traded" (14–15), futile readers reject that foundation. Like the afropessimist, futile readers hold "out no hope for dialectical synthesis" between themselves and the nation that reads them not as a person but as a sign of "accumulation and fungibility" (29, 59). But futile readers go further than the pessimist to divest themselves from the dyad of self and nation altogether. Their emptying out of the meaning of the object is not meant to indicate its hidden or melancholic importance to them: it empties out and nothing more.

What comes from futile reading is a depiction of the nation as an imagined community that cannot—and will not—transcend its problems. Futility, even more than dread, is marked by "an absence of faith in the political" (James 692). Indeed, whereas dread may relinquish faith in the political, futility is the relinquishing of faith altogether. As a result, futile reading's conviction is based on its lack of conviction in its object. It performs a reading that calls it as futile readers see it: perhaps angry, perhaps disgusted, but above all, resolute in the firmness of their conclusion. If, as Sean Austin Grattan writes, "shock and surprise are central to reparative reading practices, and this openness to shock can be profoundly uncomfortable" (125), then by contrast futile readers are never shocked or surprised because their reading does not seek reparation. If futurity suggests that at some later point the "wretched of the earth . . . will no longer be wretched" (Ahmed, *Promise* 272), futile readers suggest that this "could-be" will never occur, and the only way to be free is to exit the relationship altogether. They have realized that "the wish that the violences of racial capitalism, neoliberal empire, and settler colonialism might be remedied is in fact part of their ordinary enduring operation" (Stuelke 218). Thus futile readers are ultimately not interested in persuading, for they know that any remedy offered is part of a broader poison. Futile readers do not show: they tell. They read not to show their reasoning for critics to unpack, nor to suggest a new or radical politics that will remedy the present one. They read to say how bad things were, how bad things are, and how bad things will forever be.

The Futile Nation

If Baldwin practiced an exceptionalist nationalism in the 1960s and incorporated elements of Black nationalism into this thinking in the 1970s, *Evidence* reflects Baldwin's turn to futile nationalism. If Baldwin walked with Martin Luther King Jr. and admired Eldridge Cleaver, the Baldwin of *Evidence* is one who realizes that, regardless of whether Americans saw the figures of the civil rights movement as heroes or villains, the nation would prefer to see these figures as past tense: Baldwin writes that King became acceptable to many white Americans only after "the publicly and privately willed event that transformed him into a *corpse*" (88, emphasis in original). The American that Baldwin depicts in *Evidence* is uninterested in genuine reform: instead, it is interested in hiding behind trite celebrations of now-deceased leaders as a way of disconnecting them from the radicality of their thoughts and actions. In this way, the nation claims a façade of equality even as it sustains and further entrenches inequality.

Futile readers take the perspective as "the eyes to see" that nothing has changed and nothing will change to perform a reading that demonstrates "reinforcement, adornment, and closure" (Hirschman, *Rhetoric* 57–58). The result is that futile reading, like the reading produced by other strong nationalisms, is both broad and thin, seeking in this case to expose the futility of the whole and to reinforce its conclusions through a style of adornment that is synecdochically deictic. If only I can put this in front of your eyes, you too will see the pointlessness, futile readers say through their narrative construction. And because no one is ever merely half-futile, futile readers examine the object deemed futile with a "dogged circumlocution" to "excavate its totalizing scale" (Eburne 264). To perform a futile reading is to read with a scope that is "global and absolute" (274). It is a reading that sees the nation as what it was, as what it is, and as that which can be nothing more. It has a past and a present but no future. As such, the nation is a threat that must be exited lest it render the reader futile, too.

Evidence is the culmination of a turn that emerged in Baldwin's writing in the late 1960s. Jessica Hurley notes Baldwin's changing rhetoric as the 1970s unfolded: "He continues to foretell disaster for America," she writes, "but he no longer seems able to bear the conviction that things will improve" (96). This turn occurred at the same time as new strong nationalisms, in particular Black nationalism, offered a more intense incitement,

based not on tolerance and moderation but instead on "masculine symbols of the panther and the gun" (Field 462). In a 1969 essay, Baldwin
writes that "this country's white population impresses me . . . as being beyond any conceivable hope of moral rehabilitation" (*Cross* 97). There is a
ring of condemnation in this diagnosis, which does not foresee incremen-
tal change or progress but dismisses all modes of change or progress as
unrealizable. By the beginning of the 1980s, Baldwin was at futility's precipice. In a 1980 essay entitled "Notes on the House of Bondage," he writes
with increased certainty that "American institutions are all bankrupt in
that they are unable to deal with the present" (*Collected Essays* 801). Baldwin became so certain of his diagnosis that specifics need not be mentioned: "American institutions" need not be named because they are "all
bankrupt," much like its people, who "see nothing but dark and menacing
strangers" at home and in the world (801). The America he envisions is
not only ignorant but hostile, not only insular but intolerant. His writing
demonstrates the conclusion, as George Shulman aptly summarizes, that
"whites invent fictions of race and sustain melodramas of black pathology
to justify domination and to protect an innocence expressed in repeated
claims to moral virtue and an exceptional—liberal—nationalism" (144).
Baldwin sought to depict an "American pattern for all the years I have
been on this earth, and, of course, for generations before that" (*Collected
Essays* 803). The textual work of Baldwin's final years was to persuade
readers that this has always been so—and would always be so.

Yet Baldwin, at this point on the precipice, still surmises that if African
Americans could stick together, there is a sliver of hope. Even if the nation is a "house of bondage" that destroys white America's "moral sense
except in relation to whites," he implores African Americans to bond together in their awareness of whiteness's fictions (*Collected Essays* 805).
He still tries, at the beginning of the 1980s, to find a way in which young
and old can work together, even if the elder is "schooled in adversity and
skilled in compromise" and the youth is more prone to public protest
and its risks of imprisonment. "I may have to visit [the youth] in prison,
or suffer with him there—no matter," Baldwin writes (807). He holds out
that old and young can "sustain each other a very long time and come
a long, long way together" (807). This is the way African Americans
can escape the "house of bondage" and achieve a new nation that rec-
onciles Baldwin's generation of activists with the Black Panther generation. It is through intergenerational communion that Baldwin aspires

to synecdochically yoke together disparate movements, some nationalist, others not, as followers of the same cause, insisting in the essay's
conclusion that the house of bondage would be no more. If anything,
such communion will be proof, he concludes, that "we have all survived,
children, the very last white country the world will ever see" (807). Such
rhetoric relies on what Jennifer C. James describes as a twofold process
that first entails a "rhetoric of revelation" and is followed by a "strain
of hopefulness" that remedies what has been revealed (see 690). That
Baldwin concludes "Notes from the House of Bondage" with the figure
of the child—calling all his readers his children—is a telling sign that
Baldwin still envisioned some form of a national future. As the "children"
who survive "the very last white country the world will ever see," we are
positioned as both witnessing the death of something and a birth of a new
mode of life.

But by 1985, Baldwin's twofold rhetoric had vanished and was replaced
by one narrative path without recourse. Instead, what Baldwin writes of in
The Evidence of Things Not Seen is how the murders and subsequent trial
demonstrate the futility of the American national project. They serve for
Baldwin as the site in which "our deepest fears about this country—what
we in fact *know* about this country—are not ruptured or remade in these
moments and are instead *confirmed*" (James 691, emphasis in original).
Baldwin's prose reflects the rollback of 1960s promises, the denial of
1970s tribulations, and the stark embrace of whiteness as the "rigidity,
machismo, and conservatism" that defined the nation of the 1980s (Vogel
61).[6] In the speeches of Ronald Reagan, the "ethnic poor" were marauded
as "stigmatized moochers of the welfare system, while black men became
the face of crack addiction and inner-city crime" (15). Under such a regime, "the struggle was now less about fighting discrimination than it
was about convincing people that discrimination against minorities still
existed" (6). Reagan expanded national inequality, retranslating race and
class issues into "inequality in the genes" or "inequality in defective culture," both beyond national solution (Robinson 119). In this he was start-
ingly successful, even among African Americans: Baldwin writes with
scorn that his "old running buddies, some of who I trusted, with perfect
confidence, with my life" had voted for the Republican (*Evidence* 79).
Those who had voted for Reagan, "from the schools to the labor unions,
to say nothing of the churches, or yesterday's Liberals, the Negro's friends"
showed in their endorsement of neoconservatism that "our countrymen

have never loved us, nor ever, indeed, considered us to be their countrymen." Going further, Baldwin insists to "have this on my record" his belief that "the Reagan vote was an anti-Black/Black vote absolutely." It was not just that the nation had turned to the right; it was that those who had been victims of the right willingly joined its ranks, which to Baldwin seemed like a betrayal of one's personhood.

Why did Baldwin want his belief publicly known? The phrasing "anti-Black/Black vote" is telling. Baldwin was highly skeptical of Wayne Williams's guilt: "the accused may be guilty, for all I know, but I fail to see his guilt as proven," he asserts (*Evidence* 56). But it is not the trial that leads to his loss of faith altogether. His futility comes from what he could not ignore: that the suspect and probable culprit of the serial murder of Black children was himself a Black man. Williams was to Baldwin the epitome of the "anti-Black/Black." Williams's guilt—proven or otherwise—becomes for Baldwin the foreclosing of any hope that African Americans could unite together for a better nation. Williams was the physical manifestation of antiblackness, a self-hate so virulent that it drove him to murder Black children. Not only did he destroy their futures, but he broke the futurist logic that asserts children can achieve the nation we cannot. He killed not only children, but the future of Black life and thus, to Baldwin, the future for any national life.

Baldwin attempts to negotiate this by disavowing Williams as an authentic African American. "We didn't want to believe that this was happening, that one of *us* could do this," one of his informants tells him, to which another responds, "They got us. They win—when a Black person can do this!" (Baldwin, *Evidence* 9, emphasis in original). The Atlanta murders proves to Baldwin that the trauma induced by whiteness can turn African Americans against each other to destroy the future generation in which Baldwin had placed so much hope. In effect, the crime was a betrayal. It had brought the white world of serial murder into African American life, and it had done so in such a way that made whites look like victors once Williams was apprehended and tried, thus confirming the very pathologizing of blackness that Baldwin saw as key to the perpetuation of whiteness's fictions. Some of Baldwin's informants attempted to resist this by telling him that "mentally, Wayne is White" (*Evidence* 120). And Baldwin's own depiction of Williams—"authoritative and puny, so demanding and remote"—makes him sound more like a stereotypically uptight white man than a member of the African American community

(19). Despite Willliams's attempts to appear media savvy (claiming to be a talent scout) or street smart (claiming to be a crime photographer), his most prominent affect was, as Baldwin put it, that of a "wise-ass" (112). Baldwin ultimately describes Williams as a "chubby, weak, arrogant boy . . . a profoundly lazy boy" (75). He is neither a sex-crazed killer perpetuated by panicked moralists nor the "Black Homosexual" stereotype perpetuated by national journalists and local gossips, but your "bachelor uncle, or your slightly kinky nephew," a member of the family who is eccentric but ultimately impotent (19). "He is probably not sexual at all," Baldwin concludes, describing him as "sheltered, somehow, from the storm of puberty" (19, 112). What was most tragic about him, Baldwin writes, was that Williams "never learned to love himself" (19).

Williams's conviction confirmed Baldwin's futility. For Baldwin, the trial had been far too hasty, was more of a confirmation of a decade's moral panic, and was ultimate proof that Reagan-era America's façade of law and order would come at the cost of actual justice. "The judgment did not release, but exacerbated an intolerable tension," he writes (Baldwin, *Evidence* 13). It confirms to him that to be Black in America is a "kind of doom" (6). *Evidence* works to support this conclusion through its synecdochical reading of the trial as one small part of a broader portrait of national futility. This reading operationalizes the "sense of dread that comes with that burden of *knowing*" that racial justice has been repeatedly set aside throughout American history (James 691, emphasis in original). The murders and trial are to Baldwin the literal manifestation of "black foreboding: the feeling of inevitability coupled with the fact that the calamitous racial 'event' could occur anywhere at any time" (James 694). In *Evidence*, Baldwin synecdochalizes this burden of knowing, shows the source of his foreboding. And because futility is synecdochical, his reading is not just local or national, but transhistorical and international in scope. The whole that Baldwin constructs is, in the negative sense of the word, awesome, not only in its size, but also in its reach.

The choice of an African American judge to preside over the Williams trial only proves the point to Baldwin: "it was never said, in so many words, but everyone appeared to suspect that this particular computer had had its own reasons for selecting this particular judge" (*Evidence* 1). To him, even the computer, which can only think within the parameters of its programming, is complicit in creating a theater-like atmosphere to the trial, proof that "the circus and the audience are absolutely indispensable to the hygiene of the State" (2). To him, the presence of an African American judge on the Williams trial, or the presence of an African American mayor in Atlanta, does not offer any relief: they are a "concession masking the face of power, which remains White" (26). No judge, no mayor: nothing individual, communal, or local can change that "Atlanta belongs to the state of Georgia" and "Georgia belongs to the United States" (4). Indeed, it is the federal structure of the nation and the white hegemony it was founded upon and protects to this day that spurs his futile reading. "Cities, in any event, are controlled by the states, and these United States are controlled by the real aspirations of Washington," he writes (27). "All governments, without exception, make only those concessions deemed absolutely necessary for the maintenance of the status quo; and if one really wishes to know how highly this Republic esteems Black freedom, one has only to watch the American performance in the world" (27). Atlanta may be seen by many as a "Black Mecca," but it "belongs to," as if it were owned by, the state. And thus the federal government dictates to the state government, and the "real aspirations of Washington" are the aspirations of a corrupt few who profit from the nation as it is. It will not accede to popular opinion—nor will it facilitate freedom—but it will protect its hegemony and go no further. Its values, which are not "our" values, are evident in how it does not "esteem Black freedom" but also in how it treats other nations, what Baldwin loosely writes as "American performance in the world." Baldwin insists that the "links"— the fiber evidence in particular—that established Williams as a suspect are the same sort of "links" that connect Atlanta to Georgia to the United States. In doing so, he suggests that the federal structure of the nation works to find Williams—or anyone, for that matter—guilty by design. Synecdochically, the nation is not a source of liberty but of potential and eventual imprisonment. Baldwin's futile reading chains deixes together, pointing out how each element is connected in a way that ultimately perpetuates the insidious magnitude of white power in the nation.

Such reading demonstrates the broad expanse of negativity that futility fosters. "The spirit of the South is the spirit of America," Baldwin notes, a nation where "whoever was murdering the children, then, could literally have been anyone" (*Evidence* 7–8). This is a nation built not upon mutual trust but mutual distrust, a nation where everyone is a suspect, "from the teacher to the preacher to the cop to the bus driver to your neighbor to you" (7–8). It is a nation that constantly encroaches, from its community leaders to the carriers of justice to any fellow citizens, with the potential for violence. And its spread is not just inward but outward as well, moving from the regional "spirit of the South" to the "spirit of America" and ultimately to the world. This is how Baldwin concludes, "The auction block is the platform on which I entered the Civilized World. Nothing that has happened since, from South Africa to El Salvador, indicates that the Western world has any real quarrel with slavery" (45–46). Baldwin links the Reagan administration's support of apartheid regimes abroad to an endorsement of apartheid at home, and its support of neocolonial dictatorship abroad to its reliance on the exploitation and trafficking of all people, including its fellow citizens and Baldwin himself. Ultimately, Baldwin's futility transcends time and space altogether, as he concludes that "the American Dream can be taken as the final manifestation of the European/Western/Christian dominance" (124). As part reveals part, the whole of futile reading grows: the slashes in *Evidence* work as quick glue to attach the Atlanta murders to a transhistorical problem and to textually reproduce a permanent, wide-reaching battle between us/them that is for the futile reader a foregone conclusion. There is not much need to identify the specifics of the problem when one concludes, "The Western world is located somewhere between the Statue of Liberty and the pillar of salt" (82).

Baldwin used the "bricks without straw" adage in the *Playboy* essay to describe the dire situation of class-based antagonism among African Americans. This adage takes on an even more bleak cast in *Evidence*—the miracle that would allow bricks to be made without straw has not happened, and Baldwin expresses doubt that it ever will. "The hour is too late, the facts too blatant, and there *is* no straw," he writes (*Evidence* 92, emphasis in original). He concludes that "the present social and political apparatus" of the United States "cannot serve human need," and it is beyond a miracle that the nation will ever move forward (124). "He who collaborates" with America, Baldwin writes at the book's conclusion, "is doomed, bound forever in that unimaginable and yet very common condition which we weakly suggest as Hell. In that condition, and every American walking should know it, one can never again summon the breath to cry *let my people go!*" (125, emphasis in original). It is tempting to take the essay's last four words as a plea for a sort of future. But that would be too aspirational a reading. What Baldwin concludes is much more dire—that if being an African American is a form of doom, life is doom for all Americans. This conclusion is a description of the nation as a hell in which "we" are all accomplices in its perpetuation.

Evidence concludes far—very far—from the murdered youth of At-lanta from 1979 to 1981. And it concludes far from Wayne Williams and his guilt or innocence. And perhaps most importantly, it concludes far from the "we better take it from here" call to action that concludes Bald-win's *Playboy* essay. What Baldwin depicts in *Evidence* is a nation that is no source of individual or community agency, no source of freedom or liberty. It is a place where destiny has reached its end, and nothing is left. His conclusion tells much of where futility goes, but also, how far it goes in its incitement to read the nation. Its scope of reading may be global, encompassing everything it encounters, but in a fundamental way, its synecdochical expanse only serves to reinforce its damning convic-tion that the object is beyond redemption. Having poured the meaning out of its object, futile readers exhaust their explanatory power. Baldwin's conclusion shows, as he understands it, how "the expulsion itself becomes the 'truth' of the reading of the object" (Ahmed, *Cultural Politics* 87). The only way for his people to be let go is if they let go, as he has, of the nation.

Conclusion: Exit, Voice, and the Nation

As Albert O. Hirschman writes, when the disparity between ourselves and others—he is particularly thinking of the relationship customers have with products and the relationship voters have with candidates—is real-ized, we face three choices. We can remain loyal despite the disparity; we can voice our discontent in the hope that doing so will hasten reform; or we can exit the relationship altogether. Of these three options, Hirschman was most fascinated by the role of voice. The opportunity for voice, he notes, enforces loyalty: the more we talk about something, even in com-plaint, the further we create our connection to it. Voice takes time and it takes energy, but with voice comes an unpredictable and often original creativity, as clients attempt to make their voices heard. As such, voice "is essentially an art constantly evolving in new directions" (Hirschman, *Exit* 43). It is voice that insists that the nation "be made into the ideal place which one wants it so passionately to be" (114).

James Baldwin, to many, fulfilled this conception of voice. To return to the Jonathan Yardley review with which I began this chapter, it is worth noting how his dismissal of *Evidence* is based upon his presumption of what Baldwin's voice was supposed to be—a "startling voice from a land called black America that white America scarcely knew" (242). To him, Baldwin's was "a voice that sought to reason with us even as he exposed our hypocrisies and cruelties. He was angry, with ample reason, but he appealed to the decent and humane in us; he tried to make us understand that we were all in this business together" (242). This was what, to Yardley and many others, the voice of James Baldwin was supposed to be. For Walter Lowe Jr., this was the voice of Baldwin that made the author "a legend, a hero, someone we'd like to measure up to one day" (54). To deviate from that voice was a terrific risk, as Yardley's review shows. And when Baldwin did, critics did not respond in kind. Even Henry Louis Gates Jr., in his retrospective of Baldwin's career, insists that *Evidence* was the voice of an author who "contradict[ed] his own greatest achievements."

But what if the author is no longer interested in this voice? What if he has found this voice to be futile? What if he is no longer interested in seeking to reason with white critics or white people, or whiteness altogether? What if he no longer cares if he has produced "ample reasons" that justify his anger to critics, or expended energy appealing to the "decent and humane" when those appeals go perpetually unenacted? What if he does not want to be together with "us"? And, ultimately, what if he no longer believes that white America, or America entirely, is worthy of his patience, his intellect, his identity, or his voice?

Evidence is Baldwin's affective exit from America. It is a rejection of loyalty to the nation that does not nurture but only threatens him. As Hirschman writes, the "paradigm of loyalty—'our country, right or wrong'—surely makes no sense whatever if it were expected that 'our country' were to continue forever to do nothing but wrong" (*Exit* 78). *Evidence* is Baldwin's writing out the proof that America did exactly this. As Baldwin told Quincy Troupe shortly before his death, he had tried to "tell the truth and it takes a long time to realize that you can't—that there's no point in going to the mat, so to speak . . . there's no point in saying this again" (Troupe 282). It was not that Baldwin's futile thinking was the problem: it was that the nation, by design, could never accept his diagnosis. And just as futility chides those naive enough to believe that change is possible, Baldwin chided himself for even having tried. He described himself to Troupe as a "broken motor" that could no longer gather the power to explain one more time the nation he saw: what he had to say had "been said, and it's been said, and it's been said," ultimately to no avail (282).

Of America, Baldwin told Studs Terkel in a 1985 interview, "there's nothing anyone can do about it . . . we have reached a culmination point, we have reached a point of no return" (Terkel).[7] Having textually enacted that point of no return in *Evidence,* Baldwin exited. As he saw it, white America would not budge from the myths that entrapped not only African Americans but whites themselves. "They know [the myth] is not true. They know it," he implores in the Terkel interview. What *Evidence* shows is Baldwin's rejection to being, as Wilderson puts it, the "property of enjoyment" by his critics (89). In *Evidence,* Baldwin refuses to "speak from the point of view of the victim" for "the victim can have no point of view for precisely as long as he thinks of himself as a victim" (78). He refuses to deal melancholically or pessimistically with the nation that perpetually wants to "confirm the authority of the jailer" through "the sound of the victim's moaning." He refuses, in effect, to supply the voice that "we" expect to hear from him, the nation "we" expect him to produce. What futile readers do, ultimately, is debase our loyalty by pointing to the selective knowing or willed ignorance that is its foundation. They are no longer interested in supplying this opiate to us.

When exit is favored over voice, strong affect follows. And when exit is favored over nation, strong nationalism manifests in the "jolt provoked by clamorous exit" (Hirschman, *Exit* 117). If the strongest weapon those who voice discontent have is "the threat to resign under protest," then the futile reader has done exactly this (116). Baldwin was aware of the effect of such emptying. When Terkel asked him, "What is a nation?," Baldwin responded, "I don't know what it is anymore." Futility says what we are afraid to say: that the nation's foundation is poor, its purpose hypocritical, its imagined community hostile to its own citizens and to anyone who insists that the nation live by its ideals. Baldwin, in the last years of his career, did not know what a nation is because he knew the truth of what the American nation is. His futile reading of the nation asks questions that its elect are afraid to answer: it makes sense where nonsense is preferred. Thus in place of the critical tirades that surround the book, critics might think of Baldwin's futile reading in the plural: not only in how his exploration in *Evidence* leads him to find futile that which he once saw as exceptional, but how in his doing so, he exits from the charade of American exceptionalism and comes upon a final, resolute voice.

4

Resentment

J. D. VANCE'S *HILLBILLY ELEGY*

THE ISSUE of who is the "truly representative" American is at the forefront of J. D. Vance's *Hillbilly Elegy*. The book's foundational premise is that Vance's life is representative, not just of one swath of the nation—the "hillbillies" who migrated to the industrial North in the 1950s—but of their succeeding generations, their abandonment of progressive politics, the struggles of Rust Belt and blue-collar Americans more generally, and ultimately of an entire nation in decline. Vance's premise allows him to take on multiple voices, sliding from exemplary hillbilly to concerned middle-class citizen, from atypical to typical American.[1] His narrative is dependent upon his strategic pivoting from one synecdoche to the other, exhorting the collapse of urban communities on the one hand while indicting suburban consumerism on the other hand, all the while claiming to represent an ultimately undefined—yet truly "American"—morality that is beyond exhortation or indictment. The effect of such synecdochical sliding is that it quickly—and deliberately—becomes impossible to discern the whole that Vance, as a part, exactly represents.

And while this ambiguity gives Vance tremendous explanatory power across the political spectrum, it also reveals the underlying affects that motivate it. Take, for instance, the book's positive review in *National Review*: summarizing the section of the book in which Vance's mother seeks the help of a therapist, its author cannot help but add, "Chances are she wasn't footing the bill" (Andrews). The reviewer picks up on how the book engages readers to go further than the text itself to resent the mother as a representative of wasteful welfare spending. (The right resents the left.) This engagement is bipartisan: as Frank Guan writes, liberals have found in Vance "a trustworthy local interpreter from Trump Country—one willing to confirm that poor white Appalachians were degenerate, bigoted, and to blame for putting a degenerate bigot in the White House" (10). Guan picks up on how the book engages readers to go further than the text itself, which concludes before the 2016 election and never mentions Donald Trump, to resent hillbillies as representatives of "Trump Country." (The left resents the right.) These readings demonstrate that *Elegy*'s appeal across the political spectrum comes from the way in which Vance's memoir validates the resenting of others.

If *Elegy* asks us to feel, it asks us to feel resentment. Pick any character in the memoir: they have a resentment. Pick any part of America that Vance describes: it brims with resentment. It is impossible to read *Elegy* without activating resentment as integral to its understanding. Curiously, as much as the author supposedly aspires to speak for an entire nation, the book's rhetoric strives to expel some of its constituents by encouraging them to resent others. How does J. D. Vance claim to speak for America while reducing large swaths of its population to non-Americans? He does so by mobilizing the representational powers of synecdoche to limit who can be seen as truly representative of the nation. It is through the synecdochical winnowing of the nation—by denying the possibility of comradeship with those he characterizes as unjustly entitled—that Vance aspires to limit the conception of America to a vertical society in which poverty is the manifestation not of economics or politics but of individual moral flaws and bad choices. The purpose of Vance's synecdochalization is not to construct a diverse country but to "*drag the others down*" so they no longer represent it (Solomon, *Passions* 295, emphasis in original).[2] This "dragging down" through synecdoche does rhetorically what the memoir captures affectively: the complex politics of resentment, a politics based on denying others the power to represent the whole. The strength of *Elegy* is its use of a feigned weakness to substitute for solutions to national problems.

Positioning himself as the glue between hillbilly and elite, Vance may well think his memoir creates "sympathy among equals that doesn't demean or condescend" (Rothman). But his peculiar use of synecdoche reflects that he is not interested in depicting the entire nation but rather in limiting who counts as an American. Ultimately this reveals that Vance is only able to derive explanatory power through others whom he can judge as superior or inferior to him. Herein is the darker premise of the memoir, for if it is possible for Vance, the hillbilly turned elite, to resent both hillbillies and elites, then the rhetoric of his memoir does not bring people together. Instead, the memoir offers a rhetoric that sustains "a feedback loop of mutual contempt" between them (Rothman). What the memoir posits is a world of strong affect anchored in a national morality that "always first needs a hostile external world" and whose "action is fundamentally reaction" (Nietzsche 473). The nation is no longer a horizontal space where common ground is imagined and articulated, but a site of endless, defensive derision.

This feedback loop is sustained by the memoir's predominant affect. As Robert C. Solomon writes, the work of resentment is to "judge another person as superior but at the same time condemn him" (*Passions* 225). To do so, resentment constructs a relationship between parts and wholes that enables such conclusions to be drawn. Resentment's discourse is synecdochical, for it is both "keen on every point" and "virtually global," simultaneously obsessed with the part and the whole (291). Such a discourse is a prime example of what Michel de Certeau sees as the danger of synecdoche, that "synecdoche makes more dense: it amplifies the detail and miniaturizes the whole" (101). In this curious way, resentment amplifies and miniaturizes simultaneously: out of the parts it uses to construct—and amplify—a larger story, it simultaneously dismisses—and miniaturizes—the morality of what it has amplified.

In this chapter, I examine *Elegy*'s resentment as a strong nationalism. The memoir's use of synecdoche reinforces strong affect by describing a nation of us/them: of who is entitled to it (the resentful) and who is not (the resented). In this way, the memoir's use of synecdoche reinforces the strongly affected, corrective, and exclusionary reading of the nation that has been a mainstay of conservative thought since the 1960s: the feeling that others are getting what "we" deserve, an injustice that can be corrected only by excluding "them" from the nation. *Elegy* is thus both a memoir of Vance's life and, more broadly, an outline of a reading strategy that showcases how others are to be read in order to blame them for the national predicament that conservatism perceives. And it is here where the book proves insidious, for its explanatory power rests on an assumption that resentment is intuitively American. What Vance emotes is not the egalitarian "fierceness" of an American's "roused resentment," which insists that a democratic nation has room for mechanics as well as farmers, poets as well as presidents (Whitman 617). Instead, Vance's resentment insists that the nation be divided into factions of the worthy and the unworthy. The unfortunate message of his memoir is that "to feel love for the nation . . . is to feel injured by these others, who are 'taking' what is yours" (Ahmed, *Cultural Politics* 1). To do so, he posits a national way of life that is under duress by the supposedly entitled: he suggests that resentment toward the entitled is the most patriotic response. Vance's use of synecdoche reveals that the "truth" of conservative nationalism is ultimately an affect, and the more it relies on resentment as "truth," the uglier that nationalism becomes.[3] In its use of synecdoche to reinforce resentment, *Elegy* displays how conservative nationalism's "only truth is the resentment we feel when we contemplate others" (Snyder 114). Such "truth" aspires to rewrite the national narrative as an elegy brimming with resentment, one in which retribution toward the injustices inflicted by the supposedly entitled is taken as the "common sense" of national life.

Resentment: A Strong Affect

Classical rhetoricians from Aristotle to Quintilian warn that resentment is a "bitter, eruptive, undignified force" requiring containment (Engels, *Politics* 4). Such warnings continue throughout modern philosophy and contemporary political theory. Robert C. Solomon describes resentment as far worse than hatred in its insatiability: even hatred "treats the other on an equal footing" in ways that resentment does not (*Passions* 264). For him, resentment is "the villain of the passions" (290). Rather than seeking actual triumph over that which has wronged it, resentment seeks triumph in exclamations of how it has been denigrated. Its power is not in action but in explanation, for resentment never "want[s] to cure the evil: the evil is merely a pretext for the criticism" that follows (Scheler 51). Resentment's power comes from perpetually assigning guilt and blame to people or institutions, without ever accepting, nor ever proposing, a remedy that would mend whatever harm the supposedly guilty party has performed. Through synecdochical tactics, resentment seems to explain more than it actually does, generating, unlike the sudden intensity of hatred or the harmless inferiority of envy, a steady, continuous fuel of hostile negativity (see Solomon, *Passions* 248). Thus it frequently poses as other affects, such as indignation and pity, but ultimately lurks in a defensive posture, where everyone else (the whole) is to blame, and everything about it (the part) is the proof. Its power comes from its ability to perpetually, endlessly, critique.

To do so, resentment gains explanatory power by its ability to conflate categories upon which comparisons are made. "The main achievement of *ressentiment*" is the falsification of "the values themselves which could bestow excellence on any possible objects of comparison" (Scheler 58, emphasis in original). The comparative work of resentment brings together categories that would not otherwise connect to form a critique that "feels right" more than it is accurate. With a unique monomania, resentment encourages a turning inward, a reducing of the political to the personal, because the affect is "a way of ruminating on our anger and misfortune like an extended reproach to the world and to those around us" (André 96).

Thus the work of resentment is synecdochical in how it fuses parts together to create whole "others" who are the plight and the problem, as much as it fuses together the "we" who is injured by those others. The politics of resentment erases complex concepts such as fairness and reduces deliberation to the inventorying of grievances. In other words, resentment's construction of a moral world is designed to sustain strong affect. According to its logic, those who have suffered the most are not those who have actually suffered, but those who have been aggrieved by the suffering of others. Thus other's suffering is reframed as a lesser suffering that is not worthy of a correction that may entail a change of our life; indeed, any change would only create more blame. Blame has tremendous explanatory power in the politics of resentment, for it not only substitutes for complex action to remedy an issue, but also substitutes for the deliberative process that would expose solidarities. Blame reduces the social to the personal. As a result the "resentment that should be directed *ad ratio* goes in search of an interpersonal cause, becoming resentment *ad hominem*" (Engels, *Politics* 146). Ultimately, resentment is "less about finding consensus and more about achieving expiation, less about giving reasons and more about plotting revenge" toward others (Engels, "Politics" 304). Resentment does not seek to achieve justice: validation only perpetuates it.

Resentment has the dangerous ability to keep itself alive. It sustains itself through ruminations that guarantee its persistence, enabling the reader a "sentimental career with no interest in justice in the abstract or the majesty of the law" (Dore, Connor, and Sinykin). Resentment resentiments an issue, a cause, a people, with strong affect. As a strong affect, resentment reduces people to a "them" to be resented. It cannot construct an imagined community of a democratic "us" but instead validates an antidemocratic "flexible absolutism" that "frame[s] new and internally diverse cultural positions as 'eternal absolutes'" that the other can never shed (Harding 275). As such, synecdoches of resentment cease being figural: they become literal. People are no longer complex individuals who are part of "us" but instead the physical embodiment of a resentment: a person is no longer a person, but a living entitlement who takes something from you and whose education, lifestyle, or residence threatens your life and livelihood.

Resentment and Representation

Vance positions himself as both an outsider and an insider by developing a conceit anchored in synecdoche. His purpose in writing *Hillbilly Elegy,* that he is "not a senator, a governor, or former cabinet secretary," that he has "a nice job, a happy marriage, a comfortable home, and two lively dogs," relies on the conceit that he has "achieved something quite ordinary, which doesn't happen to most kids who grow up like me" (1).[4] Vance's life is worthy of a memoir because he was once an other, one of those who "face a grim future—that if they're lucky, they'll manage to avoid welfare; and if they're unlucky, they'll die of a heroin overdose, as happened to dozens in my small hometown just last year" (2). To validate his claim that he is a synecdoche, Vance must prove that he is an exception to a rule and is therefore exceptional, even in his ordinariness. His claim to speak for those others is predicated on being a part of that which, according to Vance, cannot represent itself: "I was one of those kids with a grim future. I almost failed out of high school. I nearly gave in to the deep anger and resentment harbored by everyone around me" (2).[5] Yet Vance is one of those with a "grim future" only by proximity, as he "almost failed" and "nearly gave in" to their resentful ways. Through its slippery phrasing—by claiming to both represent and not represent the people he describes—Vance shifts the resentment felt by "kids like me" as a reaction to a structural phenomenon—the economy and its "grim future"—to an emotion that is harbored, kept secretly, given a home by an individual who could otherwise, like Vance, overcome it. The effect may seem merely rhetorical. But in its obfuscation Vance is able to blame—that is, to perform resentment—upon the people whose resentment he claims to represent.

Vance's obfuscation is also apparent in the way he attempts to avoid his affiliation with the elite. Much like his description of those with a "grim future," he constructs for himself a category by evoking the others who he is not. "I may be white," he writes, "but I do not identify with the WASPs of the Northeast. Instead, I identify with the millions of Americans with Scots-Irish descent who have no college degree. To these folks, poverty is the family tradition. . . . Americans call them hillbillies, rednecks or white trash. I call them neighbors, friends and family" (3). Vance's claim to represent is based on a strange admixture of race ("white"), ethnicity ("Scots-Irish"), and class ("no college degree"). It is also based on a fatuous presumption that all those who fit this admixture are "white trash" for whom "poverty is the family tradition." The more important matter is that we "identify" as one or the other: in Vance's formulation, the "them" of the WASP or the "us" of the hillbilly. The word he uses to accomplish this is "identify." And when being a "hillbilly" is a matter of self-identification, anyone can believe themselves to be a hillbilly, even if they are, like Vance, an Ivy League–educated lawyer once employed by a multi-millionaire urbanite. (Even a city person can say they are "country at heart.") Ultimately, Vance's use of synecdoche serves as a way for him to both identify himself as a hillbilly and to screen himself from his actual identity—as he told a reporter for the *Financial Times*, "I react viscerally to this idea that I am a member of the elite, even though it's objectively true" (Donnan). The way in which Vance constructs an identity out of what he feels, rather than who he is, avoids what he knows is "objectively true." This is a telling example of what Robert C. Solomon sees as the "deviousness" of resentment: the way in which resentful readers torque the external world so that they can refute their personal history, in order to affectively build a nation in which they can hold others back (*Passions* 292).

The narrative that follows at times seeks to expose the hidden underside of hillbilly life in the Rust Belt but uneasily pivots into a rags-to-riches narrative in its second half as Vance leaves behind southwestern Ohio for military service in Iraq, Yale Law School, and elite life. Still, the memoir chronicles a lifetime of resentments. It is the preadolescent summers at his "home in the holler" of Jackson, Kentucky, that Vance remembers most positively, whereas growing up in Ohio was merely an "address" where "I was the abandoned son of a man I hardly knew and a woman I wished I didn't" (11, 13). Most of Vance's family strife comes not from a "revolving door of father figures," but from his mother, who he claims absorbed the turbulence of his grandparents' midlife and spent much of her youth either suicidal or suffering from addiction (88). He struggles throughout his adolescence for an identity. He dabbles in the Pentecostal faith of his father, in which "[e]volution and the Big Bang became ideologies to confront, not theories to understand. . . . I felt like a persecuted minority" (96–97). As his mother's addiction accelerates, he begins to realize that he and his sisters were "conditioned to feel that we couldn't really depend on people" (104). By the seventh grade, Vance feels perpetually "on guard" (123). Rotating between living with his sister, his mother, and his grandmother, he suffers from "an intense, indescribable anxiety" throughout most of his adolescence (150). His mother's turbulent relationships with her various husbands offer Vance no security, and his grandmother's declining Middletown neighborhood "had a kind of desperate sadness" (142). Yet living his last two years of high school with his grandmother gives him resilience. A stint in the marines provides self-confidence and a structured life; an internship in the Ohio State Legislature brings him eventually to Yale Law School. Yet even at Yale, Vance laments that "though we sing the praises of social mobility, it has its downsides. The term necessarily implies a sort of movement—to a theoretically better life, yes, but also away from something" (206). Perhaps such ruminations provided the spark that kindled the book, for in its final chapters, Vance reconnects with his family, particularly his mother, all the while attempting to negotiate the gulf between his past and present lives.

Adopting himself as its representative, Vance maps a narrative of American cultural decline into every facet of his life. Vance's representation of himself—and his family—supports a view of the hillbilly as the embodiment of "the American dream gone berserk" (Albert Votaw qtd. in Harkins 177).[6] His Uncle Pet, responding to a truck driver calling him a son of a bitch, "pulled the man from his truck, beat him unconscious, and ran an electric saw up and down his body" (Vance 14). And it is his grandmother, Mamaw, who intervenes throughout Vance's life to protect him, even from his own mother, such as when she takes him into her home despite her daughter's protests: "Mamaw told me that if Mom had a problem with the arrangement, she could talk to the barrel of Mamaw's gun" (78). These individual moments of strong affect construct a narrative of an entire people "going berserk." By equating family trauma with regional character, Vance conflates pathology with culture. The stories he hears as a youth during family reunions in Kentucky "made me feel like hillbilly royalty, because these were classic good-versus-evil stories, and my people were on the right side. My people were extreme, but extreme in the service of something—defending a sister's honor or ensuring that a criminal paid for his crimes" (17). The strong affects of these stories enable Vance to define himself as different from, and superior to, others: he is not a mere hillbilly, but rather royalty. His country is one where "us" and "them" is a matter of good and evil. It is a world of emotional extremes where a "potent, radically inclusive love, in other words, goes hand in hand with violently exclusive hate" (Huehls 332). Extremism is a means to achieve justice: extreme feelings demonstrate the authenticity of his patriotism.

Elegy shows how resentment is a representation that resentiments what it claims to represent with strong affect. Through anecdotes like these, Vance conveys that the right way to be an American is to be resentful. It is supported by a mode of reading the nation that cannot resist lengthy descriptions of the injustices it perceives, cannot stop obsessing over the manifold ways that guilt and blame can be assigned to the other. And at the textual level, it cannot stop supplying adjectives (minorities are "persecuted," anxiety is "indescribable," sadness is "desperate") to embellish the descriptions of its dramatic conflict with those deemed not "us" but "them." Later in the memoir, Vance reflects that "I'm the kind of patriot whom people on the Acela corridor laugh at. I choke up when I hear Lee Greenwood's cheesy anthem 'Proud to Be an American'" (189–90). From hillbilly justice to Lee Greenwood, the contours of the nation that Vance maps amplify conservatism as the only source of genuine national affect. What counts as true American feeling is often laden with a moralizing that is corrective, defensive, and visceral (Vance feels "on guard" as an adolescent; he "chokes up" at the Greenwood song). Such strong affects prove more important to the resentful than the delineation of accurately complex categories—or the envisioning of synecdoches that are truly representative of all citizens of the nation.

It is the degree of reaction that Vance intuits as distinctly American, from stories of violent but righteous "hillbilly justice" to his family's dysfunctions to Mamaw's nightly routine in which she would "watch *Law & Order,* read the *Bible,* and fall asleep" (85). Intense feelings of right and wrong, of pride and shame, coalesce in Vance's claim that his people are the nation's true representatives. "Mamaw always had two gods: Jesus Christ and the United States of America," Vance writes (189). If people like Mamaw are mocked for their extremism, this denigration is the sign of their authenticity. This is how Vance's resentments become most political. His enjoyment of family stories—of how his family represents themselves—as evidence of their being "extreme in the service of something" recalls Barry Goldwater's 1964 Republican National Convention acceptance speech, in which he proclaimed that "extremism in the defense of liberty is no vice. And let me remind you also that moderation in the pursuit of justice is no virtue." Such strong affect not only gives Vance a way to read the nation through a lens of resentment; it also gives him affective fuel for a conservative politics that actively endorses those resentments to perpetuate a campaign of enmity toward others.

How to Read Resentfully

As Jeremy Engels notes, "the mark of the politics of resentment is to capture and direct civic resentment . . . toward scapegoats" (*Politics* 101). Vance's synecdoches—the examples he chooses to exemplify the nation in decline—offer a rich index of scapegoats. Much of the work of resentment is to take an otherwise vague feeling of otherness and amplify it into a threat against "our" way of life, thus resentimenting that otherness with hostility. Such amplification is synecdochical in nature: individuals are interpreted as agents of the cause that threatens. Observing his father's fundamentalist preaching, Vance notes that his church's morality "was defined by not participating in this or that particular social malady: the gay agenda, evolutionary theory, Clintonian liberalism, or extramarital sex. Dad's church required so little of me. It was easy to be a Christian" (98). All it required of him was to be incurious toward those not like him, to be pridefully ignorant of science and progressive politics, to condemn people for moments of weakness. It required him to learn a "flexible absolutism" in which theories and people that are "other" to the cause are interpreted as "social maladies" that threaten your way of life and require correction. In effect, the church's politics show how resentment offers a primer, a strategy of strong affect, to read the world. As a reading strategy, resentment reduces people to a perceived, unfairly awarded entitlement, turning a part of their lives into the whole. In doing so, resentful readers become "overdetermined, monomaniacal figure[s], overly confident in what they think they recognize and know" (Huehls 336). Entitlement is taken as a core moral fault; indeed, a sense of entitlement spoils the entire person, and the resentful delight in narrating this fault. Entitled people, in effect, are not "good" citizens and should not only have their

entitlements withdrawn but should be expelled from the "us" that constitutes the nation.[7]

Early in the memoir, Vance describes "Bob," a fellow employee at a
tile warehouse where Vance works before enrolling at Yale Law School.
While Vance "collected as many overtime shifts and extra hours as I
could," lifting heavy boxes of floor tile onto shipping pallets, Bob proves
uninterested in overtime, much less his job (5). Vance does not fully explore the reasons behind Bob's disinterest; instead, he sees Bob's frequent
break taking and absences as signs of a flawed person, and eventually
of a flawed people, in terms of not only his work ethic but other ethical
areas as well. "Bob was nineteen with a pregnant girlfriend. The manager
kindly offered the girlfriend a clerical position answering phones. Both
of them were terrible workers," Vance writes (6). Eventually the manager
fires first his girlfriend, then Bob.

From this example, Vance claims to have a better understanding of
people who react to "bad circumstances in the worst way possible," that
Bob's story reflects "a culture that increasingly encourages social decay
instead of countering it" (7). Such a reading relies upon the synecdochical
assumption that Bob's life represents national "social decay": Vance parallels Bob's lack of work ethic with his lack of sexual and moral restraint.
This reading makes sense only in contrast to Vance's hard work and his
employer's beneficence. It is, for Vance, not a matter of economics but a
matter of people who are "warned to change [their] habits repeatedly"
and fail to do so (6). Vance never pauses to reflect on why a man with
a pregnant girlfriend may be late or miss work. Instead, Vance extrapo-
lates from Bob a story of a cultural failure that is separate from a story
of labor: "The problems that I saw at the tile warehouse run far deeper
than macroeconomic trends and policy," he insists (7). The problem, as
Vance sees it, is "too many young men immune to hard work. Good jobs
impossible to fill for any length of time." Bob's position, as Vance sees it,
makes no sense: "a young man with every reason to work—a wife-to-be
to support and a baby on the way—carelessly tossing aside a good job
with excellent health insurance." But what elicits strong affect in Vance
is not so much Bob's work ethic but how Bob responds to losing his job,
from which Vance intuits the full degree of a national problem. Vance
opines, "More troublingly, when it was all over, he thought something
had been done *to him*. There is a lack of agency here—a feeling that
you have little control over your life and a willingness to blame everyone

but yourself" (emphasis in original). As Vance sees it, Bob's predicament "is distinct from the larger economic landscape of modern America." Bob feels, unjustly Vance tells us, entitled.

Notice what Vance amplifies—and what he does not. In cordoning off economics (Bob's problem runs "deeper than macroeconomic trends" and is "distinct from the larger economic landscape") from consideration, Vance amplifies Bob's morality to make it the only component of the story, the part from which a resentful reading can be made (7). And notice how Vance amplifies Bob's morality: not by interpreting it, but by ruminating on it through repeated use of the same words (Bob is "immune to hard work" and he has "every reason to work;" Vance repeats twice that the job is "good"). Vance does not interpret: sentence by sentence, he only moralizes Bob's problem. Vance reduces the warehouse to a setting through which these affective amplifications occur. Each successive sentence fails to explore Bob's predicament further; instead, it repeats what is said before in a stronger and more "troubling" register. And as it continues, Vance deprives him of agency by mocking his perception of lacking agency. Bob himself becomes smaller; all the while, Vance blames Bob by insisting that Bob blames "everyone but [him]self."[8]

Bob's story is a source of rumination because it merely confirms what Vance already knows: that Bob is morally flawed. The problem is not Vance's—nor that of the "larger economic landscape"—but one of Bob's own making. What Vance first describes as Bob's carelessness, his poor work ethic, his apparent disinterest in work to support his girlfriend and soon-to-be family becomes a matter of his attitude, his "willingness to blame everyone" but himself. It is not that the job lifting boxes of flooring tile is backbreaking or that it pays sixteen dollars per hour—by Vance's own admission his employers find it impossible to keep any long-term employees—it is that the nation's young men are "immune to hard work," a disposition that implies that someone, or some culture, has vaccinated them against labor. Bob's failures, and his sense of entitlement, come to serve as a synecdoche for a declining American workforce, a declining nation.

Bob's story works as a synecdoche to verify conservative complaints. Vance tells Bob's story in a way that encourages readers to resent Bob for his feeling of entitlement. His pregnant girlfriend, in particular, is an almost irresistible ploy that activates the resentful attention of those who think that others are "eating their share of the pie" of government benefits

(Cramer 6). Bob's story is thus also a synecdoche that verifies contemporary conservative complaints of "overly entitled young people" (Skocpol and Williamson 72). As Theda Skocpol and Vanessa Williamson discovered, this specific complaint has significant credence in Tea Party circles. Whereas rank-and-file members of the Tea Party see themselves as having earned entitlements such as Social Security and Medicare/Medicaid, they simultaneously "connected worries about the deteriorating behavior of young people directly to fears about wasteful entitlement spending" (73). Entitlements are wasted on youth because they encourage dependency: as members of the Tea Party frame it in pedagogical terms, "rather than learning how to contribute to society, young people are being taught that they deserve support from the government" (73). Vance's construction of Bob's story validates conservative suspicions of young people: their lack of morality, their disinterest in hard work, and their feelings of deservingness as unfounded entitlement. Here the slide in the use of the word "entitlement" by conservatives is key: young people do not deserve entitlements (government assistance) because they feel entitled (expectant) of it. The only way to morally oppose the latter, according to conservative logic, is to deprive them of the former. And Vance's story provides readers with a moral scapegoat (in Bob and his girlfriend) for doing so: because they are unrepresentative of American morality, he implies, they should not receive "American" entitlements.

Vance gradually extends this resentful reading to the entire United States as a nation in which almost everyone (aside from fellow conservatives) has an entitlement he or she has not earned. By doing so, Vance shows how resentment's synecdochical work turns others into scapegoats in a broader narrative of national decline, even when those scapegoats are close to home. Examining his family, Vance finds that while "my grandparents embodied one type: old-fashioned, quietly faithful, self-reliant, hardworking," his "mother and, increasingly, the entire neighborhood embodied another: consumerist, isolated, angry, distrustful" (148). In his mother—who experiences a lifetime of instability, is unable to nurture her family, and moves from one drug dependency to another—he does not see a figure who needs a lifetime of help as much as a figure who, even in the throes of addiction, feels "entitled." When his mother asks for his help to fake a urine test, Vance notes that above all, "Mom's demand came with a strong air of entitlement. She had no remorse, no sense that she was asking me to do something wrong. Nor was there any guilt over the fact that she had broken yet another promise to never use drugs" (130). The scene is traumatic—"something inside me broke," Vance writes—but ultimately Mamaw persuades him to provide his mother with the urine she needs to pass the drug test required for her nursing license (132). In this moment, any resentment would be justified. Yet Vance does not "regret relenting" because he interprets giving his mother the urine as a demonstration of hillbilly values: "Giving Mom that piss was wrong, but I'll never regret following Mamaw's lead" (131). The urine becomes a synecdoche of Mamaw's "hope," which "allowed her to forgive Papaw after the tough years of their marriage. And it convinced her to take me in when I needed her most" (131). It also works to forge a chain of resentment between family members, as Vance's urine substitutes not only for his mother's, but for her moral failures.

Synecdoche can take waste and endow it with meaning. Synecdoche can also take meaning and turn it into waste. It is the alchemical power of synecdoche to extrapolate wholes from parts, to read what families do as reflective of a culture, and that culture as reflective of a nation. In such moments, the premises of resentment as a strategy for reading become apparent. At its core, being entitled, according to Vance, means not having remorse, not having guilt. As such, it becomes a judgment in the eye of the beholder without an honest exploration of genuine inequality. It means that those who are "entitled" have done something for which they should feel remorseful, something they should feel guilty about. Feeling entitled means breaking promises. And as Vance theorizes, the person who resents knows what is right: that the other who feels entitled is wrong. Resentment becomes a way of setting aside conflicting positions for the false righteousness of moral absolutes.

Vance's mother once again succumbs to addiction, and the author finds himself back in Middletown to manage her finances. He asks of himself, "How much of our own lives, good and bad, should we credit to our personal decisions, and how much is just the inheritance of our culture, our families, and our parents who have failed their children?" (231). For Vance, this question is not only national but personal: "How much is Mom's life her own fault? Where does the blame stop and the sympathy begin?" (231). The questions Vance asks are the fundamental questions of synecdoche: How much am "I" part of a whole: a family, a community, a culture, a nation? How much of "me" is a part of these wholes? How many wholes are parts of "me?" As such, these are questions well worth asking. Yet throughout *Elegy,* these questions are asked not to earnestly uncover their complex and ambiguous answers, but to perpetuate resentment through synecdoche. Vance asks not about individual luck or cultural practice; he asks not about social, economic, and government policies that inevitably shape one's life and livelihood. Instead, he asks these questions to establish fault and blame. What Vance provides, time and time again throughout *Elegy*, is not a genuine answer to these fundamental questions. Instead, he insists that structural issues be reduced to individual morality. The answers to the questions Vance raises are not meant to provide closure. Quite the opposite: they are meant to keep the wound open so it can be filled with a penumbra of resentments.

Resentment thus provides Vance with a way to read his position in the world by noting that weak others have unjust power over him. A job in a grocery store during high school "taught me a little more about America's class divide . . . it also imbued me with a bit of resentment, directed toward both the wealthy and my own kind" (Vance 139). That the store's owners allow wealthy patrons to keep lines of credit infuriates Vance, who "hated the feeling that my boss counted my people as less trustworthy than those who took their groceries home in a Cadillac. But I got over it. One day, I told myself, I'll have my own damned tab." (It is telling that Vance subscribes to a fundamentally neoliberal financial identity; that is, that the sign of one's success, even one's identity, comes from the ability to manipulate debt.)[9] He also sees that synecdochically "most of us were struggling to get by, but we made do, worked hard, and hoped for a better life" in the face of "a large minority [that] was content to live off the dole." Even worse, Vance notes, "every two weeks, I'd get a small paycheck and notice the line where federal and state income taxes were deducted from my wages. At least as often, our drug addict neighbor would buy T-bone steaks, which I was too poor to buy for myself but was forced by Uncle Sam to buy for someone else." Vance paints this resentment melodramatically: people like him—the silent majority—not only work, but work hard. The paychecks they earn are small because their taxes subsidize drug-abusing others who in turn abuse benefits to purchase symbols of elite life, such as T-bone steaks. Vance, though, is "forced" by a synecdoche for the federal government—"Uncle Sam"—to subsidize an ambiguous but "large minority" who, through entitlements, are "content to live off the dole."

Resentment presumes the affects of others: "we" are exhausted while the other is at ease; "they" are content while we are discontent. And those presumptions reveal a veritable index of conservative resentments:

the abuse of the welfare system and wages eaten by the high taxes caused by entitlements. Vance's analysis endorses a reading of liberal social policy as perversity: the idea that such policies "produce the exact contrary of the objective being pursued" (Hirschman, *Rhetoric* 11). The "perversity thesis," as Albert O. Hirschman notes, is "admirably simple, whereas the claim being made is rather extreme."[10] Vance presumes that the drug addict neighbor in Middletown is a "welfare queen" abusing the system, which reinforces a "resentment toward cities" that serves as the "glue between anti-government and small-government attitudes" (Cramer 154). Vance's presumption depends on a particular way of reading: to read for other people's entitlements is to indulge in slips of synecdochical thinking, requiring resentment to fill in the blanks. Such reading extends to multiple domains of conservative sensemaking. As Katherine J. Cramer notes in her study of resentment in Wisconsin, "people tended to meld together different levels of government—local, county, state, national—when they talked about the government. Complaints about one level seemed to flow right into complaints about another" (160). Throughout *Elegy*, Vance performs a similar melding: the resentments of his family flow into condemnations of his neighbors and ultimately the entire nation. Resentful reading is thus ideological reading, for resentment legitimizes certain visibilities as it manufactures invisibilities. It is where the "perversity thesis" substitutes strong affect for any potential solution to the problem it outlines: after all, if policy produces a contrary effect, then any policy makes the problem worse. This allows Vance to write about class as if it is totally separate from economics. As a cultural problem, it lies outside the sphere of policy altogether. It does not produce a nation that can reduce or eliminate its inequalities. Ultimately, it cannot imagine a way to connect the "us" and the "them" together in a meaningful exchange, or meaningful policy, that would lead to a "we." What resentment makes visible has no solution. As Dore, Connor, and Sinykin note, in *Elegy*, "feelings accumulate anecdotes, and anecdotes shade silently" into nonpolicies. At the same time, Vance's affects only perpetuate more resentment-producing synecdoches, which makes it impossible for anecdotes to cohere into a policy and fuels the strong affect that substitutes for narrative coherence.

Examining Mamaw's neighbors—a woman whose house is ruined due to her drug abuse, an obese neighbor who never says hello, another who is neglectful of her child—Vance writes: "This was my world: a world of truly irrational behavior" (146). In synecdochical fashion, he goes on to

assert that his world is our world; that ours, too, is one of irrational behavior. "We spend our way into the poorhouse. We buy giant TVs and
iPads. Our children wear nice clothes thanks to high interest credit cards
and payday loans. We purchase homes we don't need, refinance them for
more spending money, and declare bankruptcy, often leaving them full of
garbage in our wake." From this, Vance asserts that "thrift is inimical to
our being." The problem, as he sees it, is that Americans "spend to pretend that we're upper-class. And when the dust clears—when bankruptcy
hits or a family member bails us out of our stupidity—there's nothing left
over." Notice the synecdochical slide that occurs in this passage: Vance
first looks at a declining neighborhood and projects that neighborhood
onto the American middle class writ large. Indeed, he complains in this
passage that economic decline is a synecdoche of moral decline: excessive
spending, Vance suggests, reflects bad character. But Vance's theory of
decline ignores the issue of how such money is acquired in the first place:
through markets that support the payday loans and offer the high-interest
credit cards. And any misuse of the market is a moral failure—Vance
cannot see why someone would need to refinance a house other than to
"spend to pretend" and maintain facades. Strangely, what Vance ruminates on is not the actual impoverishments of Mamaw's neighborhood
but the moral impoverishments he sees in middle-class life, which to him
represents a lax morality. He sees a nation worthy of resentment because
he, unlike them, manages his debts—an easy task to achieve for a person
with military benefits, an Ivy League education, a job at a Silicon Valley
law firm. In depictions of America like this, Vance's analysis always skirts,
even when the problem is right in front of him, economic actuality for
moral accusation.

The resentment that drives these synecdoches obscure exactly who is
doing what: it is a prose whose subject and object get lost in the rhythm
of its resenting. It is a pattern throughout *Elegy* that Vance often begins
with a brief statement—"This was my world: a world of truly irrational
behavior"—a part that serves as a thesis, and then follows it with a glo-
balizing embellishment, an always-undefined "we" that amplifies the part
to represent the whole. Vance's explanatory power is as ruminative as it
is repetitive ("we spend;" "we buy;" "we purchase") often repeatedly di-
gesting its own resentment ("truly irrational;" "inimical to our being;"
"bails us out of our stupidity") as a symptom of the other, even as it con-
torts that other into something different than it was at first (Vance 146).

Vance conflates his family traumas with national character: Mamaw's neighborhood represents an entire world, but the "we" that he evokes is not the problem of Rust Belt poverty but the problem of bourgeois life-styles. The lower and middle classes merge in their efforts to "pretend that we're upper-class." Yet this conflation reduces the structural to the personal: the "world" he describes is not one of markets that encourage risk and profit in other's impoverishment, but of "irrational behavior," of people making mistakes for which they can be blamed, people to whom, the passage suggests, nothing should be given when "there's nothing left over."

The Resentful American

It is through synecdochical reading that Vance offers a theory of the nation, one that, through exclaiming the laxities of the entitled, resentfully restricts the "we" of the nation so that it aligns exclusively with conservative values. Given resentment's monomania, it should not be surprising that Vance sees himself as representative of the nation and, accordingly, that he sees the nation much like he sees himself. "I am a hill person," he writes, claiming that "so is much of America's white working class. And we hill people aren't doing very well" (22). And if the reader does not buy Vance's conflation of his "people" with the entire "white working class," Vance also insists that the "plight" of his hometown has "gone mainstream" (21). Vance's narrative of cultural decline implies that mainstream America has become the hillbilly: Americans are the Uncle Pets and Mamaws, the fathers and mothers whose lives are under the duress of entitled others and whose politics are not policies but affects. Vance's memoir claims that all of its participants—"us" included—are resentful readers. And through this synecdochical sleight of hand, Vance asserts that resentment toward entitled others is central to American identity. His "people," and by extension Americans writ large, are resentful.

As the explainer of hillbilly culture, Vance writes: "Nothing united us with the core fabric of American society. We felt trapped in two seemingly unwinnable wars . . . and in an economy that failed to deliver the most basic promise of the American Dream—a steady wage" (189). He laments that the "white working class" is no longer "the core fabric of American society," which has been taken over by others. The pinnacle of this change, Vance writes, is Barack Obama, who serves as a synecdoche of the other who is resented for the power he has over them. "Nothing about him bears any resemblance to the people I admired growing up," Vance writes. "His accent—clean, perfect, neutral—is foreign; his credentials are so impressive that they're frightening; he made his life in Chicago, a dense metropolis; and he conducts himself with a confidence that comes from knowing that the modern American meritocracy was built for him" (191). Vance frames Obama as the epitome of the other through the very American traits he possesses: his accent is both "neutral" and "foreign," his training is both "impressive" and "frightening," his experiences are urban, not rural, and by inference, his "confidence" is the feeling of entitlement, of knowing the nation was "built for him" while Vance's "people" remain "trapped." At the same time, Vance acknowledges that the president "is a good father while many of us aren't. His wife tells us that we shouldn't be feeding our children certain foods, and we hate her for it—not because we think she's wrong but because we know she's right" (191). It is the work of resentment to paint a gulf between others through acknowledging the other's rightness and goodness. As Vance explains it, American resentment toward Obama is due to his being "right." It is not that the president does not represent the nation; it is that he represents it too well. The president is, therefore, the epitome of the other who is resented for the superiority they have over "us." Obama is the "them" to Vance's "us," a bifurcation that separates the president from the people, and in doing so cements an impervious divide between the representative and the represented. He has, Vance does not deny, earned his achievements. But it is the powerlessness of those who lack what Obama represents that propels Vance's resentment. And it is how Vance explains Obama's successes, reducing him and his wife to synecdoches of an America his people do not have access to, that reinforces how the "politics of resentment stems from and reinforces political differences that have become personal. In a politics of resentment, we treat differences in our political points of view as fundamental differences in who we are as human beings" (Cramer 211).

Vance insists that race has nothing to do with his hometown's perception of Obama as alien; that their "reasons have nothing to do with his skin color" (191). Further, Vance writes that anyone who blames Obama for their woes needs "to live in an environment that forces him to ask tough questions about himself," suggesting that such scapegoating is an easy way to avoid one's personal problems (194). Yet the focus of his memoir, which goes to great length to both center the American narrative around "working-class white Americans of Scotch-Irish descent" and to justify the idea that "there is no group of Americans more pessimistic than working-class whites," inevitably reads Obama's race to be as foreign as his successes (3, 194). Perhaps this is why Vance never suggests that his "people" should aspire to become Obama. Indeed, becoming Obama would be the opposite of the political life Vance has in mind for the resentful American to lead.[11]

The conclusion to *Elegy* is a reminder of the entitled others Vance cannot imagine serving as models for the community in which he was raised. It is a theory of the nation derived from not living like others. "We don't need to live like the elites of California, New York, or Washington, D.C.," Vance writes (256). "We don't need to work a hundred hours a week at law firms and investment banks. We don't need to socialize at cocktail parties. We do need to create a space for the J. D.s . . . of the world to have a chance. I don't know what the answer is, precisely, but I know it starts when we . . . ask ourselves what we can do to make things better."

Perhaps it is the epitome of synecdoche that Vance uses without irony the phrase "the J. D.s of the world"—the presumption that he himself represents a whole swath of the nation. But it is the monomania that comes with resentful reading that Vance affects in his claim to represent the entire nation exclusively. What such a space might look like is deeply synecdochical—a place where people like Vance, the "J. D.s of the world," can have opportunities—as much as it is framed through a resentment toward various synecdochical elites: where they live; their line of work; how they socialize. Intriguingly, Vance's own life suggests that it is through elites that one becomes successful: as he notes in the memoir, after military service and college, Vance went to Yale Law School, where he was mentored by "Tiger Mom" Amy Chua and contributed to *National Review*. Indeed, as Dore, Connor, and Sinykin note, Vance has become "a very familiar version of a political conservative who advances policies that promote class inequity." While there are numerous moments in *Elegy* in which Vance describes his rise into the elite, he does not conceive of his life as a model for others to follow. Vance does not see himself as representative of where hillbilly folk can go. Indeed, he sees the elites as others whom he views with "a primal scorn" for their ease as much as for their vocabulary. In what might be the ultimate sign of resentment, Vance notes, "I have to give it to them: their children are happier and healthier . . .

their church attendance higher, their lives longer. These people are beat-
ing us at our own damned game" (253).[12] There is no greater a resentment
than the feeling that you are being beaten at your own game by those with
more power than you. For the resentful American, this is a way of avoid-
ing how these people may be more like you—and more like what you
want to be—than what your rhetoric will let you think.

Elegy reveals the rhetorical and political limits of the resentful American, one who ruminates to such an extent that he cannot see how he himself is the antagonist of his own reading, a reading that restricts being able
to see how the other's game is also yours. To do so would require abandon-
ing the strong affects that encourage a flexible absolutism. And it would
require a more genuine use of synecdoche, not one that reduces, but one
that broadens the nation: not one that sees others as entitled, but one that
sees all as worthy of entitlements. Resentful readers are locked in a script
whose rhetoric is familiar to them but one that increasingly isolates them
from the nation. And they are locked into a perverse sense of freedom,
one that "means to be free from the burden of other's vulnerability—to
be free from recognizing one's complicity in making others vulnerable"
(Anker 8–9). It would be inappropriate to pity such bad faith: it is central
to the conservative definition of what it means to be an American. It is
the elegiac quality of such resentment that should repel us from its synecdochical impress.

Conclusion: Nationalism's Elegy

There has always been something elegiac in the figure of the hillbilly, a
figure that "elicit[s] a mixture of ridicule and empathy" for its "complacent poverty and geographic and social stasis" (Harkins 168, 51). And
there is an explicit promise in the title of Vance's book that such an elegy
will be performed, complete with the complex affects that would support
his thesis that "no single book, or expert, or field could fully explain the
problems of hillbillies in modern America. Our elegy is a sociological
one, yes, but it is also about psychology and community and culture and
faith" (145). Indeed, titling the book *Hillbilly Elegy* reveals the close proximity of resentment to elegiac sadness. "Resentment and sadness are very
close," writes Christophe André (97). "Often . . . what causes resentment
could just as easily have caused sadness. Indeed, sadness is almost always present, underneath the anger" of resentment. What is elegiac about

Elegy is how Vance, only once he is about to graduate from Yale, realizes that resentment is what "caused those in my family to hurt those whom they loved" (225).

There is also something elegiac in the hillbilly that makes him a powerful conduit of resentment. As Max Scheler notes, resentment "can never emerge without the mediation of a particular form of impotence . . . one of the phenomena of 'declining life'" (60). In *Elegy*, resentment is synecdochalized as the primary "communal sense of loss," a victimization that "is often instrumental in founding and fostering the nation-state" (Ramazani 603). The plight of the resentful hillbilly serves in Vance's memoir as the "abstractive monument" that mirrors the "fictive nature of the national community" it aspires to construct (602). By making hillbilly life a subject worthy of elegy, Vance synecdochically attributes the hillbilly's loss to a decline of American life caused by other people's entitlements. In doing so, he simultaneously shifts the explanation of the nation to an index of conservative resentments. In effect, *Elegy* constructs conservative resentments as the very foundation of American life. Vance's intention is, at its core, a conservative one: to construct through the hillbilly "a philosophy of the national past" with an attendant "temporality of the traditional" that must be preserved against attack from others (Schwarz 54). This is how *Elegy* enacts a politics of resentment, one that substitutes "democratic desire" for strong affects of victimization and blame that serves to defend the tradition he has invented (Engels, *Politics* 23). Throughout the book, Vance's deployment of synecdoche seeks to affirm that American life is resentful in not a figurative sense but a literal one. In a world where feeling becomes fact, such injustices cannot be resolved, nor can such a decline be halted. Reducing his people to an elegy amplifies the very politics of resentment that Vance ultimately embraces. His memoir shows how contagious resentment can be, helping to produce "precisely the type of subject neoliberalism desires: one that is forever reacting and never acting, a subject consumed by a violence that cannot be escaped because it has been psychologically internalized" (Engels, *Politics* 130). It is little wonder that critics, on both the left and the right, have parroted his resentments: they have internalized its contours just as readers are asked to do throughout the memoir. As subjects of an elegy, Vance's people serve only as conduits of strong affect that, by design, cannot read the nation with complexity. Vance may understand his own trauma as structural, but the deployment of synecdoche to validate his resentment does not allow him to see the structures—the changes to the economy and society—that would bring about its resolution for others. Thus *Elegy* aspires to recast the elegy of the nation as an elegy of resentment, turning the national story into one with the resentment of entitled others at its origin. With its substitution of complex politics for stereotyped others whose entitlement is to be exposed, conservatives' ability to explain the nation's problems by reducing them to a shorthand of scapegoats verifies and sustains strong affect in place of a more honest exploration of the nation.

Thus *Elegy* offers a reminder that there has always been something elegiac in the figure of the American as well. Especially in Vance's depiction of the contemporary American, there is a sense that what is desired is something from the past that will not be seen again in the future. Vance's insistence that the definition of a successful American means a good job—a middle-class lifestyle, moderation of conspicuous consumption, and family values—has a nostalgic quality given the contemporary economy. The very qualities of the good life that would, in theory, mitigate resentment require the very structures that Vance writes against: the good life is dependent, in ways both visible and invisible, on entitlements. At the same time, he advocates throughout the book for a "libertarian mistrust of government policy" that would work only to deny the subsidies and programs that give middle-class citizens a foothold in the economy (193). That Vance does not notice this points to resentment's reductive power, one that "serves to shift the blame away from long-term solutions toward handy scapegoats who are chimeric 'bad' elites and their supposed allies among the lazy, sinful, and subversive parasites located in the lower margins of society" (Berlet 58). Vance's memoir affirms such a view and outlines a method through which that view can be endlessly sustained.

Vance has no solutions to national problems because his use of synecdoche reduces options for national renewal. His lack of solutions shows how "resentment rationalizes its position, but it remains stuck there" (Solomon, *True* 110). Once confident in its rightness, "resentment just sits and sulks," certain that its lack of action is its very power. Where the righteousness of resentment will take readers is hard to say. If Vance offers any insight, it is that synecdoche will continue to be mobilized by conservatives, not for the sake of representing the nation, but for the sake of sustaining strong affect in ways that deny the very possibility of a representable nation in the first place. Above all, what *Elegy* works to claim as mainstream is what others have noted are key indicators of resentment: "(1) a belief that rural areas are ignored by decision makers, including policy makers, (2) a perception that rural areas do not get their fair share of resources, and (3) a sense that rural folks have fundamentally distinct values and lifestyles, which are misunderstood and disrespected by city folks" (Cramer 12). Given its origins and trajectory, it could be argued that contemporary conservatism mobilizes synecdoche to turn the nation into a bastion of resentments, whereby resentment serves as the "common sense" of economic policies that transfer wealth to the richest while slashing services to those in need, which will only generate resentment all the more, rendering the nation prey to the endless trauma of strong affect. To follow the trajectory of such policies—their reductive synecdoches, their attendant strong affects—to their conclusion may mean that the nation will someday be the subject of a much more catastrophic elegy than the one Vance's resentments enable him to write.

5

Depression

ON THE evening of the 2016 presidential election, David Sedaris finds himself in the bed of a Portland, Oregon hotel. He stares at the ceiling as he hears that Donald Trump has received the electoral college votes necessary to become the president, trying to find, quickly, another imagined community to replace the one from which he has been torn asunder. "I suddenly think of Cher," he writes, "and realize that what I'm feeling, she's feeling as well. So are millions of other people of course. . . . Oddly, it's this woman I've never met or seen in person who brings me comfort" (189). It is only in feeling that he is part of something larger than himself, that he is connected, as are many others, to a prominent figure that allows Sedaris a few hours of restless sleep before waking to wander the city "in a daze, my eyes bloodshot." The only way he makes it through the day is to repeatedly think to himself *I'm not alone. I've got Cher*" (emphasis in original).

The humor shows the need: the need for an imagined community, the comfort that can be found in knowing that while you may be in a new place and surrounded by people you do not know, you are not alone. The humor also warns of what happens if this is unfulfilled: if one cannot find a part of the nation as it is, one wanders in a daze not because the surroundings are unfamiliar but because, without a feeling of communion, one's surroundings are now illegible. And finally, the humor exposes how personal the impersonal work of synecdoche can be: Sedaris must have a figure through which he can share a sense of identification with others, a figure who represents not only himself, but a community, the conduit through which he knows others feel as he does, in order to know those others as much as know himself.

But the humor also obscures. That Sedaris takes a celebrity as a leader, much like those who voted for Donald Trump did, is a substitution that goes unexamined. Further, Sedaris's quick switch to another icon as leader performs a kind of passive defection—he does not protest Trump's worthiness or fight the injustice of an election in which the popular vote was clearly not won by the recipient of the office—he instead replaces one figure for another when that figure no longer suits his purpose. It is a kind of devaluing of the presidency. It is the political equivalent of lying in bed, staring at the ceiling, while others march.

For Sedaris, the evening of the election is one of "A Number of Reasons I've Been Depressed Lately," an essay first published in the *Paris Review* in 2017 and reprinted in his essay collection *Calypso*. "Reasons" tracks the rise of Donald Trump and his entry into the White House. The essay's "reasons" index how, through Sedaris's eyes, Trump's rise from fringe candidate to party nominee to president—his rise from part to whole—affects strangers, friends, family, and, ultimately, himself. The essay reveals the ways in which Trumpism brings extremisms together and, in doing so, not only destroys those it sees as enemies but also inspires distrust among friends. Thus the essay tracks the rising of a particularly noxious form of strong nationalism, one that through its marshaling of strong affect leaves no room for plurality, moderation, or even imagination.

The "depression" that Sedaris, "reason" by "reason," comes to feel is not only the political impress of a president and an electorate that dismisses him as a person; it is also the widening rift between people that Trumpism fosters. If nationalism is the work of attunement, as Sara Ahmed writes, then it is the work in which "you identify with the nation not only by making it the object of feeling, but by becoming attuned to national rhythms" ("Not in the Mood" 22). As the essay unfolds, it becomes apparent that Sedaris cannot find himself attuned to a nation that is finding itself increasingly supportive of Trump—and at the same time, that Sedaris cannot find himself attuned to those who are not. Sedaris's essay illustrates how his deepening refusal throws him out of tune entirely, even to those who are his intimates. Even worse, the essay shows how the tools Sedaris has at his disposal—his wit, his irony, his humor—fail to counterbalance Trumpist strong affect. As the election unfolds and its aftermath roils, Sedaris utterly fails to persuade Trump's adherents, including members of his own family, to change their minds. Even worse, by the essay's conclusion, Sedaris's attempts to rouse his own allies leads only to disaster. Trump's election, therefore, is not only a political failure to Sedaris— the feeling that one's allies will vote for a candidate who openly opposes your way of life. It is also a failure of figurative language—the depression that comes when one's rhetoric proves impotent in the world. The election shows that wit, irony, and humor prove futile in the face of Trumpist strong affect. And as Sedaris's essay shows, the continued use of these during the Trump presidency only shows how humor cannot substitute for the direct dissent of the demagogue who is now president.

Depression can be conceived of as the feeling that one is a part without a whole. It can also be conceived of as the strong affects that follow from such feeling, the inward anger one feels when one finds oneself disconnected from the whole. It is apparent when one's humor ceases to be gentle, when one relies upon stereotype and caricature to make others laugh, when one's irony is no longer pedagogic but "militant" (Northrop Frye qtd. in McClennen). The result is a turning inward that proves to be self-isolating, which only perpetuates further inward turning: a militant ironist is still a militant. What Sedaris captures, then, is one way of responding that sustains the conflict on which Trumpism thrives, a way that resigns those who oppose his regime to being immured in the demagogue's strong affect.

Trumpism is synecdoche at its most venal, but the pleasure it brings its practitioners should not be underestimated, not only for its vitriolic performativity but for the illiberal pedagogy it foists upon the whole nation: what Trumpism shows is how "the scraps, patches, and rags of daily life [are] repeatedly turned into the signs of a national culture" to which most Americans do not subscribe (Bhabha 297).[1] Indeed, Trumpism is a way of synecdochalization that does not bring the scraps, patches, and rags of daily life together but leaves them in tatters. Trumpism may construct a "we" for some, but what it is most effective at is sustaining vicious conflict while it dismantles the conventions through which an "us" can be seen, or can be desired to be seen. What makes it depressing is that what Trumpism builds never exceeds what it destroys.

Depression as Strong Affect

Affect theory seeks to complicate Freudian and neurobiological models of depression. Tomkins, for example, was fascinated by the depressive's emotional lability more than by any attempt to categorize depression per se. To him, the depressive oscillates between "intimacy and his controlling, judging, and censuring of the other" (*Affect* 3:325). Indeed, the oscillation is the point, for it is through the depressive's lability that the depressed person becomes capable of a comedy that "holds a bitter-sweet mirror to his audience . . . his humor is gentle and loving, biting and contemptuous, at once" (3:328). The depressive's willingness to see himself as he sees others is what gives him his particular affective cast as "the one who wishes to be loved and respected for the loving contempt he turns on himself, his audience, and on others more generally." The depressive is as likely to point out the fault of others as much as himself and, in doing so, expects that his contempt will be seen as a mode of love.

Tomkins's understanding of depression is a reminder of its individuating experience. What pains depressives is that their connection to others proves to be in vain, either because it is not perceived for its loving intent, or because it fails to correct the situation that has elicited their contempt. Depressives are thus highly aware of the degree of attunement they have with their object, aware of the "unfathomable distance between me and any other human being" and the desperate need "to be able to bridge that gap, to seek a true human world between two people" (Gail Hornstein qtd. in Ratcliffe 10). Depression intensifies when modes of communion become unavailable, when communities cannot be imagined. It is an acute sensitivity to the negative changes "in the kinds of possibility that are experienced as integral to the world and, with it, a change in the structure of one's own overall relationship with the world" (Ratcliffe 2). And as these negative changes increase, depressives enter a "downward spiral of hope-lessness [and] withdrawal" that leads to "the erosion of self" (Karp 91).

Depression is an affect so strong that it induces a "disappearing under the weight of daily life" (Cvetkovich 59). Should its partly contemptuous, partly loving reading of the world be ignored, the reading continues nevertheless, but directed upon the self, making depressives ever more scrutinous of themselves, all the more critical of others, all the less likely to participate in the world. Depression becomes a "blockage or impasse" that "can literally shut down or inhibit" a person or a movement (20). "Like physical pain," Ann Cvetkovich writes, depression "kept me fixated on the immediate present, unable to think about other things" (35). Depression leaves one "confused about what to do because I no longer knew how to avoid it or how to imagine it ending." To be a depressive in liberal times is hard enough: there is already ample material upon which depressives can practice their mix of love and contempt. But in illiberal times, the kinds of possibility imagined by depressives only leads to more blockages. This is what Trump does to his opponents: he keeps them entangled in squabbles of his own invention as he erases democratic principles in the short term and wrecks its foundations in the long term. One cannot imagine it ending because one can no longer tell where such destruction began, much less where it will end.

If affect is, as Sara Ahmed writes, the "sticking" of signs to bodies (*Cultural Politics* 13), depression can be thought of as the affective situation that emerges when one becomes stuck in the demagogue's language. Words do not create communities but separate them; they do not allow for imagination but facilitate condemnation. The loving contempt that comes with depressives' humor no longer teaches but only criticizes. Above all, depressives' rhetoric no longer provides them with agency, no way to escape from the present in which they find themselves. Depression is a strong affect because depressed readers are stuck in their reading, stuck with their reading, from which no good can come.

Witness to an Encroaching Trumpism

David Sedaris emerged in the late 1990s from the crowd of writers for the radio series *This American Life* and became known for a style of humor in which "his intensely human, flawed, self-inflated identity—whose impulse is to continually mock others, but who compulsively learns to check himself first—lampoons essentialist pieties" (Cardell and Kuttainen 109). The typical formula of a Sedaris essay, according to Dan Brooks, is that of "a befuddled, anxious person [who] gets into various situations in which he is intellectually, socially, or experientially unable to deal, muddling through with a series of asides" that come to synecdochically illustrate "the funny quality of how things really are" (Brooks). Sedaris aspires, as Kevin Kopelson writes, to tell the truth of a situation with a wry smile rather than the use of blunt contempt (see 2). His gambit is to remind readers of wit's harsher options in order to show the unnecessariness of "the vicious or inhumane things we could do, can imagine doing, or imagine having been done by someone else" (255). Sedaris's narrative style is "at once temporally distanced, intimately aware of his own foibles, and sincerely credulous" (Roof 34). It is a narrative style that thus closely aligns with the love-contempt combination that Tomkins sees as constituting depression.

"Reasons" begins with a question from the audience at a Greek literary festival: "What do you think of Donald Trump?" (Sedaris 185). In attempting to answer, he compares Trump to the Hamburglar of McDon-ald's commercials, with whom the Greek audience is unfamiliar. Sedaris realizes that Trump "has always been in the background, this ridiculous blowhard, part showman and part cartoon character" (186). He tells the Greek audience that there is no cause for alarm as Trump's campaign is "just another commercial for himself." In this, Sedaris's view is represen-tative of most mainstream liberals who presumed that Trump was an outlier who would withdraw from the campaign, or be defeated by the Republican establishment in the primaries, or be found so unpalatable by the voting public that victory would never be within his reach. And in this, Sedaris anticipated what would become a major problem with treat-ing Trump humorously, that "he already seemed like an impersonation. Trump's performative style, braggadocio, and basic lack of understanding of the workings of U.S. government all combined to throw challenges" to humorists and critics alike (McClennen). As Sophia A. McClennen writes, "If satirists' invective is their hammer, how were they to use it on a figure who was already a bombastic bully? If another of their skills is parody, what to make of someone who was already parodic?" Even in comparing Trump to the Hamburglar, Sedaris approaches the difficulty of censuring someone unashamed of their obscenity—the Hamburglar's name is bound up with his acts: it is the core of his identity. In this way, Sedaris points to the difficulty of ironizing a candidate who is the culmi-nation of the "Reaganite tendency to fetishize both the offensive example and the patriotic norm" (Berlant, Queen 7).

Sedaris finds, on his return to the United States, that Trump's bragga-docio has found more appeal than he anticipated. Chauffeured from Phil-adelphia to New Jersey, Sedaris listens as his driver laments, "I just feel that for guys like us, white guys of our age, if we need any help—housing or food stamps or whatever—it's the back of the line" (186). The driver provides almost verbatim what Philip S. Gorski and Samuel L. Perry de-scribe as the "deep story" that many Trumpists take as fact: that "people like them" have been "patiently waiting in line for the chance of the American Dream," only to "see people cutting in line—immigrants and minorities and other people who haven't paid their dues" (3–4). As Gorski and Perry note, this "deep story" leaves unstated a fundamental and false assumption that "white people were here first" and are therefore more de-serving than others (4). What the "deep story" offers is an affective scape-goat: that "we" are patiently waiting while "they" are jumping the queue, and what "we" need is an authority who will "send those people to the back of the line where they belong" (4). It is to say that "we" are white and "they" are not; that "we" are American and "they" are not. In effect, the "deep story" allows strong nationalists to feel as if they are polite abiders of the rules even as they vote for a figure who will break the rules for their benefit.

Sedaris's inward response, "well, isn't that sort of where the line forms?," is a typical Sedaris tactic of allowing people "to convict themselves of their own failings through their word choice, which he merely reports to his readers" (Sedaris 187; Pugh 152). His question exposes the "deep story" for what it is, an attempt to bypass democratic norms by way of race-based grievance. And Sedaris sees the driver synecdochically as part of "a group I've been hearing a lot from lately. White men who, following eight years of a black president, feel forgotten" (187). He correctly intuits the "deep story" the chauffeur has provided him—all the while not directly engaging with him. Instead, Sedaris practices what Cvetkovich critiques as "tolerance in the sense of putting up with conflict" (7). As much as he refuses to be interpellated as "guys like us" in this particular way, his wit remains a private matter between himself and the reader. He opts for the textual equivalent of a wry smile, thus preserving himself as outside the driver's group but also leaving the synecdoche the driver has evoked unquestioned—for all the driver knows, Sedaris is one of the "guys like us." This foreshadows a recurrent problem in "Reasons": Sedaris's reading does little to challenge the strong affects of "fear and anger about the loss of status" that propel Trumpist reading (Rowland 16). What Trump promises, and what many white men find appealing, is to restore their status by his very election to office: a key rhetorical move of Trumpist discourse is to "arouse a sense of threat and then resolve it by providing an answer in the form of himself" (25). The candidate-then-president promises that he will "generate massive changes through force of will" (33). As such, Trumpism offers a "fairytale that his election would produce almost immediate massive job and income gains." And as a fairy tale, it offers a narrative of magical intervention to achieve moral retribution and the permanent enshrining of status for its believers. It is a reading of the nation, then, of "us" and "them," true and false representatives, good and evil people, and of a demagogue whose power is divinely given and destined to destroy the other. Sedaris's silence might reflect his trademark anxiety and befuddlement, but it does not counter the fairy tale that lurks throughout his conversation with the driver, nor the strong affects that fuel it.

Sedaris's strategy of wry distance in the face of increasing extremism pays ever-worsening dividends once Trump is nominated by the Republican Party. Trumpism appears in friends of the family, one of whom tells him over the phone that the Clintons are members of the Illuminati and are remotely implicated in the death of the singer-songwriter Prince. "My friend gets almost feverish," Sedaris notes, "when he talks about these people and the way they're all connected: Queen Elizabeth leads to Jay-Z leads to the Center for Disease Control leads to the faked Sandy Hook shooting and the way the government handled 9/11" (188). In this moment, Sedaris's suspicion of essentialist pieties may have very well saved him from being "red-pilled," or indoctrinated into the conspiratorial thinking championed by Trump-supporting online entities such as QAnon that "portray state governments or state-run agencies either as independently motivated bad actors . . . or instruments in the thrall of criminal transnational organizations" (Packer and Stoneman 260). The "fever" Sedaris hears in his friend is the strong affect that motivates such conspiracism, "the near-reverential, quasi-fatalistic" affects adherents of QAnon feel "with respect to the state and symbols of state power" of which they claim to be the true representatives, in the face of a global elite so craven and evil that it tortures children in the basements of pizzerias, a nation that can only be saved if one properly reads Reddit pages for signs of the "Trump-directed counterinsurgency or counterconspiracy" underway to save democracy and humanity itself from a global—and perhaps reptilian—cabal (Packer and Stoneman 260, 259). To its fellow believers, QAnon provides a synecdochical web of people and events that point toward a sole source of malicious power, parts that build up to an insidious whole whose truth only they, as members of the *hoi oligoi*, can discern.

"You're kidding, right?" Sedaris asks the friend of the family (187). He checks his temptation to laugh and waits a beat for his friend to laugh and say, "Just kidding!" But the friend instead gives him the link to a website that hails Donald Trump "as a man of peace . . . the ones they hate are George Soros, of course, and surprisingly, Bill Gates, who has murdered more innocents than even the Clintons, apparently" (188). That Sedaris at first presumes the friend of the family to be joking also suggests how extremism has come to be masked as humor, and how this is manipulated for Trumpist ends. Indeed, the alt-right plays a "duplicitous rhetorical game" wherein the claim of "just kidding" serves as a shield under which much damage may ensue, where the alt-right's conflation of extremism with humor functions "as a sort of ideological lubricant to slide from the seemingly innocuous world of online lulz to serious harassment to, occasionally, brutal street violence" (Sienkiewicz and Marx 153). When the alt-right is presented as the hate groups they actually are, they often defend themselves by claiming "there's a sense of humor to this, there's an irony, there's a sarcasm to this," when in fact there is none at all (Gavin McInnes qtd. in Sienkiewicz and Marx 147). What the alt-right truly desires is the zealot's fantasy of a nation where "everything is familiar, everything is intelligible, and you don't feel alienated" because those deemed other by those in power have been forcibly excluded (Stern 55). The alt-right's lack of a rich inner life is evident in its facile and violent assumption that contentment can be achieved through enforcing racism, sexism, and classism. Nationalism, in the hands of such extremists, is never an "angle of participation in processes larger than ourselves" (Massumi 214). If the question "What is America?" requires an honest, multifaceted engagement to answer, the alt-right is uninterested. Indeed, as Thomas J. Main finds in his interviews with the alt-right's major figures, all show "little familiarity with relevant facts, no effort at research, no ability to entertain criticism, and a willingness to distort or suppress inconvenient evidence" (164). And it is through these that the alt-right can come to its major conclusions: that "politics is all about advancing the interests of your race," that only a select group of "wise people" should be allowed to vote, and if this is not possible, that the nation should be dissolved into "homelands" with walls similar to those once in Berlin and now in the West Bank (see Main 172, 147, 206).

Such nationalists are not genuinely interested in the transitive, generative power of synecdoche. Their use of synecdoche is deliberately limited to confirm the terrible severity of their us/them thinking. As Main notes, the alt-right often attempts to differentiate between the "United States" and what the movement claims is the "real America" they represent. But what doing so shows is how the alt-right uses synecdoche only to play a terrifying shell game that ultimately fails to conceal the distance between them and the nation as it was founded and as it currently exists. The alt-right rejects the premises of the Declaration of Independence, the *Federalist Papers,* and the United States Constitution. Alt-right supporters attempt to suspend the thinking of Jefferson, Hamilton, and Lincoln at specific points in time that favor their arguments, setting aside the evolution of these figures' thinking and their ultimate conclusions. Alt-right synecdoche is sophomoric semantic play: they may claim to be "pro-American" yet also claim to "hate the actually existing political entity known as the United States of America"; they may claim to be "pro-American" but only if that America is "the American nation as it had evolved up to 1960" (see Main 197, 200). The alt-right is not "American" at all—in the synecdoches it deploys, the ambiguities it abhors, the people it constructs. Indeed, it lacks the ability to imagine and wonder beyond the narcissism it holds itself in. The alt-right's affective palette is minimal: feelings of strength only through bullying and violence, feelings of pleasure only through the terrorizing and destroying of others, feelings of pride found only in adoration of the leader and the success of his petty squabbles. It is not only a poverty of thought but a poverty of affect. What Trumpists consider ecstasy is the unleashing of negative affect upon those deemed not "us."

When figurative language serves as a patina for violence, rhetoric no longer functions as a mode of genuine communion. It no longer works to open minds but to keep them closed: it does not open doors but closes them. First a stranger, then a friend of the family: what Sedaris's essay tracks is the gradual immurement those opposed to Trump increasingly feel, at first inwardly to the driver, then skeptically toward the friend of the family who he hopes is not serious but is "just kidding." The sphere in which one can practice a more plural form of nationalism increasingly begins to constrict as one goes from being indirectly to directly challenged, as one encounters first vague resentment then conspiracist vitriol. As Sedaris increasingly recognizes, Trumpism is a never-ending encroachment of strong affect into our lives. It aspires to override our readings of the nation with its own. The banalities of everyday life—riding in a car, talking to a family friend, surfing the web—become sites of Manichean dramas in which pressing economic and social issues are reduced to a single cause and solution, in which the nation becomes a site that is subsumed to the demagogue's dictates. What Sedaris indexes throughout "Reasons" is how the nation's parts become charged with strong affect in service of the Trumpist whole. Strong affect becomes inseparable from popular culture and daily life. The spheres that allow for a more honest, multifaceted engagement with the nation begin to disappear as the driver laments his status and as friends of the family feverishly foam at the mouth. Sedaris is increasingly weary, irritated, exhausted, isolated. And, ultimately, betrayed. On election night, cocooned in the Portland hotel room, Sedaris can only look at his television screen and say "Fuck you" when he sees the final results (189). This is what Trumpism does to both its adherents and its critics: it boils the "us" of the nation down to either total identification or utter disidentification.

The election does not end this bifurcation: Trumpist strong affect continues to encroach, no longer through a friend of the family but in the family itself. At Thanksgiving dinner, Sedaris and his father get into a "screaming fight" after his father tells him that "Donald Trump is not an asshole!" (190). Indeed, Sedaris's father claims that Trump "is the best thing that's happened to this country in years!" Sedaris's father has bought into Trump's positioning of himself as a redeemer of national value. He has absorbed the limited "dictionary of dignity" that Trumpists use, an almost senseless repeating of words such as "salute; respect; stand up; stand united" (Schaefer, "Whiteness" 9). Such rhetoric bonds the adherent's fears and hopes to the success of the leader. Yet it induces family shouting matches not only because members of a whole (the family) are divided, but also because Trumpism demands families, workspaces, and everyday places be divided between Trumpists and non-Trumpists. His father is so enamored by the president and his limited lexicon that he ignores his slack morality, his deprivation of the rights of women and minorities, his desire to turn homophobia into federal policy. His father believes in Trump so much that he is willing to vote for the man who seeks to injure, legally or otherwise, his own son. Sedaris's response to his father—"I thought the president-elect's identity as a despicable human being was something we could agree on. I mean, he pretty much ran on it" (190)—only activates more of his father's strong affect. "Reasons" in this way charts the diminution of language itself—gone is the wit and irony, the wordplay that weak affects find useful. Instead, it is replaced with a litany of curses—a sure sign that reflexive strong affect is in play. The potential for violence, even among family members, increases. Indeed, Sedaris's father proves to be one of many who bought into the candidate's construction of a "we" not as "a collective term for organizing political action through shared agency" but of a "we" that endures only through "survival as a violent struggle" (Johnson 196). As Paul Elliott Johnson notes, Trump's 2016 speech to the Republican National Convention featured a four-to-one ratio of descriptions of violence versus descriptions of stability—it was the imagining of a nightmare that "primed" the audience more for fear than security (see 191). Being an "asshole" to those marked other by the Trump regime became a sign of one's commitment to the cause—this is why Trumpism is what Lisa Duggan calls an "optimistic cruelty" that values meanness and greed, "the libido-infused desire for heroic achievement through contempt for social inferiors and indifference to their plight," a "moral economy of inequality" (xv, 10). In such a regime, "identification—am I the one inflicting the pain or the one suffering the pain?—becomes a form of nationalism" (Song 72). The Trumpist asshole's delight in making others suffer is also seen in their delight in obstruction, which takes the "thrill of contempt" and turns it into moments of personal glory (see Schaefer, "Whiteness" 6).

Such strong affects are proof that Trump's power is often more important to his followers than the honest truth.[2] For example, even though Trump lied about a supposed wiretap ordered by the Obama administration, Ohio Trump supporters saw it as exactly what they elected the president to do. "He's ruffling every feather in Washington he can ruffle," one supporter said, "So: yeah! I like it. I think it's a good thing. I want to see them jump around a little bit. He makes them uncomfortable, which makes me happy" (Dale). Some saw it as machismo: "Trump did that to freak them out—they were giving him bad times, so he gave them bad times. Mess with their brains . . . we've had so much crap in Washington for years, and now we have someone shaking 'em up really good" (Dale). Others saw Trump's lying as deliberately confusing the elite to draw them out—"when they're confused, they don't know what they're doing, they're going to make a mistake, and he's going to grab them" (Dale). In each of these responses, supporters provide the coherence that the candidate-then-president himself did not—they do the synecdochical work of connecting the parts of his erratic behavior to a whole political strategy. In effect, Trumpism gives its supporters the opportunity to place themselves as the conduits of transfer—they become the transitivity—between Trump and the national body. In each of these responses, there is an imagined physical parry between Trump and some undefined "them" who is the object of revenge for a never-announced slight. This is the performance of what Sara Ahmed notes of the strong nationalist maxim "spare the rod, spoil the nation" (*Willful Subjects* 130). Trump "ruffles," he makes others "jump" and "freak out," he "grabs" them, "shaking 'em up really good." Trump becomes a body in conflict with the body of government: he not only outwits but browbeats, sucker-punching at traditions and norms. This is presidential leadership by physical abuse—this is an ugly penchant for violence, manifested as a fight between demagogue and democracy. Trumpists need Trump to act as their body: in this way, Trumpists believe that they are invigorating the national body as theirs alone. What Trumpism offers its adherents is "a sense of confidence that is inseparable from arrogance" (Ben Anderson, "We Will Win").

Trumpism relishes "hate as a passionate attachment closely tied to love" (Ahmed, *Cultural Politics* 43). It is their nation to discipline and to admire, Trump and his adherents believe. And Trumpism offers its followers a nation in which "love means mutual idealization" (Berlant, "Trump"). Roderick P. Hart writes of how "Trump completes himself in others and people sense that" (54). Hart calls this a "needy populism" in which the candidate openly asks for his supporter's love and tells them in return, "I like you too. I love you" (Trump qtd. in Hart 55). It is a love, as "Reasons" shows, that obligates Trumpists to love their leader and in return feel anger at the leader's others, including one's own children. It is a love consumptive of its subject. As such, Trumpism is a strong nationalism that "perceives power and freedom in delusional self-buttressing from world destruction that they contribute to disproportionately" (Anker 158). What Trumpists want is a nation that is "national only insofar as it feels unmarked by the effects of national contradiction" (Berlant, *Queen* 4). In such conceiving of the nation, a physical constricting of the nation into "we," "us," and "them" can be profoundly felt. The walls are constructed that include or exclude through increasingly specific criteria that define true or false representatives.

The Depressed Reader on Inauguration Day

Trumpism is a nationalism in which the nation exists only in the most venal way: as a sign of support or dissent for the leader. America, in the Trump regime, becomes reduced to him as a person, his long-remembered slights and petty squabbles, which he takes the presidency as an opportunity to settle. The nation is about him and no one else. William E. Connolly describes Trump as the embodiment of "aspirational fascism": a mode of politics that is not necessarily fascistic but one that takes on its affective displays to encourage certain modes of attunement with an "authoritarian, narcissistic figure who aspires to squash critics and solicit unquestioned acclaim from subordinates and followers" (13). The "we," "us," and "them" of Trumpism is not defined by its citizens but by the demagogue. In this way, Trumpism is a diminution of language: it is the enactment of a nation that need not imagine itself because the leader does that for them. Not only does Trump's venal nationalism rob citizens of their acquaintances, friends, and family members. It also aspires to rob everyone of the language through which the nation can be imagined otherwise.

Its effects are profound. Falling from a loft on Christmas morning, Sedaris fractures eight ribs, which leaves him feeling "remarkably similar to how I felt after the election" (192). While the ribs eventually heal, he notes that "I will never be the same as I was before . . . the damage is permanent" (192–93). What Sedaris feels in his body is the physical pain through which depression is often manifested. But it is also the feeling of an individual being permanently outcast from the social body of the Trumpist nation. Sedaris's depression culminates on Inauguration Day, when an old friend emails him an image of an anti-Trump sticker from Japan. "As a joke," Sedaris responds, "'Dear Lyn, I'm sorry you're so opposed to change, or too small-minded to move past your narrow assumptions. In the future, I'd appreciate your keeping things like this to yourself'" (193). Who is Sedaris writing to in this email? Is he wryly jibing his friend about her emotional intensity—one that he feels, too? Or is he mimicking the Trump voter who, like his father, sees the president as a much-needed change? What Sedaris finds, depressingly, is that it doesn't matter. Perhaps insecure about the complex tone he has effected via email, he sends a follow-up that says "Just kidding," only to find that his email bounces back. Lyn, after thirty-eight years of friendship, has blocked him. (Here, Sedaris uses the same phrase that he wanted to hear his conspiracist friend of the family say, and that, even worse, is a key phrase used by the alt-right to justify their violence.) His militant use of irony—his irony of appearing a Trumpist militant among friends—fails. His attempt at humor has cost him a friend. "The news will spread and by morning I'll be ruined," Sedaris fears (193). "But it was just a joke, I say to myself in the dark room. A horrible, horrible joke." The "horrible joke" is not just the humiliation that Sedaris may endure as his friends learn of how he unintentionally severed his friendship. It is also the depression that comes from knowing that the distance between one and another is now unfathomable, that a gap can never be bridged, that one's wit has become not a source of communion but an impasse that cannot be unblocked. Depression may very well be the feeling of knowing that one's connection to others proves to be in vain, that in the attempt to elicit love, what is elicited is contempt. In this way, Sedaris shows how the course of the election ultimately leaves him misattuned.[3]

"Reasons" shows the risks of weak responses in strong nationalist times. On the one hand, it shows how the depressive's approach to reading further fuels a downward spiral of self-isolation and despair. While it manifests the slogan "Depressed? It Might Be Political!" in the most direct of ways, "Reasons" also shows how depression, in contrast to what some critics intuit, does not offer "sites of publicity and community formation" (Cvetkovich 2). In fact, Trumpism's peculiar affective calculus makes it impossible for depression to achieve this. Anger, perhaps, but Sedaris is not angry. Outrage, perhaps, but Sedaris's outrage has a particularly inward cast. Even when using himself as the object of irony, he finds himself all the more isolated: everything he does sheds friends. The gentler effects of irony do not suffice in demagogic times. As Sophia A. McClennen writes, "Because reality during the Trump era was already so deeply ironic, it became increasingly hard to find the right angle to expose the folly, farce, and fears brought on by the Trump presidency." There is always the danger that one's irony will be taken unironically even under normal circumstances: at a time in which the alt-right claims to use sarcasm and irony, this is even more dangerous. Indeed, as Linda Hutcheon writes, irony is always more likely to be misinterpreted than interpreted correctly. "Those whom you oppose might attribute no irony and simply take you at your word; or they might make irony happen and thus accuse you of being self-negating if not self-contradicting," Hutcheon notes (16). Yet even "those with who[m] you agree (and who know your position) might also attribute no irony and mistake you for advocating what you are in fact criticizing. They may simply see you as a hypocrite or as compromised by your complicity with a discourse and values they thought you opposed. They might also, of course, attribute irony and interpret it precisely as you intended it to be."

But the latter option is just one of many, and none of those Sedaris encounters in "Reasons" see it this way. The rise of Trump shows how those who love figurative language become utterly literal, how reasonable people become unreasonable, how friend can no longer read friend.

Depression's admixture of love and contempt no longer teaches in a nation where love and contempt are proffered by the demagogue's needy populism, his aspirational fascism. Irony no longer offers communion. If anything, its use in precarious times makes the user a horrible joke all their own. "Reasons" ends with Sedaris in physical pain and entirely alone, risking ruin, depressed in the loss of his confidants and in the loss of the language that made him a distinctive commentator. Humor, as Sedaris uses it in "Reasons," may help one "figure out what lines we desire or can bear" (Berlant and Ngai 235). But at the same time, "Reasons" shows how what once elicited laughter now only elicits tears, how it now creates the physical pain and mental anguish one is forced to bear when one's nation is reduced to a demagogue's antidemocratic desires.

Conclusion

Life in America seems a horrible joke after the election of Donald Trump. Going through the election, we got to know each other in a way we did not want. We became too much of ourselves for others to handle with any camaraderie or nuance. We found ourselves in the position of being depressed, not just emotionally, but politically. As Hannah Arendt writes at the end of *The Origins of Totalitarianism,* the work of dictatorship requires "destroying all space between men and pressing men against each other" (478). When people are pressed together they become violent—this is what the demagogue delights in. When people are pressed together there is no time to imagine—this is what the demagogue wants. Friction is not only inevitable but demanded in the Trump years—if we did not become glued together under the impress of the demagogue, then we would certainly vanish. The goal of it all was to make us feel as lonely as Sedaris does at the end of the essay, for the world of the demagogue is a world in which "nobody is reliable and nothing can be relied upon" (Arendt 478). And the goal of it all was to rob us of the language that makes democracy possible, for the world of the demagogue is one without ambiguity, irony, or humor: it is a world "whose only content is the strict avoidance of contradictions."

Such a world is the sum of interpellation. The world the Trumpist wants is one where "gestures of discomfort and alienation do not register" (Ahmed, *Promise* 42). Every day, the demagogue refreshes the drama between "us" and "them," giving old enemies new nicknames, praising the latest sycophants through an endless "game of bad metaphors" (Esty ix).[4] Quickly the nation becomes not *one* "we" imagine but *the one* the demagogue imagines for "us." It is a nation where our own affects are subordinate to our place as conduits in the demagogue's body. In such a nation, in the minds of each lives not a fellow member but instead lives the image of the demagogue. This is where strong nationalism leads, and for many who support Trump, the idea that democracy must be set aside for such an unambiguous nation to be built is appealing. Sedaris's exasperation, his impatience, his pain, his fatigue: all of these are responses to the "normalization of a frenetic chaos and hyperactivism" that characterizes the nation under Trump (Grossberg, *Under the Cover* 3). Strong affect is complicit in this chaos and hyperactivism: raising the volume, creating more noise, raising the stakes in ways that erode norms and attract extremists, in the creation of a time in which "no crisis that has come has passed" (Ogden 17).

Trumpism is far from a joke. When in power, it does exactly what it promised to do: it defines who is and who is not a person, who has and does not have rights, who is and who is not a citizen—definitions that are the utmost serious. Indeed, the glib, snide, simple way in which Trumpists bandy about such terms shows their ugly insouciance toward those who fought hard to earn such designations. Strong nationalism depresses other forms of nationalism, then extinguishes them, and in doing so robs citizens of an inclusive, varied, plural nation—weak in all the best senses. Sedaris's "Reasons" shows how irony in the face of demagoguery saves no one and only condemns oneself: the essay shows indeed how depressing is all that comes with Trump. And what the depression that manifests in the essay shows is the truth of strong nationalism, that the strength of strong nationalism gets the nation nowhere.

CONCLUSION

The Nation Needs Reading

Throughout this book, I have examined how strong affect produces a nation of "we," "us," and "them" that is counter to the premise of the nation as a diverse, imagined community. From Steinbeck's hawkish reading of the Vietnam War, which leads him to demagogic conclusions, to Thompson's bilious reading, which poaches from populist discourse without ever constructing a truly popular vision of the nation; from Baldwin's insistence of, and investment in, the nation as a site of futility, to Vance's promulgation of a politics of resentment that seeks to establish the nation as a bastion of neoconservatism, and finally to Sedaris's attempts to ironically distance himself from Trumpism, which ultimately distances himself from everyone—what we see in these narratives is how the reduction of the nation creates not a nation at all. Lacking the full diversity that comes with real community, these texts mutter among themselves, certain in how they have defined something that no one text, nor any one person, can define.

That strong nationalists accomplish this through reading parts for wholes to answer the question "What is America?" is thus to pinpoint the problem—but also the promise—of reading itself. Strong nationalist texts are a reminder that the nation is always in need of reading, not by those who illiberally claim to be its only true representatives, but by those whose very presence challenges such limiting representations. Strong nationalist texts also remind us that unless critics draw attention to the shoddy synecdochical construction of their narratives and the monochromatic affective intensities that emerge from them, more diverse forms of imagining the nation remain inchoate and unspoken. Critics need to counter what strong nationalists insist the nation is by dismantling the affective construction of their insistence. The nation needs critical reading, a reading that exposes its strong nationalism's hasty construction and the ersatz confidence that comes from their use of synecdoche not to create but to contain. Such a criticism asks: How do these texts attempt to limit and foreclose what is imaginative and ambiguous?

Does the use of synecdoche open up the field of participants, or does it close it down? How do these texts engineer a feeling of certainty that is uninterested in democracy? Do they offer new intensities or maintain already existing ones? Critics need to read narratives of strong nationalism for the "particular solidarities" of nationhood their language unfurls (Benedict Anderson 133).

At the same time, the nuances of critical reading practices will be what saves us from falling into the strong nationalist's trap, for just as strong affects produce narrow readings of the nation, just as worrisome, they also encourage the production of even narrower readings in response. Affect theory helps stanch this encouragement, for its innovation comes from its reminder that "binary divisions between positive and negative affects don't do justice to the qualitative nuances of feeling that are only crudely captured by such designations" (Cvetkovich 6). There is always something more at work in a text that claims to be the sole true representative or claims to identify false ones. Indeed, to see something as good or bad, as rational or as emotional, as friend or foe, is to narrow the circle of inquiry into something reflexive, diagnostic, and myopic—which is exactly what the strong nationalist wants. But affect theory encourages critics to read across such divisions, not to salvage them but to think otherwise. In eschewing simple classifications, affect theory sets aside the crudeness of strong nationalist prose for a more thorough probing of the nationalist's narrative work, and in doing so, it captures the dishonesty—the simplifications, shortcuts, stereotypes—that saturates such narratives. It is our very attention to affect and how affect suffuses interpretation, how it is lodged in the words we use and the synecdoches we evoke, that refuses to be contained by a single leader or a definitive answer. Affect theory is ultimately a reminder that synecdoche is not the mortar that builds walls but is instead the "metonymic slide" from person to person that proves greater than any one person, and greater than any one definition, of the nation (Ahmed, *Cultural Politics* 44).

Affect theory shows critics how strong nationalisms can be alluring. After all, strong affect sacrifices a more problematic understanding of the nation for short-term ideological satisfaction, bartering away democracy for the cheap thrill of intense personal conviction. Yet more importantly, affect theory critically undermines strong nationalism's legitimacy by reading for its unsteady premises and impermanent satisfactions. And affect theory offers the constant reminder not to succumb to strong nationalist frenzy or to let it depress us into apathy. To probe the strong nationalist's emotionality is to unravel the knot of ugly feelings, the ugly freedoms that have turned into a theory of the nation. I would go so far as to suggest that affect theory is both a prelude to and a manual for alternative solidarities than the type the strong nationalist offers. The way in which strong nationalists use synecdoche should remind us of how we can use rhetoric to read—and build—communities of our own. What strong nationalists make barren we can make fertile by deploying figurative language not to imprison but to liberate. For what strong nationalists cannot fathom is that "to identify with something is not to be identical with it" (Felski, "Identifying" 80). What they cannot fathom is what critics should do: read and study and offer a nation that is "the rough ground of resemblance rather than pure sameness" (80). The strong nationalist's ugly use of language should compel us to seize it back, if only to remind ourselves, and those with whom we commune, that words matter. And in this way, the question "What is America?" is not a fanciful or mundane one but one that harkens to the defamiliarizing power of language itself. The nation is always more encompassing, more plastic, more democratic than what the strong nationalist wants. The great myth of strong nationalism is that it is the only form of nationalism. Yet there are many other forms of imagined communities that await our reading of them.

The nation is always worth reading. And it is always in need of reading. As Martin Griffin and Christopher Herbert write, "A representative democracy, in which we permit others to speak on our behalf, allows the pride of empowerment when we are pleased with the state of affairs; but just as often it provides us the option for plausible deniability when we are dismayed" (xiii). The nation is pliable: it can be the container for virtually anything we wish it to contain, or virtually anything we wish it not to contain. Indeed, it is because the nation can stand for so many things (or the very absence of those things) that endows it with both feeling and meaning. The nation is at its least democratic—its least representative—when its interpreters are motivated by strong affect to boil complex problems down to one demagogic solution. The nation is at its most democratic—its most representative—when the narratives that seek to answer the question "What is America?" are crude, general, and weak enough for them to be perpetually revised and ever expanded, and when the answer captures enchantment and disenchantment, pleasures and displeasures, the sum of ourselves and others.

If the question is "What is America?," the answer to that question is "Affect." And not just one affect, but a penumbra of affects. The synecdoches that emerge in an honest answer to this question do not bracket the nation to one ugly feeling.[1] The plurality of affects the nation evokes is a reminder that no one conception of the nation has omnipotence: it may at times induce strong affects of fanaticism or frenzy but more importantly induce moderate affects of "mutual responsibility, significant interaction, and a cooperative spirit" (May 170). To discern the nation's affective variegations requires an "uneasy copresence of theories, methods, and modes which might enable both a granular complexity of response as well as an enlarged terrain of the critical encounter" (Coviello 87).[2] Thus to study nationalism through affect is to realize and celebrate how "the United States is neither New York nor Texas nor Main Street. It is, somehow, scattered among all of these" (Grossberg, *Dancing* 129). What is needed to see this is a way of reading that is like, as Lawrence Grossberg suggests, "driving by the billboards that mark the system of interstate highways, county roads, and city streets that is the United States" (*Dancing* 128). To read for a strong nationalism is to read for the starkness of the signposts on display, for the narrowing road that inevitably leads to a terrible destination. But to read the nation as a site of alternative solidarities is to read equipped with the lens of affect, to see the beaming and sorrowful faces of its citizens, to hear the whoops and yawps of all those who live there, and to realize that narratives are never final destinations but the beginnings of the voyage to visit one's fellow neighbors and learn the myriad ways of being "we." Thus the nation is always more than what strong nationalists say it is, feels it to be. We need to resist their tendency to simplify the nation's affective spectrum into one dull color: we need to see the promise in what they dismiss when they write of the nation as a mere "interpretation of predicaments" (Ngai, *Ugly Feelings* 3). When strong nationalists insist that the nation be a "daily plebiscite," we should be prepared to counter their urgency with a calmer, confident response (Ernest Renan qtd. in Bhabha 310). What I have tried to do in this book is show how theories of affect help do this. And in doing so, I offer that reading these texts for their affects is a way to not only understand what the strong nationalist says, but to create the space in which critics and others can restore the scales to what the strong nationalist has imbalanced, so that we all may more carefully weigh nationalism and its protean ambiguities.

NOTES

INTRODUCTION

1. Brooks's concerns are not exactly new. As Natasha Zaretsky notes, concern for "behavior codes" percolates throughout American nonfiction, particularly in books such as Christopher Lasch's *The Culture of Narcissism*, which conflate upward mobility with hedonism and a "crisis of accumulation" that can only be tamed by more prudent consumption and sterner father figures (221). Nor is the concern about the smothering mother a new one: as Zaretsky also notes, it was brought into plain view in books such as Philip Wylie's *Generation of Vipers*, which assert that "America's democratic ideals were under threat by mothers who wielded too much power" (8).

2. Perhaps this is why Brooks has become known as "the liberals' favorite conservative," for through his synecdochical writing, he ultimately positions himself as spokesman for a "polymorphous opposition" who is able to "articulate the discontents it held in common" (Kinsley; Kazin 274). He may be its favorite because he does this so badly.

3. Brooks's article was lambasted after its publication. Caitlin Dewey of the *Washington Post* reminded readers that the Mexican food that Brooks and his friend ultimately agreed to lunch upon could be just as elite and expensive as the Italian eatery they departed: "lower-class ≠ Mexican," she effectively diagrammed (Dewey). Others took the "Ruining" article as an opportunity to revisit a study of Brooks's writing by the *Philadelphia* magazine journalist Sasha Issenberg, who, following up on claims made in his 2004 book *Bobos in Paradise*, found that "many of his generalizations are false" and that some of the material he passed as fact (business names; purchasing data) "were entirely manufactured" (Issenberg). Issenberg found it "increasingly hard to believe that Brooks ever left his home."

4. Brooks's writing in particular frequently descends into what Jed Esty calls "declinism," a genre of writing that claims to offer proof of American decline through "moralized narratives" that rely upon thin evidence: as Esty notes, their potency is more in their theory of reading for decline, as "how-to manuals about how to recognize or reverse the loss of superpower status" than the supposed decline they document (2).

5. As Cynthia Enloe notes, "even when they have been energized by nationalism, many women have also discovered that, in practice, as women, they

have often been treated by male nationalist leaders and intellectuals as symbols—patriarchally sculpted symbols—of the nation. . . . being reduced to a symbol has meant that women have not even [been] treated as genuine participants (with their own ideas, goals, and skills) in nationalist movements" (87).

6. Orwell notes a similar effect in his essay "Notes on Nationalism," though he frames it not affectively but instead ethnically, as a "dislocation" in nationalist writing that shows an "indifference to reality" (12).

7. Synecdoche is the substitution of a part for a whole such that "a reduction is a *representation*" (Burke 507, emphasis in original). As Kenneth Burke notes, synecdoche is "present in all theories of political representation, where some part of the social body . . . is held to be 'representative' of the society of the whole" (508). And while he acknowledges that "there are many disagreements within a society as to what part should represent the whole and how this representation should be accomplished," Burke also notes that "representation automatically implies a synecdochic relationship (insofar as the act is, or is held to be, 'truly representative')" (508). Thus synecdoche, as a representation, is inherently political because the extent to which any synecdoche is "truly representative" is always under debate.

8. As the philosopher Kate Manne writes, for example, the strong affects that drive misogyny frame individual women "as interchangeable and representative of a certain type of woman . . . standing in imaginatively for a large swathe of others" (58). The only way this can persuasively function is if the misogynist's rhetoric is "punitive, resentful, and personal, but not particular" (59). Misogynists, like strong nationalists, poach synecdoche's tactics but ultimately derive something quite different than representation from those tactics: the production of types instead of a complex, diverse people.

1. HAWKISHNESS

1. Paradoxically, Steinbeck proposed using napalm at the same time as the American public was becoming aware of the weapon's gruesome effects. As the American press began circulating images of Vietnamese women and children who were permanently scarred by napalm, self-labeled "housewives" began blocking the factories that produced it. Steinbeck makes no mention of the protests in his letter to Valenti: one wonders, given Steinbeck's notorious chauvinism, if he saw at all the "reputably dressed" women "wearing high heels, stockings, gloves, and pearls" (Wells 85).

2. The long course of Steinbeck's nonfiction merits its own study. However, it is worth noting that the "Letters to Alicia" (published in book form as

Steinbeck in Vietnam) depart from his previous writing in two fundamental ways. First is Steinbeck's departure from use of synecdoche to produce positive affect. For instance, in *Bombs Away* (1942), Steinbeck inventively uses synecdoche to focus each chapter on an individual member of an air force bomber team, from basic training to their first sortie. In his use of synecdoche, he shows how each member of the bomber team is necessary for the success of the whole, and how these individuals will "once, established, remain as a unit," having developed a bond that transcends propaganda, fascistic indoctrination, or "manufactured" comradeship (154, 156). In the "Letters," by contrast, Steinbeck's use of synecdoche produces negative affect either by thorough bellicosity toward the Vietcong, contempt for the South Vietnamese, or condemnation of the war protestors at home. Second is Steinbeck's departure from a self-conscious sense of tolerance. In his *A Russian Journal* (1948) for instance, he begins the travelogue by writing, "We knew there would be many things we couldn't understand, many things we wouldn't like, many things that would make us uncomfortable. But we determined that if there should be criticism, it would be criticism of the thing after seeing it, not before" (4). In effect, Steinbeck deliberately suspends his disbelief in order to depict a nation that was quickly becoming the United States' main rival. The effect is to produce a travelogue that, by his own words, "will not be satisfactory either to the ecclesiastical Left, nor the lumpen Right" (212). There is no similar self-statement of tolerance in the "Letters." Steinbeck did not go to Vietnam to suspend his disbelief: he went to find proof of what he believed.

3. For the purposes of this chapter, page numbers are derived from *Steinbeck in Vietnam* and appear parenthetically. Dates of publication in *Newsday*, when included in Steinbeck's book, appear in the notes. These quotes were published in *Newsday* on May 20, 1967; March 4, 1967; January 7, 1967, respectively.

4. "Hawkishness," *Oxford English Dictionary* (https://www.oed.com/). The "war hawk" has been a figure of American politics from its inception (see Hickey). But it was not until the Cuban Missile Crisis that the word "hawk" and its opposite, "dove," were thoroughly popularized through the journalism of Stewart Alsop and Charles Bartlett, who identified the president's advisers according to these attributes in an influential *Saturday Evening Post* article (15–21). The hawks "favored an air strike to eliminate the Cuban missile bases, either with or without warning," while the doves "opposed the air strike and favored the blockade" (20). Later, the hawk/dove distinction would be used by pollsters to frame support for the Johnson administration's Vietnam policies. The political scientists Philip E.

Converse and Howard Schuman, for instance, asked those surveyed to position themselves as hawks who "believe that the US did the right thing in attempting to stem the tide of Communism in Southeast Asia and that the nation should now escalate its military efforts to achieve victory" or as doves who "rue the fact that American troops ever became involved in Vietnam and demand their immediate withdrawal" (20).

5. As Charles DeBenedetti writes, the American public "were willing, but they were not purposeful" in their war-making efforts (209). And as William Conrad Gibbons notes, even when support for the war was at its highest, a Gallup Poll in June 1967 reported that only 48 percent "had a clear idea of what the Vietnam War is all about" (692).

6. January 7, 1967. Steinbeck's characterization of the Degar worrisomely parallels their fictional depiction in Robin Moore's 1965 novel *The Green Berets*. As "the symbolic opposites to the Vietnamese and the French," the Degar are presented in Moore's book much like contemporary accounts of the Native American, "as premoral creatures . . . generous, accepting, and loyal, they are also given to riotous ceremonies and undisciplined blood lust" (Hellmann, *American Myth* 62). Seeing them as noble savages, Americans are entrusted to "protect them from the communists as well as from the Royal Laotians and the South Vietnamese" (62). For Moore, "the Montagnards embody the natural drives that the Green Berets must use, restrain, and indulge in a controlled manner for larger ends" (62). The Montagnard thus comes to embody the instincts of the Berets themselves, albeit unrestrained by military discipline and ideological superiority. The Montagnard is reduced to the id, the Beret to the ego, of the American psyche.

7. January 7, 1967.

8. February 27, 1967.

9. February 27, 1967.

10. As Richard Slotkin notes, the "cowboy" and "frontier" metaphors were prevalent throughout the Kennedy and Johnson administrations. Agents deployed by the CIA to undermine the Castro regime were nicknamed "cowboys," and Johnson told soldiers going to Vietnam to "bring the coon skin home and nail it to the barn" (496).

11. December 31, 1966.

12. April 15, 1967.

13. February 20, 1967.

14. In doing so, Steinbeck offers evidence of General Maxwell Taylor's claim that "there is no George Washington in sight" among the South Vietnamese leadership (see Slotkin 542).

15. By this, Ngai means the ascribing of value to "that which seems to differ, in a yet-to-be-conceptualized way from a general expectation

or norm whose exact concept may itself be missing" (*Our Aesthetic Categories* 112).

16. April 15, 1967.
17. February 11, 1967.
18. February 11, 1967.
19. December 31, 1966.
20. February 4, 1967.
21. January 19, 1967; February 9, 1967.
22. February 11, 1967.
23. February 11, 1967.
24. The domino theory evoked a cascade of metaphors. John F. Kennedy told the American Friends of Vietnam in 1956 that the country "represents the cornerstone of the Free World in Southeast Asia, the keystone to the arch, the finger in the dike" preventing "the Red Tide of Communism" from overtaking the continent (618).
25. February 11, 1967.
26. The costs of hawkish policy are as literal as they are metaphorical. In a January 1966 letter to Ambassador Henry Cabot Lodge, Secretary of State Dean Rusk laments that the war was costing the U.S. government "some $120,000 per Viet Cong" casualty, yet he ultimately concluded that it would be "worth any amount to win in Vietnam" (see Gibbons 172).
27. As Jennifer R. Mercieca defines it, demagoguery is the weaponization of communication such that leaders prevent themselves "from being held accountable, from being questioned, debated, from having to give good reasons and persuade" and thus avoid and ultimately disregard "a commitment to the democratic process" by refusing to "respect political opposition, discourage violence, and protect civil liberties" (270).
28. January 7, 1967.
29. January 7, 1967.
30. January 7, 1967.
31. January 7, 1967.
32. January 7, 1967.
33. January 7, 1967.
34. Privately, Steinbeck brooded over the possibility of defeat. To him, losing Vietnam would be proof that "we cannot win this war, nor any war for that matter" (*Life in Letters* 848). He confided to his longtime editor Elizabeth Otis in August 1967, "We seem to be sinking deeper and deeper into the mire. . . . When we have put down a firm foundation of our dead and when we have by a slow, losing process been sucked into the texture of Southeast Asia, we will never be able nor will we want to get out" (848). But this is not so much an admission of the impossibility of the American

mission in Vietnam as it is an example of how hawks read defeat in the same escalating, reactive ways that they do victory. It is also a position that is more reflective of Steinbeck's interpretive impasse to which his use of hawkish synecdochalization leads. Even if his personal opinion evolved, he continues to ignore the growing number of war protestors—his "we" being sucked into the mire does not seem to include them—all the while refusing to formulate an exit strategy.

35. As Maria Ryan notes, hawks from across the political spectrum who endorsed the second Iraq war blamed the Bush administration instead of questioning their endorsement. "Whereas the neocons believed that their project was strategically essential but ruined by Bush's incompetence, the liberal hawks still conceived of the invasion as an idealistic endeavor, just one that had gone wrong" (689).

2. BILE

1. Though he does not mention specifics, one presumes that Booth has in mind two infamous incidents that Thompson provoked while on the 1972 campaign trail: in March, Thompson gave his press pass for the Edmund Muskie campaign to an accomplice who boarded Muskie's train and harassed its occupants throughout their travels in Florida (see *Campaign Trail* 88–91). The next month, Thompson invented a rumor that Muskie's poor performance during the Democratic primary was due to his addiction to an esoteric West African stimulant named Ibogaine, which led him to be "almost paralyzed by hallucinations at the time that he looked out at the crowd and saw gila monsters instead of people," suggesting that "his mind completely snapped when he felt something large and apparently vicious clawing at his legs" (135).

2. Thompson's fascination with Wallace continued into the 1972 campaign. Attending a Wallace rally, he notes, "The air was electric even before he started talking, and by the time he was five or six minutes into his spiel I had a sense that the bastard had somehow levitated himself and was hovering over us" (*Campaign Trail* 139). In one of the book's weirdest mixed metaphors, Thompson writes that the frenzy felt by Wallace's blue-collar, proto-conservative audience of "beer-drinking factory workers" "reminded me of a Janis Joplin concert" (139). And as a friend might suggest that one go to a band's concert, Thompson encouraged readers to "go out and catch his act sometime . . . it was a flat-out fire & brimstone *performance*" (139, emphasis in original). Thompson could not help but make a jab at Wallace's populist theatricality—perhaps thinking back to how he saw himself as its authentic progenitor in his campaign for sheriff—but in

doing so, he gave more subcultural cache to Wallace than anyone would have otherwise imagined.

3. Thompson's commitment to public displays of outrage and his promise to turn everyday life into an ongoing antagonizing of the mainstream "they," when read without its humor, is not only the problem of George Wallace–style populism but presages the problem of twenty-first-century Trumpism, which sees itself as the "face of white nationalism" that "revels in taboo performances, nihilism, sadism, masochism, death, lawlessness, and cathartic acts of violence" (Kelly 2).

4. And in almost winning the sheriff's race, Thompson would cement himself as part of Aspen's mythology, proof that the village was "politically progressive and full of unique characters," with "adult forms of fun and entertainment, namely drugs and a more libertine approach to sex" (Stuber 43, 39). Yet he would cement himself in mythos alone: the cost of living in Aspen continued to climb as the "messy vitality" of the 1960s and early 1970s became a core part of its expansive corporate brand (Stuber 41). In contemporary terms, the sociologist Jenny Stuber notes that "an individual earning $300,000 a year—a member of the top 1 percent in many US communities—qualifies for subsidized housing in Aspen" (55).

5. The result of bilious reading is a false equivalency that led to errors in its attempts to expose the "terrible logic to it all" (Thompson in Torrey and Simonson 182). Even in September 1972, when the polls had Nixon ahead by an epic landslide, Thompson wrote that McGovern would probably lose by 5.5%: in a footnote written after the election, he noted—in a rare moment of understatement—that "I was somewhat off on this prediction. The final margin was almost 23%" (*Campaign Trail* 386).

6. Of Nixon, see "Fear and Loathing in the Bunker"; "Fear and Loathing at the Watergate"; and "Fear and Loathing in Washington." Of Gerald Ford, see "Fear and Loathing in Limbo," and for Ali, see "Fear and Loathing in the Near Room" and "Fear and Loathing in the Far Room," all anthologized in *The Great Shark Hunt*. See also "Fear and Loathing in Sacramento" in *Songs of the Doomed* and "Fear and Loathing in Elko" in *Kingdom of Fear*.

7. The ability for the "American Dream" to arouse strong affect might be more clearly seen in its opposite, the trope of the "American Nightmare," which, Pamela Hunt Steinle writes, became just as commonplace by the mid-1960s. The usage of these phrases, Steinle notes, reflects midcentury "increasingly distanced" cultural ideals: the rhetoric of the Dream posited a nation that was "destined to guide the world as a democratic nation of regenerative innocence, selfless individualism, and consequent ingenuity," while the rhetoric of the Nightmare "focused on extremes of social order and chaos, individual alienation and increasing conformity, monolithic

unity and the threat of impending nuclear annihilation wrought by our own technological ingenuity" (156).

8. It is the trouble of bilious reading that any event seen in retrospect, personal or critical, can be made to justify their reading and thus keep the feedback loop of negative attunement alive. (Thompson would read his 1990 arrest for drug possession and sexual assault as his being "on trial for Sex, Drugs, and Rock and Roll," as if his indiscretions were being used to adjudicate an entire generation [*Songs of the Doomed* 336–37]). For instance, it may be tempting to assert that Thompson wrote of an early version of what became known as "Californian ideology," posited by Richard Barbrook and Andy Cameron as the mixture of cultural bohemianism and private enterprise which leads to both staggering economic inequality in the state and a naive national faith that the "electronic marketplace can somehow solve America's pressing social and economic problems without any sacrifices on their part" (Barbrook and Cameron). But to do so is to give bilious reading an insight it did not possess at the time, and an interest in the future that its focus on sustaining strong affect does not have.

3. FUTILITY

1. In this way, Yardley unfortunately participates in a critical tactic that, as Sarah Winstein-Hibbs notes, Baldwin endured throughout his career: of being scapegoated as "the flaming figurehead of a politics too 'young'" and of a temperament "'too 'angry' to be taken seriously" (296).

2. As Lowe notes, Baldwin was told by an "old friend" that the suspect in the Atlanta murders was a member of "an underground of black closet homosexuals, many of whom were firmly entrenched political and financial power brokers in Atlanta" (54).

3. Baldwin notes that such wild theorizing continued even once Wayne Bertram Williams was identified as a suspect. The cold dynamics of the Williams family was explained in a popular theory that "the father, subsequent to some grim scandal involving boys, sodomized the son, thus giving the son a lethal blackmail power over him, this accounting for their (allegedly) icy relationship" (*Evidence* 72).

4. Here Baldwin adopts a synecdochical perspective on the institution of American slavery also held by Malcolm X that "there are two kinds of Negroes. There was that old house Negro and the field Negro. And the house Negro always looked out for his master. When the field Negroes got too much out of line, he held them back in check. He put them back on the plantation" (*Evidence* 63). To Malcolm X, the house Negro would do anything to help the master even if doing so brought death to the field

Negro: he associated himself with the field Negro who, if the master became ill, would pray for his death.

5. We may be tempted to read futility as pessimism if only because, as Oliver Bennett reminds us, pessimism is a familiar component of the critical tradition: from Arthur Schopenhauer to Max Weber, from Sigmund Freud to Horkheimer and Adorno, much of what we call critique is based upon a pessimistic worldview (see 1–20). It is also a familiar component of the American literary tradition, as Dienstag notes, present in the works of Melville, Twain, Henry Adams, and W. E. B. DuBois, all of whom were influential upon Baldwin's style (see 45). In other words, critics are highly conversant in pessimism: many a monograph has focused on how decline, however defined, can form the beginning, middle, and end of a critical problem.

6. Reagan's rise also aligns with the resurgence of white supremacy, as in the 1970s "Klansmen and neo-Nazis united against communism at the same time that elements of the left fractured and collapsed under the pressure of internal divisions and government infiltration" (Belew 60). Such groups often targeted veterans for recruitment, using the failure of Vietnam to point toward national failure and using Iran-Contra to point to the emergence of a "New World Order" bent on destroying individual liberty. By the end of Reagan's presidency, a militia movement had grown alongside a national white power movement that "bridged regional and class identities," intertwining "antigovernment paramilitarism" and "overt racism" (192).

7. Baldwin's claim would be supported by scholars such as Dean E. Robinson, who notes that both civil rights actions and Black nationalist movements continue to lack a comprehensive, national audience. "In contrast to the March on Washington in 1963, the Million Man March [1995] had no clear policy agenda. . . . If anything, Farrakhan and the March reproduced conservative tendencies" (Robinson 125). Its appeal came not in a universalizing message but in its adoption of the Reaganite presumption that systemic race and class barriers are instead cultural and individual issues. "The marchers agreed that black men had particular responsibilities in need of address; and in this and other respects, the Million Man March articulated sentiments not unlike those of the evangelical Christian men's group the Promise Keepers, who are determined to reassert themselves as proper heads of their households and who root that alleged mandate in scripture" (125).

4. Resentment

1. There is no shortage of books, popular or scholarly, that take aim at Vance's characterizations of "hillbillies." In addition to Harkins (*Hillbilly*) and Isenberg (*White Trash*), see Catte (*What You Are Getting Wrong*). Nor is there a shortage of texts that examine the deployment of racially charged resentment to shore up conservative political power: in addition to Skocpol and Williamson (*Tea Party*), see D. Carter (*Politics of Rage*) and C. Anderson (*White Rage*).

2. Similarly, as Søren Kierkegaard writes, the goal of resentment is to "belittle" the superior so that it is no longer "distinguished" (26–27).

3. One should never underestimate resentment's willingness to bite the hands that feed it. As one journalist observed of Vance's 2022 campaign for the United States Senate, he "is still framing himself as a conservative champion of the dispossessed—one who's no longer fixating on the perceived failings of the people he grew up with, but on the professional class to which he ascended" (van Zuylen-Wood).

4. Vance is at present a United States senator for Ohio. How this affects the premise of his memoir he has not commented on.

5. That Vance describes this in terms of personal affect ("deep anger") instead of terms of structural social and economic inequality is telling. As Anthony Harkins writes, the stereotype of the hillbilly is bolstered by capitalists who use it as a "foil for industrial exploitation" to depict a "diseased, illiterate, undernourished, sexually promiscuous, and degenerate people" in need of corporate paternal benevolence, a "hopelessly isolated and irrationally violent" people who could be tamed through manual labor (56).

6. Harkins notes that the word "hillbilly" is a combination of the words "hillfolk" and "billie," a Scots-Irish synonym for "fellow" or "companion" that first appears in print in the 1900s, though its use likely began decades before (48). As a cultural type, the hillbilly is an amalgam of earlier stereotypical characterizations of "mountain folk" prevalent since the American Revolution: "rural rube[s]" whose conduct and way of life run counter to civil society (21). Of particular note are the hillbilly's unrestrained affects—their sudden swings from apathy to violence in particular—which are often depicted in such characterizations for comedic effect.

7. As Rachel Sherman notes in her study of the anxieties of the affluent, even among the wealthy, being a "good person [is] not to be entitled" (23–24).

8. The insights produced from such resentful rumination are at best partial: while reflection seeks to understand a problem, rumination only seeks to judge it (see André 44).

9. This also explains Vance's positive portrayal of payday lending in the memoir, which, for him, solves an "important financial problem" for hill-billies when he writes a check for his rent without depositing his paycheck and uses a payday loan to cover the check (185). The "few dollars of interest" to the payday lender enable him to "avoid a significant overdraft fee" from the bank: in effect, Vance has enough money to play one bank against the other and come out on top (185). As Dore, Connor, and Sinykin note, Vance's description of Ohio legislation to curb payday lenders shows less the legislator's "appreciation" of Vance's problem than it does lobbying and regulatory evasion. Eventually, "All the lenders that might have been covered by the act reclassified themselves and went on lending at outrageous rates."

10. It is also a tactic that Hirschman sees at work in one of the few texts that Vance cites in his memoir, Charles Murray's *Losing Ground,* which Hirschman describes as "a slight toning down of nineteenth-century coloratura" attacks on the welfare state (*Rhetoric* 29).

11. Carol Anderson notes that "the trigger for white rage, inevitably, is black advancement" (3). Obama, as a synecdoche for Black advancement, embodies "blackness with ambition, with drive . . . that refuses to accept subjugation, to give up" (Carol Anderson 3–4). It is worth noting that Obama is marked as alien in *Elegy* not only for his race, but for his affects in which resentment is not dominant. And it is also worth noting that the whites Vance describes in *Elegy* use resentment—a false sense of being subjugated by entitled others—to critique and denigrate those who refuse to give up. Resentment thus stokes the fire of rage and culminates in spite.

12. Indeed, it seems that Vance has successfully beaten his fellow Ohioans at their own game, weaponizing "their resentments and cultural dysfunctions" in his 2022 campaign for the United States Senate, which was "fueled by the money of others who would never deign to live in the Midwest" (Nichols).

5. Depression

1. By this I mean the popular vote count of both the 2016 and 2020 elections, as well as Gallup Poll data that shows Trump's presidential approval rating was as low as 34 percent at times and never in his four years exceeded 49 percent (Gallup).

2. In this way, Trump's supporters are another point on a political-cultural trajectory of "post-truth," a phrase that originated, as Roderick A. Ferguson explores, in the discourse surrounding the Iran-Contra scandal to describe the Reagan-Bush administration's "deliberate subterfuge and

misleading of the American public" (55). As part of a conservative-driven "social turn away from truth," Trump supporters, much like their preceding Reagan supporters, "look to our government to protect us from the truth" as part of their "demoting of empirical knowledge [and] the unseating of historical and cultural knowledge about racial, gender, and sexual minorities and its potential to disrupt the coherence of subjects privileged by . . . the innocence of the U.S. nation state" (53, 54).

3. One should not underestimate Sedaris's power to misattune. Take, for instance, his December 6, 2020, appearance on *CBS News Sunday Morning*, in which he suggests that Americans should be able to perform a "citizen's dismissal" of service employees. "It's like a citizen's arrest, but instead of detaining someone, you get to fire them!" he intones. The humor of the bit may stem from Sedaris's repeated firing of those he encounters as he shops, akin to how Donald Trump "fired" contestants from *The Apprentice*. But the response to Sedaris's appearance was negative, to say the least. As Geordie Gray of *The Brag* notes, "Despite being completely void of humor, something about a man that makes $2 million a year churning out a bit about firing retail employees that are probably struggling to survive on an unlivable wage left a bad taste in the mouths of us mere working class" (Gray). One can only assume that if Sedaris's humor follows this particular trajectory, his humor's tendency to shock readers under the guise of "just kidding" could easily slide into an endorsement of reactionary politics.

4. As Gorski and Perry note, Trump produces an entire discourse to castigate his adversaries and encourages his allies to repeat (if not chant): "Crooked Hillary," "Sleepy Joe," "Lyin' Ted," "Little Marco," "Low Energy Jeb," and so forth (91). And as Gorski and Perry also note, such rhetoric encourages other ideologues to revel in a particularly juvenile discourse of either invective or pride, such as that of a polemicist turned felon (subsequently pardoned by Trump and then turned polemicist again) who, despite the intellect that comes with an Ivy League education, joyously describes himself as a "butt-kicking Republican, Christian, right-wing American capitalist" (Dinesh D'Souza qtd. in Gorski and Perry 44).

Conclusion

1. Too much literary and cultural study of American nationalism perpetuates a worrisome tendency, as Dana D. Nelson describes it, of "thinking self-confirmationally" (e7). Critics too often synecdochically boil nationalism down to one thing—a bad, emotional thing—that is the contrary of the good, studied voice of criticism. There is a pleasure in doing this, but I suspect it is an ugly us/them feeling, the pleasure of not having to

"let our familiar attachments go" because "we can't stop finding the same thing" (e5). This works to sustain critical ambivalence: as Lauren Berlant put it, the situation when "we want and we don't want what we want" (*On the Inconvenience* 36). But it is in actuality a repetition compulsion: not so much a pleasure but a reenactment of a darkness that, if it were brought into the light, would be better for us all.

2. I agree with Nelson that our predominant critical attachment to the nation has been that of the critic as hero versus the nation as villain, a drama that Nelson calls the "Bad America without which we would hardly know ourselves as a field" (e5). "Bad America" is the nation "we can't stop being angry at, can't stop surveying in total disgust, can't stop countering with the help of our canonical superheroes," either literary or theoretical, that keeps us locked into an adversarial relationship with the nation so that we may look, at least to ourselves, as disciples of justice, freedom, and equality (e5). The criticism that comes from such a perspective rather openly demonstrates how the critic "want[s] parts but not wholes and resent[s] the hidden freight" that comes with them (Berlant, *On the Inconvenience* 36). Certainly there are "Bad Americas" like the ones I have examined in this book. But to see all Americas as "Bad Americas" is really to serve one purpose, to identify other critics who see the same "Bad America" as fellow members of the elect, "permanently on the vanguard" as separate from the supposed dupes who have emotionally invested themselves in the nation (Castronovo 243). This is an ugly purpose because it activates, according to Russ Castronovo, a sort of morality play in which critics "willingly cloak themselves with a hair-shirt logic that makes their own penance about American nationalism a prerequisite for progressive critique." This critical penance reduces American nationalism to one thing, and as I explore in this book, American nationalism is many things. If we are to truly understand the nation whose texts we study, we must do more than penance to do justice to the object we study.

BIBLIOGRAPHY

Ahmed, Sara. *The Cultural Politics of Emotion.* 2nd ed. New York: Routledge, 2015.

———. "Not in the Mood." *New Formations* 82 (2014): 13–28.

———. *The Promise of Happiness.* Durham, NC: Duke University Press, 2010.

———. *Willful Subjects.* Durham, NC: Duke University Press, 2014.

Alsop, Stewart, and Charles Bartlett. "In Time of Crisis." *Saturday Evening Post,* December 8, 1962, 15–21.

Althusser, Louis. "Ideology and Ideological State Apparatus (Notes towards an Investigation)." In *Lenin and Philosophy and Other Essays,* edited by Frederic Jameson, 85–126. New York: Monthly Review Press, 2001.

Altman, Rick. *Film/Genre.* London: British Film Institute, 1999.

Amis, Martin. *The Moronic Inferno and Other Visits to America.* New York: Penguin, 1996.

Anderson, Ben. "Affect and Critique: A Politics of Boredom." *EPD: Society and Space* 39.2 (2021): 197–217.

———. "Becoming and Being Hopeful: Towards a Theory of Affect." *EPD: Society and Space* 24 (2006): 733–52.

———. "'We Will Win Again. We Will Win a Lot': The Affective Styles of Donald Trump." *Society and Space,* February 28, 2017. https://www.societyandspace .org/articles/we-will-win-again-we-will-win-a-lot-the-affective-styles-of -donald-trump.

Anderson, Benedict. *Imagined Communities: Reflections on the Origin and Spread of Nationalism.* New York: Verso, 1991.

Anderson, Carol. *White Rage.* New York: Bloomsbury, 2017.

André, Christophe. *Feelings and Moods.* New York: Polity, 2012.

Andrews, Helen. "An Eroded Culture." Review of *Hillbilly Elegy: A Memoir,* by J. D. Vance. *National Review,* August 15, 2016. https://www.nationalreview .com/magazine/2016/08/15/jd-vance-hillbilly-elegy/.

Anker, Elisabeth R. *Ugly Freedoms.* Durham, NC: Duke University Press, 2022.

Arendt, Hannah. *The Origins of Totalitarianism.* New York: Schocken Books, 1951.

Baldwin, James. *Collected Essays.* Edited by Toni Morrison. New York: Library of America, 1998.

———. *The Cross of Redemption: Uncollected Writings.* Edited by Randall Kenan. New York: Vintage, 2010.

———. "The Evidence of Things Not Seen." *Playboy*, December 1981, 140–42, 308–16.

———. *The Evidence of Things Not Seen*. New York: Henry Holt, 1985.

Balfour, Lawrie. *The Evidence of Things Not Said: James Baldwin and the Promise of American Democracy*. Ithaca, NY: Cornell University Press, 2001.

Barbrook, Richard, and Andy Cameron. "The Californian Ideology." Imaginary Futures: From Thinking Machines to the Global Village. Hypermedia Research Centre Archive, April 17, 2007. http://www.imaginaryfutures.net /2007/04/17/the-californian-ideology-2/.

Barden, Thomas E. Afterword to *Steinbeck in Vietnam: Dispatches from the War*, edited by Thomas E. Barden, 157–68. Charlottesville: University of Virginia Press, 2012.

Belew, Kathleen. *Bring the War Home: The White Power Movement and Paramilitary America*. Cambridge, MA: Harvard University Press, 2018.

Bennett, Oliver. *Cultural Pessimism: Narratives of Decline in the Postmodern World*. Edinburgh: Edinburgh University Press, 2001.

Benson, Jackson J. *John Steinbeck, Writer: A Biography*. New York: Penguin, 1984.

Berlant, Lauren. *On the Inconvenience of Other People*. Durham, NC: Duke University Press, 2022.

———. *The Queen of America Goes to Washington City: Essays on Sex and Citizenship*. Durham, NC: Duke University Press, 1997.

———. "Trump, or Political Emotions." *The New Inquiry*, August 5, 2016. https://thenewinquiry.com/trump-or-political-emotions/.

———. "Unfeeling Kerry." *Theory & Event* 8.2 (2005). https://muse.jhu.edu /article/187843.

Berlant, Lauren, and Sianne Ngai. "Comedy Has Issues." *Critical Inquiry* 43 (Winter 2017): 233–49.

Berlet, Chip. "Reframing Populist Resentments in the Tea Party Movement." In *Steep: The Precipitous Rise of the Tea Party*, edited by Lawrence Rosenthal and Christine Trost, 47–66. Berkeley: University of California Press, 2012.

Best, Joel. *American Nightmares: Social Problems in an Anxious World*. Berkeley: University of California Press, 2018.

Bhabha, Homi K. "DissemiNation: Time, Narrative and the Margins of the Modern Nation." In Bhaba, *Nation and Narration*, 291–322.

———, ed. *Nation and Narration*. New York: Routledge, 1990.

Billig, Michael. *Banal Nationalism*. Thousand Oaks, CA: SAGE, 1995.

Booth, Wayne C. "Loathing and Ignorance on the Campaign Trail: 1972." *Columbia Journalism Review* 12.4 (November/December 1973): 7–12.

Braunstein, Peter, and Michael William Doyle. "Historicizing the American Counterculture of the 1960s and '70s." In *Imagine Nation: The American*

Counterculture of the 1960s and '70s, edited by Peter Braunstein and Michael William Doyle, 5–12. New York: Routledge, 2002.

Brennan, Timothy. "The National Longing for Form." In Bhabha, *Nation and Narration* 44–70.

Brooks, Dan. "The Unrelenting Glibness of David Sedaris." *Gawker,* May 31, 2022. https://www.gawkerarchives.com/culture/david-sedaris-happy-go-lucky-review.

Brooks, David. "How We Are Ruining America." *New York Times,* July 11, 2017. https://www.nytimes.com/2017/07/11/opinion/how-we-are-ruining -america.html.

Brooks, Peter. *Reading for the Plot: Design and Intention in Narrative.* Rev. ed. Cambridge, MA: Harvard University Press, 1992.

Bruce-Novoa, Juan. "Fear and Loathing on the Buffalo Trail." *MELUS* 6.4 (Winter 1979): 39–50.

Burke, Kenneth. *A Grammar of Motives.* 1945. Repr., Berkeley: University of California Press, 1969.

Cardell, Kylie, and Victoria Kuttainen. "The Ethics of Laughter: David Sedaris and Humor Memoir." *Mosaic* 45.3 (September 2012): 99–114.

Carter, Dan T. *Politics of Rage: George Wallace, the Origins of the New Conservatism, and the Transformation of American Politics.* Baton Rouge: Louisiana State University Press, 2000.

Carter, Jimmy. *Why Not the Best?* Nashville: Broadman Press, 1975.

Castronovo, Russ. "What Are the Politics of Critique? The Function of Criticism at a Different Time." In *Critique and Postcritique,* edited by Elizabeth S. Anker and Rita Felski, 230–51.

Catte, Elizabeth. *What You Are Getting Wrong about Appalachia.* Cleveland: Belt, 2018.

Certeau, Michel de. *The Practice of Everyday Life.* Translated by Steven Rendall. Berkeley: University of California Press, 1984.

Chafe, William H. *The Unfinished Journey: America since World War II.* New York: Oxford University Press, 2014.

Cherwitz, Richard A. "Lyndon Johnson and the 'Crisis' of Tonkin Gulf: A President's Justification of War." *Western Journal of Speech Communication* 42.2 (Spring 1978): 93–104.

Cmiel, Kenneth. "The Politics of Civility." In *The Sixties: From Memory to History,* edited by David Farber, 263–90. Chapel Hill: University of North Carolina Press, 1994.

Collins, Robert M. *Transforming America: Politics and Culture in the Reagan Years.* New York: Columbia University Press, 2007.

Connolly, William E. *Aspirational Fascism: The Struggle for Multifaceted Democracy under Trumpism.* Minneapolis: University of Minnesota Press, 2017.

Converse, Philip E., and Howard Schuman. "'Silent Majorities' and the Vietnam War." *Scientific American* 222.6 (June 1970): 17–25.

Cooper, Ken. "'Zero Plays the House': The Las Vegas Novel and Atomic Roulette." *Contemporary Literature* 33.3 (1992): 528–44.

Corrigan, Lisa M. *Black Feelings: Race and Affect in the Long Sixties.* Jackson: University Press of Mississippi, 2020.

Costello, Bonnie. *The Plural of Us: Poetry and Community in Auden and Others.* Princeton, NJ: Princeton University Press, 2017.

Coviello, Peter. "Remediations in an Emergency." *American Literary History* 34.1 (2022): 77–90.

Cox, Lloyd. *Nationalism: Themes, Theories, and Controversies.* New York: Palgrave, 2021.

Cramer, Katherine J. *The Politics of Resentment: Rural Consciousness in Wisconsin and the Rise of Scott Walker.* Chicago: University of Chicago Press, 2016.

Cvetkovich, Ann. *Depression: A Public Feeling.* Durham, NC: Duke University Press, 2012.

Dale, Daniel. "Donald Trump Voters: 'We Like the President's Lies.'" *Toronto Star,* March 26, 2017. https://www.thestar.com/news/insight/donald-trump -voters-we-like-the-president-s-lies/article_076e5349-0846-5172-b205 -ca38c4ad98d3.html.

Darda, Joseph. "Dispatches from the Drug Wars: Ishmael Reed, Oscar Zeta Acosta, and the Viet Cong of America." *Modern Fiction Studies* 64.1 (2018): 79–103.

———. *Empire of Defense: Race and the Cultural Politics of Permanent War.* Chicago: University of Chicago Press, 2019.

DeBenedetti, Charles. *An American Ordeal: The Antiwar Movement of the Vietnam Era.* Syracuse, NY: Syracuse University Press, 1990.

Dettlinger, Chet. *The List.* With Jeff Prugh. Atlanta: Philmay Enterprises, 1983.

Dewey, Caitlin. "The Real Problem with David Brooks's Sandwich Column." *Washington Post,* July 11, 2017. https://www.washingtonpost.com/news/wonk /wp/2017/07/11/the-real-problem-with-david-brooks-sandwich-column/.

Diamond, Elin. "The Violence of 'We': Politicizing Identification." In *Critical Theory and Performance,* edited by Janelle G. Reinelt and Joseph R. Roach, 390–98. Ann Arbor: University of Michigan Press, 1992.

Dickstein, Morris. *Gates of Eden: American Culture in the Sixties.* New York; W. W. Norton, 2015.

Dienstag, Joshua Foa. *Pessimism: Philosophy, Ethic, Spirit.* Princeton, NJ: Princeton University Press, 2009.

Donnan, Shawn. "Hillbilly Elegist JD Vance: 'The People Calling the Shots Really Screwed Up.'" *Financial Times,* February 2, 2018. https://www.ft.com /content/bd801c3c-fab7-11e7-9b32-d7d59aace167.

Dore, Florence, J. D. Connor, and Dan Sinykin. "Rebel Yale: Reading and Feeling in 'Hillbilly Elegy.'" *Los Angeles Review of Books,* January 10, 2018. https://lareviewofbooks.org/article/rebel-yale-reading-feeling-hillbilly-elegy/.

Douglas, John E. *Mindhunter: Inside the FBI's Elite Serial Crime Unit.* With Mark Olshaker. New York: Scribner, 1995.

Duggan, Lisa. *Mean Girl: Ayn Rand and the Culture of Greed.* Berkeley: University of California Press, 2019.

Eburne, Jonathan. "The Terror of Being Destroyed." *Critical Philosophy of Race* 3.2 (2015): 259–81.

Edelman, Lee. *No Future: Queer Theory and the Death Drive.* Durham, NC: Duke University Press, 2004.

Engels, Jeremy. *The Politics of Resentment: A Genealogy.* University Park: Pennsylvania State University Press, 2015.

———. "The Politics of Resentment and the Tyranny of the Minority: Rethinking Victimage for Resentful Times." *Rhetoric Society Quarterly* 40.4 (2010): 303–25.

Enloe, Cynthia. *Bananas, Beaches, and Bases: Making Feminist Sense of International Politics.* 2nd ed. Berkeley: University of California Press, 2014.

Esty, Jed. *The Future of Decline: Anglo-American Culture at Its Limits.* Stanford, CA: Stanford University Press, 2022.

Felski, Rita. *Hooked: Art and Attachment.* Chicago: University of Chicago Press, 2020.

———. "Identifying with Characters." In *Character: Three Inquiries into Literary Studies,* edited by Amanda Anderson, Rita Felski, and Toril Moi, 77–126. Chicago: University of Chicago Press, 2019.

Ferguson, Roderick A. "The Backdrop of the Post-Truth." In *The Long 2020,* edited by Richard Grusin and Maureen Ryan, 53–65. Minneapolis: University of Minnesota Press, 2022.

Field, Douglas. "Looking for Jimmy Baldwin: Sex, Privacy, and Black Nationalist Fervor." *Callaloo* 27.2 (2004): 457–80.

Finchelstein, Federico. *From Fascism to Populism in History.* Berkeley: University of California Press, 2019.

Flatley, Jonathan. *Affective Mapping: Melancholia and the Politics of Modernism.* Cambridge, MA: Harvard University Press, 2008.

———. "How a Revolutionary Counter-Mood Is Made." *New Literary History* 43.3 (Summer 2012): 503–25.

Frank, Adam J., and Elizabeth A. Wilson. *A Silvan Tomkins Handbook: Foundations for Affect Theory.* Minneapolis: University of Minnesota Press, 2020.

Gallup. "Presidential Approval Ratings—Donald Trump." January 20, 2017, to January 15, 2021. https://news.gallup.com/poll/203198/presidential-approval-ratings-donald-trump.aspx.

Gates, Henry Louis, Jr. "The Fire Last Time: What James Baldwin Can and Can't Teach America." *New Republic,* June 1, 1992. https://newrepublic.com /article/114134/fire-last-time.

Gerstle, Gary. *American Crucible: Race and Nation in the Twentieth Century.* Princeton, NJ: Princeton University Press, 2017.

Gibbons, William Conrad. *The U.S. Government and the Vietnam War: Executive and Legislative Roles and Relationships.* Part IV: *July 1965–January 1968.* Princeton, NJ: Princeton University Press, 1986.

Goodwin, Doris Kearns. *Lyndon Johnson and the American Dream.* New York: Harper and Row, 1976.

Gorski, Philip S., and Samuel L. Perry. *The Flag and the Cross: White Christian Nationalism and the Threat to American Democracy.* New York: Cambridge University Press, 2022.

Grattan, Sean Austin. *Hope Isn't Stupid: Utopian Affects in Contemporary American Literature.* Iowa City: University of Iowa Press, 2017.

Gray, Geordie. "David Sedaris Cops Heat over Hot Take about How People Should Be able to Fire Retail Workers." *The Brag,* July 12, 2020. https:// thebrag.com/david-sedaris-retail-employees/.

Gregg, Melissa, and Gregory J. Seigworth. "An Inventory of Shimmers." In *The Affect Theory Reader,* edited by Melissa Gregg and Gregory J. Seigworth, 1–25. Durham, NC: Duke University Press, 2010.

Griffin, Martin, and Christopher Herbert, Introduction to *Stories of Nation: Fiction, Politics, and the American Experience,* edited by Martin Griffin and Christopher Herbert, vii-xviii. Knoxville: University of Tennessee Press, 2017.

Grosby, Steven. *Nationalism: A Very Short Introduction.* New York: Oxford University Press, 2005.

Grossberg, Lawrence. *Dancing in Spite of Myself: Essays on Popular Culture.* Durham, NC: Duke University Press, 1997.

———. *Under the Cover of Chaos: Trump and the Battle for the American Right.* London: Pluto Press, 2018.

———. *We Gotta Get Out of This Place: Popular Conservatism and Postmodern Culture.* New York: Routledge, 1992.

Guan, Frank. "The Hills Have Lies." *Bookforum,* February/March 2018, 10.

Hagan, Joe. *Sticky Fingers: The Life and Times of Jann Wenner and Rolling Stone Magazine.* New York: Knopf, 2017.

Hage, Ghassan. *Against Paranoid Nationalism: Searching for Hope in a Shrinking Society.* Annandale, VA: Pluto Press, 2003.

Harding, Susan Friend. *The Book of Jerry Falwell: Fundamentalist Language and Politics.* Princeton, NJ: Princeton University Press, 2000.

Hardt, Michael, and Antonio Negri. *Commonwealth.* Cambridge, MA: Harvard University Press, 2011.

Harkins, Anthony. *Hillbilly: A Cultural History of an American Icon.* New York: Oxford University Press, 2005.

Hart, Roderick P. *Trump and Us: What He Says and Why People Listen.* New York: Cambridge University Press, 2020.

Headley, Bernard. *The Atlanta Youth Murders and the Politics of Race.* Carbondale: Southern Illinois University Press, 1998.

Hellmann, John. *American Myth and the Legacy of Vietnam.* New York: Columbia University Press, 1986.

———. *Fables of Fact: The New Journalism as Fiction.* Urbana: University of Illinois Press, 1981.

Hickey, Donald R. "'War Hawks': Using Newspapers to Trace a Phrase, 1792–1812." *Journal of Military History* 78.2 (2014): 725–40.

Hill, Leslie. *Maurice Blanchot: Extreme Contemporary.* New York: Routledge, 1997.

Hirschman, Albert O. *Exit, Voice, and Loyalty: Responses to Decline in Firms, Organizations, and States.* Cambridge, MA: Harvard University Press, 1970.

———. *The Rhetoric of Reaction: Perversity, Futility, Jeopardy.* Cambridge, MA: Harvard University Press, 1991.

Hobson, Maurice J. *The Legend of Black Mecca: Politics and Class in the Making of Modern Atlanta.* Chapel Hill: University of North Carolina Press, 2017.

Hofstadter, Richard. *The Paranoid Style in American Politics.* New York: Vintage Books, 1965.

Hollinger, David A. "How Wide the Circle of 'We'? American Intellectuals and the Problem of the Ethnos since World War II." *American Historical Review* 98.2 (April 1993): 317–37.

Huehls, Mitchum. "What's the Matter with Ohio?: Liberal Democracy and the Challenge of Irrationality." *American Literary History* 32.2 (2020): 328–53.

Hurley, Jessica. *Infrastructures of Apocalypse: American Literature and the Nuclear Complex.* Minneapolis: University of Minnesota Press, 2020.

Hutcheon, Linda. *Irony's Edge: The Theory and Politics of Irony.* New York: Routledge, 1994.

Isenberg, Nancy. *White Trash: The 400-Year Untold History of Class in America.* New York: Penguin, 2017.

Issenberg, Sasha. "David Brooks: Boo-Boos in Paradise." *Philadelphia,* April 1, 2004. https://www.phillymag.com/news/2004/04/01/david-brooks-booboos-in-paradise/.

Ivie, Robert L. "Cold War Motives and the Rhetorical Framework: A Framework for Criticism." In *Cold War Rhetoric: Strategy, Metaphor, and Ideology,* edited by Martin J. Medhurst, Robert L. Ivie, Philip Wander, and Robert L. Scott, 71–79. New York: Greenwood Press, 1998.

James, Jennifer C. "Dread." *American Literature* 92.4 (December 2020): 689–95.

Jane, Emma A. "'Your a Ugly, Whorish Slut': Understanding E-Bile." *Feminist Media Studies* 14.4 (2014): 531–46.

Johnson, Paul Elliott. *I the People: The Rhetoric of Conservative Populism in the United States.* Tuscaloosa: University of Alabama Press, 2021.

Judis, John B. *The Populist Explosion: How the Great Recession Transformed American and European Politics.* New York: Columbia Global Reports, 2016.

Kahin, George McTurnan. *Intervention: How America Became Involved in Vietnam.* New York: Anchor Books, 1987.

Kahneman, Daniel, and Jonathan Renshon. "Hawkish Biases." In *American Foreign Policy and the Politics of Fear,* edited by A. Trevor Thrall and Jane K. Cramer, 79–96. New York: Routledge, 2009.

Karp, David A. *Speaking of Sadness: Depression, Disconnection, and the Meanings of Mental Illness.* 2nd ed. New York: Oxford University Press, 2013.

Kazin, Michael. *The Populist Persuasion: An American History.* Rev. ed. Ithaca, NY: Cornell University Press, 2017.

Keller, Florian. *Andy Kaufman: Wrestling with the American Dream.* Minneapolis: University of Minnesota Press, 2005.

Kelly, Casey Ryan. *Apocalypse Man: The Death Drive and White Masculine Victimhood.* Columbus: Ohio State University Press, 2020.

Kennedy, John F. "America's Stake in Vietnam: The Cornerstone of the Free World in Southeast Asia." *Vital Speeches of the Day* 22.20 (1956): 617–19.

Kierkegaard, Søren. *The Present Age.* Translated by Alexander Tru. New York: Harper, 1962.

Kinsley, Michael. "Suburban Thrall." *New York Times:* May 23, 2004. https://www.nytimes.com/2004/05/23/books/suburban-thrall.html.

Klugman, Jeffry. "Hawks and Doves." *Political Psychology* 6.4 (1985): 573–89.

Konda, Thomas Milan. *Conspiracies of Conspiracies: How Delusions Have Overrun America.* Chicago: University of Chicago Press, 2019.

Kopelson, Kevin. *Sedaris.* Minneapolis: University of Minnesota Press, 2007.

Laclau, Ernesto. *On Populist Reason.* New York: Verso, 2007.

Lancaster, Roger N. *Sex Panic and the Punitive State.* Berkeley: University of California Press, 1991.

Levy, Ariel. "Lesbian Nation." *New Yorker,* February 22, 2009. https://www.newyorker.com/magazine/2009/03/02/lesbian-nation.

Logevall, Fredrik. *Choosing War: The Lost Chance for Peace and the Escalation of War in Vietnam.* Berkeley: University of California Pres, 1999.

Logue, Cal M., and John H. Patton. "From Ambiguity to Dogma: The Rhetorical Symbols of Lyndon B. Johnson on Vietnam." *Southern Speech Communication Journal* 47.3 (Spring 1982): 310–29.

Lopez, Nancy, "The City It Always Wanted to Be: The Child Murders and the Coming of Age in Atlanta." In *The Southern Albatross: Race and Ethnicity in the American South* edited by Philip D. Dillard and Randal L. Hall, 197–233. Macon, GA: Mercer University Press, 1999.

Lowe, Walter, Jr. "Moment of Truth in Atlanta: James Baldwin Remembered." *Emerge* 1.1 (October 31, 1989): 54.

Main, Thomas J. *The Rise of the Alt-Right.* Washington, DC: Brookings Institute Press, 2018.

Malatino, Hil. *Side Affects: On Being Trans and Feeling Bad.* Minneapolis: University of Minnesota Press, 2022.

Manne, Kate. *Down Girl: The Logic of Misogyny.* New York: Oxford University Press, 2017.

Marantz, Andrew. "Firing Line." *New Yorker,* August 2, 2021, 78–81.

Massumi, Brian. "Navigating Movements." In *Hope: New Philosophies for Change,* edited by Mary Zournazi, 210–43. New York: Routledge, 2003.

May, Elaine Tyler. *Fortress America: How We Embraced Fear and Abandoned Democracy.* New York: Basic Books, 2017.

McClennen, Sophia A. "Trump's Ironic Effect on Political Satire." *Film Quarterly* 75.2 (Winter 2021). https://filmquarterly.org/2021/12/03/trumps-ironic-effect-on-political-satire/.

McNamara, Robert. *In Retrospect: The Tragedy and Lessons of Vietnam.* New York: Random House, 1995.

Mercieca, Jennifer R. "Dangerous Demagogues and Weaponized Communication." *Rhetoric Society Quarterly* 49.3 (2019): 264–79.

Miroff, Bruce. *The Liberals' Moment: The McGovern Insurgency and the Identity Crisis of the Democratic Party.* Lawrence: University Press of Kansas, 2007.

Morrison, Toni. *Playing in the Dark: Whiteness and the Literary Imagination.* Cambridge, MA: Harvard University Press, 1992.

Müller, Jan-Werner. *What Is Populism?* Philadelphia: University of Pennsylvania Press, 2016.

Muñoz, José Esteban. *Disidentifications: Queers of Color and the Performance of Politics.* Minneapolis: University of Minnesota Press, 1999.

Myers, Thomas. *Walking Point: American Narratives of Vietnam.* New York: Oxford University Press, 1988.

Nelson, Dana D. "We Have Never Been Anti-Exceptionalists." *American Literary History* 31.2 (2019): e1–e17.

Ngai, Sianne. *Our Aesthetic Categories: Zany, Cute, Interesting.* Cambridge, MA: Harvard University Press, 2015.

———. *Ugly Feelings.* Cambridge, MA: Harvard University Press, 2007.

Nguyen, Marguerite. *America's Vietnam: The Longue Durée of U.S. Literature and Empire.* Philadelphia: Temple University Press, 2018.

Nichols, Tom. "The Moral Collapse of J. D. Vance." *The Atlantic,* July 14, 2011. https://www.theatlantic.com/ideas/archive/2021/07/moral-collapse-jd -vance/619428/.

Nietzsche, Friedrich. *Basic Writings of Nietzsche.* Translated by Walter Kaufmann. New York: Modern Library, 1968.

Nudelman, Franny. "'Marked for Demolition': Mary McCarthy's Vietnam Journalism." *American Literature* 85.2 (2013): 363–87.

Ogden, Emily. *On Not Knowing: How to Love and Other Essays.* Chicago: University of Chicago Press, 2022.

Olson, Christa J. *American Magnitude: Hemispheric Vision and Public Feeling in the United States.* Columbus: Ohio State University Press, 2021.

Orwell, George. *Notes on Nationalism.* 1945. Repr., New York: Penguin Books, 2018.

O'Toole, Fintan. "The King and I." *New York Review of Books,* March 21, 2019, 12–16.

Packer, Joseph, and Ethan Stoneman. "Where We Produce One, We Produce All: The Platform Conspiracism of QAnon." *Cultural Politics* 17.3 (2021): 255–78.

Pearcy, Lee T. "Melancholy Rhetoricians and Melancholy Rhetoric: 'Black Bile' as a Rhetorical and Medical Term in the Second Century A.D." *Journal of the History of Medicine* 39.4 (1984): 446–56.

Pilisuk, Marc, Paul Potter, Anatol Rapoport, and J. Alan Winter. "War Hawks and Peace Doves: Alternate Resolutions of Experimental Conflicts." *Conflict Resolution* 9.4 (1965): 491–508.

Polsgrove, Carol. *It Wasn't Pretty Folks, But Didn't We Have Fun? Esquire in the Sixties.* New York: W. W. Norton, 1995.

Pugh, Tison. *Precious Perversions: Humor, Homosexuality, and the Southern Literary Canon.* Baton Rouge: Louisiana State University Press, 2016.

Railton, Ben. *History and Hope in American Literature: Models of Critical Patriotism.* Lanham, MD: Rowman & Littlefield, 2017.

Ratcliffe, Matthew. *Experiences of Depression: A Study in Phenomenology.* New York: Oxford University Press, 2015.

Ramazani, Jahan. "Nationalism, Transnationalism, and the Poetry of Mourning." In *The Oxford Handbook of the Elegy,* edited by Karen Weisman, 601–19. New York: Oxford University Press, 2010.

Reynolds, Bill. "On the Road to Gonzo: Hunter S. Thompson's Early Literary Journalism (1961–1970)." *Literary Journalism Studies* 4.1 (Spring 2012): 51–84.

Robinson, Dean E. *Black Nationalism in American Politics and Thought.* New York: Cambridge University Press, 2001.

Rodgers, Daniel T. *Age of Fracture.* Cambridge, MA: Harvard University Press, 2011.

Roof, Judith. *Tone: Writing and the Sound of Feeling.* New York: Bloomsbury, 2020.

Rothman, Joshua. "The Lives of Poor White People." *New Yorker,* September 12, 2016. https://www.newyorker.com/culture/cultural-comment/the-lives-of-poor-white-people.

Rowland, Robert C. *The Rhetoric of Donald Trump: Nationalist Populism and American Democracy.* Lawrence: University Press of Kansas, 2021.

Rubenstein, Richard. *Reasons to Kill: Why Americans Choose War.* New York: Bloomsbury, 2010.

Ryan, Maria. "Bush's 'Useful Idiots': 9/11, the Liberal Hawks and the Cooption of the 'War on Terror.'" *Journal of American Studies* 45.4 (2011): 667–93.

Saint-Amour, Paul. "Weak Theory, Weak Modernism." *Modernism/Modernity* 24.3 (2018): 437–59.

Sandbrook, Dominic. *Mad as Hell: The Crisis of the 1970s and the Rise of the Populist Right.* New York: Knopf, 2011.

Schaefer, Donovan O. *The Evolution of Affect Theory: The Humanities, the Sciences, and the Study of Power.* New York: Cambridge University Press, 2019.

———. "Whiteness and Civilization: Shame, Race, and the Rhetoric of Donald Trump." *Communication and Critical/Cultural Studies* 17.1 (2020): 1–18.

Scheler, Max. *Ressentiment.* Translated by William W. Holdheim. New York: Schocken Books, 1972.

Schulman, Bruce J. *The Seventies: The Great Shift in American Culture, Society, and Politics.* New York: Da Capo Press, 2002.

Schwarz, Bill. "Conservativism." In *New Keywords: A Revised Vocabulary of Culture and Society,* edited by Tony Bennett, Lawrence Grossberg, and Meaghan Morris, 54–56. Malden, MA: Blackwell, 2005.

Sedaris, David. "A Number of Reasons I've Been Depressed Lately." In *Calypso,* 185–93. New York: Back Bay Books, 2018.

Sedgwick, Eve Kosofsky. *Touching Feeling: Affect, Pedagogy, Performativity.* Durham, NC: Duke University Press, 2003.

Sherman, Rachel. *Uneasy Street: The Anxieties of Affluence.* Princeton, NJ: Princeton University Press, 2017.

Shrum, Robert. *No Excuses: Concessions of a Serial Campaigner.* New York: Simon and Schuster, 2007.

Shulman, George. *American Prophecy: Race and Redemption in American Political Culture.* Minneapolis: University of Minnesota Press, 2008.

Sienkiewicz, Matt, and Nick Marx. *That's Not Funny: How the Right Makes Comedy Work for Them.* Oakland: University of California Press, 2022.

Skocpol, Theda, and Vanessa Williamson. *The Tea Party and the Remaking of Republican Conservatism.* New York: Oxford University Press, 2016.

Slocum-Schaffer, Stephanie. *America in the Seventies.* Syracuse, NY: Syracuse University Press, 2003.

Slotkin, Richard. *Gunfighter Nation: The Myth of the Frontier in Twentieth-Century America.* Norman: University of Oklahoma Press, 1998.

Smith, Rachel Greenwald. "The Contemporary Novel and Postdemocratic Form." *Novel* 51.2 (August 2018): 292–307.

Snyder, Timothy. *On Tyranny: Twenty Lessons from the Twentieth Century.* New York: Tim Duggan Books, 2017.

Solomon, Robert C. *The Passions: Emotions and the Meaning of Life.* Indianapolis: Hackett, 1993.

———. *True to Our Feelings: What Our Emotions Are Really Telling Us.* New York: Oxford University Press, 2008.

Song, Min Hyoung. *Strange Future: Pessimism and the 1992 Los Angeles Riots.* Durham, NC: Duke University Press, 2005.

Stanley, Timothy. *Kennedy vs. Carter: The 1980 Battle for the Democratic Party's Soul.* Lawrence: University Press of Kansas, 2010.

Staub, Michael. E. "Setting Up the Seventies: Black Panthers, New Journalism, and the Rewriting of the Sixties." In *The Seventies: The Age of Glitter in Popular Culture,* edited by Shelton Waldrep, 19–40. New York: Routledge, 2000.

Steinbeck, John. *Bombs Away: The Story of a Bomber Team.* New York: Viking Press, 1942.

———. *A Russian Journal.* New York: Viking Press, 1948.

———. *Steinbeck: A Life in Letters.* Edited by Elaine Steinbeck and Robert Wallsten. New York: Viking Press, 1975.

———. *Steinbeck in Vietnam: Dispatches from the War.* Edited by Thomas Barden. Charlottesville: University of Virginia Press, 2012.

Steinbeck, John, IV. "The Importance of Being Stoned in Vietnam," *Washingtonian,* January 1968, 33–35, 56–60.

Steinle, Pamela Hunt. *In Cold Fear: "The Catcher in the Rye" Censorship Controversies and Postwar American Character.* Columbus: Ohio State University Press, 2000.

Stephenson, William. *Gonzo Republic: Hunter S. Thompson's America.* New York: Continuum, 2012.

Stern, Alexandra Minna. *Proud Boys and the White Ethnostate: How the Alt-Right Is Warping the American Imagination.* New York: Penguin, 2020.

Stockton, Katherine Bond. *Beautiful Bottom, Beautiful Shame: Where "Black" Meets "Queer."* Durham, NC: Duke University Press, 2006.

Stuber, Jenny. *Aspen and the American Dream: How One Town Deals with Inequality in the Era of Supergentrification.* Oakland: University of California Press, 2021.

Stuelke, Patricia. *The Ruse of Repair: US Neoliberal Empire and the Turn from Critique.* Durham, NC: Duke University Press, 2021.

Tamir, Yael. *Why Nationalism?* Princeton, NJ: Princeton University Press, 2020.

Terkel, Studs. "James Baldwin Discusses His Book *The Evidence of Things Not Seen*." *Studs Terkel Radio Archive,* November 22, 1985. https://studsterkel .wfmt.com/programs/james-baldwin-discusses-his-book-evidence-things -not-seen.

Thacker, Eugene. *Infinite Resignation.* New York: Repeater Books, 2018.

Thompson, Hunter S. *Fear and Loathing in Las Vegas: A Savage Journey to the Heart of the American Dream.* New York: Vintage, 1971.

———. *Fear and Loathing on the Campaign Trail '72.* New York: Simon and Schuster, 1973.

———. *The Great Shark Hunt: Strange Tales from a Strange Time.* New York: Simon and Schuster, 1979.

———. *The Proud Highway: The Saga of a Desperate Southern Gentleman, 1955–1967.* Edited by Douglas Brinkley. New York: Ballantine, 1998.

———. *Songs of the Doomed: More Notes on the Death of the American Dream.* New York: Simon and Schuster, 1990.

Thomson, James C. "How Could Vietnam Happen? An Autopsy." *The Atlantic,* April 1968. https://www.theatlantic.com/magazine/archive/1968/04/how -could-vietnam-happen-an-autopsy/306462/.

Todorova, Maria. "Is There Weak Nationalism and Is It a Useful Category?" *Nations and Nationalism* 21.4 (2015): 681–99.

Tomkins, Silvan. *Affect Imagery Consciousness.* Vol. 2, *The Negative Affects.* New York: Springer, 1963.

———. *Affect Imagery Consciousness.* Vol. 3, *The Negative Affects: Anger and Fear.* New York: Springer, 1991.

Torrey, Beef, and Kevin Simonson. *Conversations with Hunter S. Thompson.* Jackson: University Press of Mississippi, 2008.

Trask, Michael. *Ideal Minds: Raising Consciousness in the Antisocial Seventies.* Ithaca, NY: Cornell University Press, 2020.

Troupe, Quincy. "Last Testament: An Interview with James Baldwin." In *Conversations with James Baldwin,* edited by Fred L. Standley and Louis H. Pratt, 281–86. Jackson: University Press of Mississippi, 1989.

Urbinati, Nadia. *Me the People: How Populism Transforms Democracy.* Cambridge, MA: Harvard University Press, 2019.

Vance, J. D. *Hillbilly Elegy: A Memoir of a Family and Culture in Crisis.* New York: Harper, 2016.

van Zuylen-Wood, Simon. "The Radicalization of J. D. Vance." *Washington Post,* January 4, 2022. https://www.washingtonpost.com/magazine/2022/01 /04/jd-vance-hillbilly-elegy-radicalization/.

Vendler, Helen. *Soul Says: On Recent Poetry.* Cambridge, MA: Harvard University Press, 1995.

Vietnam Study Task Force. *Report of the Office of the Secretary of Defense Vietnam Task Force.* Vol. 4. Washington, DC: Department of Defense, 1969.

Vogel, Joseph. *James Baldwin and the 1980s: Witnessing the Reagan Era.* Urbana: University of Illinois Press, 2018.

Wald, Priscilla. *Constituting Americans: Cultural Anxiety and Narrative Form.* Durham, NC: Duke University Press, 1995.

Wall, Cheryl A. "Stranger at Home: James Baldwin on What It Means to Be American." In *James Baldwin: America and Beyond,* edited by Cora Kaplan and Bill Schwarz, 35–52. Ann Arbor: University of Michigan Press, 2011.

Wells, Tom. *The War Within: America's Battle over Vietnam.* New York: Henry Holt, 1996.

Wenner, Jann, and Corey Seymour. *Gonzo: The Life of Hunter S. Thompson.* New York: Little, Brown, 2007.

Whitman, Walt. *Leaves of Grass, and Other Writings.* Edited by Michael Moon. New York: W. W. Norton, 2002.

Wilderson, Frank B., III. *Red, White & Black: Cinema and the Structure of U.S. Antagonisms.* Durham, NC: Duke University Press, 2010.

Winstein-Hibbs, Sarah. "Otherwise Charisma: James Baldwin and the Black Queer Archive of Civil Rights Historiography." *American Quarterly* 74.2 (June 2022): 295–315.

Worden, Daniel. *Neoliberal Nonfictions: The Documentary Aesthetic from Joan Didion to Jay-Z.* Charlottesville: University of Virginia Press, 2020.

X, Malcolm. *Malcolm X on Afro-American History.* New York: Pathfinder Press, 1970.

Yardley, Jonathan. "The Writer and the Preacher." In *Critical Essays on James Baldwin* edited by Fred L. Standley and Nancy V. Bert, 240–43. Boston: G. K. Hall, 1988.

Young, Marilyn B. "Two, Three, Many Vietnams." *Cold War History* 6.4 (November 2006): 413–24.

Zaretsky, Natasha. *No Direction Home: The American Family and the Fear of National Decline, 1968–1980.* Chapel Hill: University of North Carolina Press, 2007.

INDEX

affect: of hillbillies, 156n6; as incitement to read, 12–13; in "Letters to Alicia," 27–28; national decline and, 3; paradox of, 14–15; strong nationalism and, 8, 10–11, 15–19, 80, 144–46; synecdoche and, 5, 13, 14, 31, 103, 144, 149n2; theories of, 11–15, 127, 144–46; weak, 15, 135. *See also* strong affect; *and specific affects*
Affect Theory Reader, The (Gregg & Seigworth), 11
African Americans. *See* Black Americans
afropessimism, 90
aggression, 20, 25, 28, 30–32, 40, 42, 46
Ahmed, Sara, 6, 10, 13, 18, 21, 80, 85, 126, 129, 136
Alsop, Stewart, 149n4
Althusser, Louis, 5
Altman, Rick, 17
alt-right, 132–34, 138, 139
American Dream: Baldwin on, 97; Best on, 68; contradictory nature of, 7; failure of, 21, 48, 69, 70; hillbillies and, 108, 118; Keller on, 70; rhetoric of, 153n7; strong affect and, 108, 153n7; Thompson on, 61, 69, 70; Trumpism and, 130; Vance on, 108, 118
American exceptionalism, 74, 84, 86, 100
American Nightmare, 68–69, 153–54n7
Amis, Martin, 76, 79
Anderson, Ben, 49, 52, 87
Anderson, Benedict, 5–7, 20, 29
Anderson, Carol, 157n11
André, Christophe, 121
anger: bilious reading and, 21, 49, 50, 53; depression and inward feelings

of, 127; resentful reading and, 105, 106, 121, 157n11; Trumpism and, 131, 137, 139
Anker, Elisabeth R., 20
antidemocratic sentiment, 4, 10, 105, 140
antisociality, 49–54, 59, 65
anxiety, 15, 68, 108, 109, 131, 156n7
apartheid, 97
Arendt, Hannah, 140
Aspen (Colorado): cost of living in, 153n4; Edwards's campaign for mayor, 49, 55–57; Thompson's campaign for sheriff, 49, 54, 56–59
aspirational fascism, 137–38, 140
Atlanta murders (1979–81): Baldwin on, 7, 21–22, 74, 79, 81–88, 93–97; futile reading of, 93–97; synecdoche and, 77–79, 82, 85–86, 95; theories related to, 75–77, 81, 154n3; trial and conviction of Williams for, 78–79, 94–96; victim demographics, 75–77

"Bad America," 159n2
Baldwin, James: on American Dream, 97; on Atlanta murders, 7, 21–22, 74, 79, 81–88, 93–97; Black nationalism and, 21, 91–92; "Down at the Cross," 86–87; "The Evidence of Things Not Seen," 21, 74, 81–88, 98; "Nobody Knows My Name," 82; "Notes on the House of Bondage," 92–93; on Reagan, 74, 83, 85, 93–94, 97; strategic exceptionalism and, 21, 86, 88. See also *Evidence of Things Not Seen, The;* futile reading
Baraka, Amiri, 8
Barbrook, Richard, 154n8

welfare system, 93, 101, 106, 116, 157n10
white nationalism, 92, 153n3
whiteness: conservatism and, 72, 93;
    elitism and, 47, 75; power and, 96,
    155n6; stereotypes of, 94
white rage, 157n11
white supremacy, 86, 155n6
Wilderson, Frank B., III, 90, 100
Williams, Wayne Bertram, 78–79,
    94–96, 154n3
Williamson, Vanessa, 113
Wilson, Elizabeth A., 16
Winstein-Hibbs, Sarah, 154n1

Wolfe, Tom, 47
women: feminism and, 51, 76;
    misogyny and, 148n8; as
    mothers, 1, 147n1; napalm factory
    protests by, 148n1; in national-
    ist movements, 147–48n5. *See also*
    mothers
Worden, Daniel, 53
Wylie, Philip, 147n1

Yardley, Jonathan, 72, 98–99, 154n1

Zaretsky, Natasha, 60, 80, 147n1

Cultural Frames, Framing Culture

Criminal Cities: The Postcolonial Novel and Cathartic Crime
Molly Slavin

Skimpy Coverage: Sports Illustrated *and the Shaping of the Female Athlete*
Bonnie M. Hagerman

Story Revolutions: *Collective Narratives from the Enlightenment to the Digital Age*
Helga Lenart-Cheng

Institutional Character: Collectivity, Agency, and the Modernist Novel
Robert Higney

Walk the Barrio: The Streets of Twenty-First-Century Transnational Latinx Literature
Cristina Rodriguez

Fashioning Character: Style, Performance, and Identity in Contemporary American Literature
Lauren S. Cardon

Neoliberal Nonfictions: The Documentary Aesthetic from Joan Didion to Jay-Z
Daniel Worden

Dandyism: Forming Fiction from Modernism to the Present
Len Gutkin

Terrible Beauty: The Violent Aesthetic and Twentieth-Century Literature
Marian Eide

Women Writers of the Beat Era: Autobiography and Intertextuality
Mary Paniccia Carden

Stranger America: A Narrative Ethics of Exclusion
Josh Toth

Fashion and Fiction: Self-Transformation in Twentieth-Century American Literature
Lauren S. Cardon

American Road Narratives: Reimagining Mobility in Literature and Film
Ann Brigham

The Arresting Eye: Race and the Anxiety of Detection
Jinny Huh

Failed Frontiersmen: White Men and Myth in the Post-Sixties American Historical Romance
James J. Donahue

Composing Cultures: Modernism, American Literary Studies, and the Problem of Culture
Eric Aronoff

Quirks of the Quantum: Postmodernism and Contemporary American Fiction
Samuel Chase Coale

Chick Lit and Postfeminism
Stephanie Harzewski

American Iconographic: "National Geographic," Global Culture, and the Visual Imagination
Stephanie L. Hawkins

Wanted: The Outlaw in American Visual Culture
Rachel Hall

Male Armor: The Soldier-Hero in Contemporary American Culture
Jon Robert Adams

African Americans and the Culture of Pain
Debra Walker King

Against the Unspeakable: Complicity, the Holocaust, and Slavery in America
Naomi Mandel

I'm No Angel: The Blonde in Fiction and Film
Ellen Tremper

Visions of the Maid: Joan of Arc in American Film and Culture
Robin Blaetz

Writing War in the Twentieth Century
Margot Norris

The Golden Avant-Garde: Idolatry, Commercialism, and Art
Raphael Sassower and Louis Cicotello

Kodak and the Lens of Nostalgia
Nancy Martha West

www.ingramcontent.com/pod-product-compliance
Lightning Source LLC
Chambersburg PA
CBHW030947260425
25722CB00024B/693